*Ghosts
along the
Cumberland*

WILLIAM LYNWOOD MONTELL

Ghosts along the Cumberland

DEATHLORE IN THE KENTUCKY FOOTHILLS

PHOTOGRAPHS BY MIKE MORSE

The University of Tennessee Press

Publication of this book was assisted by the
American Council of Learned Societies
under a grant from the Andrew W. Mellon Foundation.

Library of Congress Cataloging in Publication Data

Montell, William Lynwood, 1931–
Ghosts along the Cumberland.
Bibliography: p.
Includes index.
1. Folk-lore—Kentucky. 2. Dead (in religion,
folk-lore, etc.) 3. Ghost stories, American—Kentucky
I. Title.
GR110.K4M66   398.2'7'097691   74-32241
ISBN 0-87049-165-2

For Richard M. Dorson

PREFACE

The lore of death and ghosts persists as a great vestige of the past in the eastern section of an area known as the Kentucky "Pennyroyal" —or, as long-time residents sometimes call it, the "Pennyrile." Located in the foothills of southcentral Kentucky near the Tennessee line, the Eastern Pennyroyal has produced a genuine folklore, handed down by generation after generation, that even today is manifested by beliefs in death omens and the recital of tales of the supernatural.

A selection of many such beliefs, as well as a body of ghost narratives, is presented in this volume as they were collected from oral tradition by the writer and his students over the period of a decade. My own collections were made from 1958 to 1968, whereas my folklore students at Campbellsville College gathered their material from 1963 to 1968.

The setting for these stories is a land where mountains to the east have given way along their western margin to a broad belt of hills and ridges whose rugged monotony is only occasionally broken by moderately rolling terrain, fertile bottomlands, and karst topography. The region is carved up by rivers and large creeks, segmented by hills and ridges, and dotted with small towns and communities on narrow, crooked roads. On the west the main area is bordered by and includes the counties of Allen, Barren, and Green; on the north, by Taylor, Casey, Lincoln, and Rockcastle counties; on the east, by Pulaski, Wayne, and Clinton counties; and on the south, by Monroe and Cumberland counties. The internal counties of the area are Metcalfe, Adair, and Russell. Very slight portions of Warren, Marion, and McCreary counties are also within the Eastern Pennyroyal.

Lying generally south of the Western Coal Field and Bluegrass regions, the Pennyroyal stretches eastward from the Tennessee

River and Kentucky Lake to the mountains and Cumberland Plateau of eastern Kentucky. A section known as The Knobs separates the Pennyroyal region from the Bluegrass area to the north, and the Kentucky-Tennessee state line forms the boundary on the south. Geologically speaking, the Pennyroyal is a major part of the Mississippian Plateau and embraces some 7,800 square miles.

An interesting example of the folk process at work is the evolvement of the region's name itself. The name is derived from a pungent member of the mint family, which grows profusely in the region and was used by many early Americans to make a tea and to treat various illnesses. To botanists, the plant is known as the American or "mock" pennyroyal (*Hedeoma pulegioides*) because of its resemblance to the true English pennyroyal (*Mentha pulegium*). Within Kentucky, however, the word *Pennyroyal* has undergone a vernacular turn-about. Apparently a folk corruption has transformed the term into *Pennyrile*, a colloquialization that has been perpetuated especially in the western sectors but has become widely used throughout the state.

The people of Kentucky, once agrarians, are slowly becoming urbanized. Before the Second World War, 50 percent of the entire state lived on farms and another 20 percent resided in rural towns. Although Kentucky is still characteristically rural, the swift pace of technology is evident, and in the Eastern Pennyroyal the economic and cultural growth has been phenomenal. Before the war, not a town in the region was more than an agglomerated extension of the surrounding rural culture. Today the construction of roads and factories, the consolidation of schools, and the increased agricultural production have made this a fairly progressive section of the state. Influences of the frontier, once so deeply ingrained in the lives of the people of the foothills, are being meshed with the powerful tempo of modern times. Traditional ties with the soil have been greatly loosened within recent years. Farms have become increasingly larger, or else deserted, as the rural population has moved to the urban areas of the North or gravitated to local factory towns where husband and wife work side by side on the assembly line. Even those who chose to remain on the farm have seen their former living patterns virtually disappear. With isolation no longer a prohibiting factor, they go to town as often as they like, usually every day. A merchant recently commented to the writer on the disappearance of the special days, common in pre-war years, when the farmer and his family would come to town to buy, sell, barter, or attend some seasonal event. Saturday, of course, was generally observed as "butter and eggs day," focusing on home-grown produce.

Despite the fascination of a new way of life, these people of the soil have managed to cling tenaciously to many of the older forms of folk traditions. For example, the employees of the Union Underwear plant in Campbellsville bring out guitars and banjos as well as their lunchboxes when the noon whistle blows, and some of the workers often gather in their homes at night to make music and swap stories, the stories running the gamut from humorous yarns to tales of the supernatural. It was the urge to collect these latter tales and other oral traditions that provided the impetus for this book.

Many of the tales were tape-recorded and thus could be reprinted word-for-word; they are indicated here by the customary use of quotation marks for verbatim material. All other texts were taken down by hand as the informants spoke, with every effort made to transcribe accurately. The students who assisted me were carefully instructed in the proper collecting techniques, whether the recording medium was tape or pencil and pad.

It will be seen that some of the texts contain much historical data as well as information which gets very personal at times. Quite a few of the informants preferred not to be identified, especially in conjunction with the stories and beliefs they imparted. Hence I have chosen, insofar as the annotation is concerned, to protect the anonymity of all informants, thus avoiding any possibility of invading their privacy. It is believed that the information provided— that is, the age, sex, and home county of each informant—will meet the needs of all readers except those folklore scholars who wish to supplement or further analyze my research; to responsible members of this latter group I will open the files at any time. The typical informants pictured in the illustrations in each case granted permission for use of their names, although even in these instances they are not linked with the specific tales and beliefs they recounted.

To simplify the annotations, I have identified the collectors of these tales and beliefs by initials only in the main body of the work, but reference to the "Index of Collectors" found in the back of the book will provide their full names and their home towns at the time of collection. Also in the back pages will be found an "Index of Tale Types and Motifs," to which I have keyed in the annotations those beliefs and tales that have motifs parallel to ones found in Stith Thompson's and Ernest Warren Baughman's folktale indexes. The phrase "previously unreported" in some annotations is used to designate items that, as far as I know, have not appeared in print before. All place names mentioned are located in Kentucky unless otherwise indicated.

In sum, the annotations supply the following information in this order: county where collected, date of collection, initials of collector (in parentheses), informant data, and, where appropriate, comments on the belief or tale itself and on previous or related reports.

The fact that the stories themselves do not generally read smoothly is indicative, of course, of folklore. The variation from one text to the next in those instances where multiple variants are presented is also characteristic of folk tradition. A student at Campbellsville College summed it up this way: "Probably the one thing, more than anything else, that makes folklore interesting is the fact that people will change a story to suit their taste, but they will not change the basic core of the story. If it were not for the fact that people do change the stories, folklore would be as dry and dusty as the historical data one gets from the County Court House."

To this student and to all the others at Campbellsville College who assisted in this project, I am indeed grateful. A word of thanks is also due Dotty Smallwood, Paula Speer Reynolds, Peggy Bradley Boaz, and Brenda Morris, my student secretaries at Western Kentucky University, who helped to annotate the tales. Beverly Slezak, who typed the initial manuscript, and Brenda Smallwood, successive administrative secretaries in the Center for Intercultural

Studies, deserve special thanks. Brenda Smallwood assisted me with editorial duties, in addition to typing the final manuscript. I also wish to thank Mike Morse, a graduate student in Folk Studies, for providing the photographs.

W.L.M.

Bowling Green, Kentucky

CONTENTS

ILLUSTRATIONS

Following page 80: A signal of a deserted dwelling; Sam Moore, storyteller of Green County; a haunted country lane in Monroe County; Montgomery mill in Green County; Marvin Moody and Clutie Bailey, gravediggers in the Sulphur Lick community; "if a rooster crows . . ."; Opal Howard, storyteller of Monroe County; Harley L. Gilmore in the Hiestand graveyard.

Following page 144: Charles Strode, Tompkinsville undertaker; the grave headstone of an early resident of the Eastern Pennyroyal; the old Strode homeplace near Tompkinsville; Mrs. Margaret Edith Tucker, storyteller, at the Hiestand house in Taylor County; a deserted cabin in Russell County; Croy Fish, Monroe County storyteller, and Lynwood Montell; a specter-haunted house in the Mt. Gilead community; a ghostly setting in the Eastern Pennyroyal.

*Ghosts
along the
Cumberland*

PROLOGUE

The Kentucky Foothills, Where Folk Belief Abounds

It was a still summer night in July during the dark of the moon when strange things are assumed likely to be seen or heard. We sat under the castor bean tree with its overhanging branches arching downward almost to the ground. Behind us and a few feet away stood the oldest log cabin in Metcalfe County, built during the 1780s. The stick and clay chimney was crumbling in decay, and the framed addition tacked onto the end of the ancient structure opposite the chimney was in need of repair. Through a small window in the log cabin, we could see the dull glow given off by a kerosene lamp which kept vigil over a very sick member of the owner's household. The background was perfect for a discussion of ghosts.

"How do you account for the appearance of so many ghosts in the Subtle Community?" I asked the host, a poor though articulate farmer nearing his fiftieth birthday, who claimed to have seen a ghost in the community only a few days prior. The farmer answered:

> Old folks say that ghosts have been here all along, but it was the War between the Democrats and Republicans over the Niggers that made it so bad. You see, back during those days brother fought against brother, and father and son were sometimes on different sides. And worst of all was the robbing and killing that took place through here by the people that wudn't on neither side.
>
> All of this was displeasing to God, and he got fed up with the people. So in order to punish them, God sent all these ghosts and haints and things into this community. You know, the Bible says that God will visit his wrath upon the third and fourth generations. But now, they don't bother me! When I hear something or see something, I just go on about my business.

Although the informant uttered those words in 1965, his style of living, virtually unaffected by modern technological advances, was reminiscent of that of the folk of at least a century earlier.

Men and women of the middle generation, such as this farmer, and those of the older generation have related most of the beliefs, tales, and practices offered in this book. There is a reason for this. Before the days of the Second World War, these beliefs and customs were prevalent throughout the Eastern Pennyroyal of south-central Kentucky. In the mid-1940s, however, technology became such a factor in the lives of these simple and unrefined rural people that the vestiges of the past became neglected, especially among the newer, oncoming generation.

The change wrought by that technological factor is apparent everywhere today, thirty years later. The children of the great depression years, the middle generation of this study, have bridged the gap between the old and the new—the antiquated and the modern. Many of them grew up with kerosene lamps, wooden milking stools, and springhouses. They knew the meaning of dirt roads and brief periods of hunger. They vowed that their offspring would know a better way of life, would be spared such deprivation, and indeed most of the offspring were. The children of the newer generation know little except modern affluence based on electrical switches that control virtually every phase of life.

Although technological advances accompanied by a relative prosperity did come to this land of abundant natural beauty, it is still possible to find people in the hillcountry who cling to beliefs in omens of death and attendant manifestations of non-malevolent supernatural creatures. It is not at all uncommon to hear utterances claiming that the dead may return to visit the scenes known by them during their lifetime on earth. Even those people who were children as late as the lean years of the 1930s, and who have since been educated at the university, recall with a fondness verging on nostalgia what it was like to sit around the fireplace on long winter evenings and listen to parents and grandparents engage in tale-swapping sessions. Many of them, adults and children alike, believed in the ghosts and haints mentioned in these stories, and the existence of family legends describing real occurrences about personal acquaintances served to reinforce such belief. These sessions might recount, for example, the time that Granny saw the

THE EASTERN PENNYROYAL
IN KENTUCKY

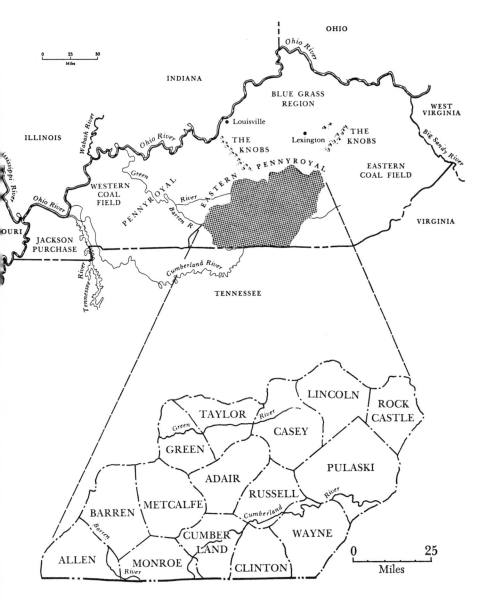

ghost of Uncle Andrew, or when Grandpa passed by the hallowed spot where the old homeplace stood and heard the cries of Little Jimmy, who had perished inside the burning structure, or when the appearance of a ghostly woman in the front yard signified the death of Mama's brother in the prime of his life.

The folk of the Kentucky foothills fear death and the mysteries surrounding the life beyond this one. They are devoutly Christian and interpret the Scriptures literally. They listen on Sunday to the preacher articulate the merits of living by faith, but on Monday they revert to certain folk beliefs and practices which have been transmitted across the centuries by word-of-mouth. Some beliefs, even, are related to paganistic times but nonetheless function to a high degree of relevancy in the lives of the occupants of this region.

Since folk beliefs and practices are so viable in the folk culture of the Eastern Pennyroyal, it is not without merit to compare these people with the Christians of the Middle Ages, who accepted the teachings of the Church on one hand but clung tenaciously to the orally transmitted beliefs in witchcraft and sorcery on the other. Christianity today teaches that the soul has returned to its Maker, and the body, now deserted by the soul, should be laid away in reverence. Pre-Christian ideas were very different. According to these, the dead continued an existence very similar to that which they enjoyed on earth (Kevin Danaher, *In Ireland Long Ago* [Hatboro, Pa., 1967], 170). Although the people of the Kentucky foothills are not oriented so strongly on this point, there is an indication that many believe that the dead remain close at hand and continue to interest themselves in the affairs of the living, either helpfully or harmfully, and sometimes appear as a sort of God-sent messenger to get an errant one to "live right." Consider the testimony of an unidentified Wayne Countian during the mid-1930s: "I always kept a horseshoe over my door to keep the evil spirits away. We live very close to the graveyard. And my boy, Ed, said he had been seeing his brother, Charlie, in his room every night. If he was livin' right he would not be seein' Charlie ever night. Charlie never bothers me! He was my boy that died and is buried in this graveyard above our house" (collected by Gertrude Vogler as a part of the Federal Writers' Project during the Roosevelt

Administration. Used by permission of the Library of Congress, Rare Books Division).

To point out the inconsistency between religious beliefs and folk practices is not an indictment in any sense of the word. The simple fact is that the people of the Kentucky foothills do not question time-honored Biblical passages, nor do they question the wise counsel inherited from their elders. Such is the way of life with these people.

The population of these counties is predominately white and, among those affiliated with churches, Protestant. In the 1970 census, whites numbered 121,057 as compared with 7,231 (6 percent) blacks. There were a few Indians, Filipinos, Japanese, and Chinese also reported living in the area, but their number was extremely small.

According to the 1973 religious census, conducted by the Glenmary Research Center, 56 percent of the 1970 population of the Eastern Pennyroyal belonged to some organized Christian denomination. The Glenmary census revealed the following data by denominations: 0.12 percent of all church members were Brethren of Christ, 1.94 percent Catholic, 2.17 percent Christian Church (Disciples), 6.75 percent Christian Churches and Churches of Christ, 1.99 percent Church of God (Anderson), 0.71 percent Church of God (Cleveland), 3.11 percent Church of the Nazarene, 0.15 percent Episcopal, 0.02 percent Free Methodist, 0.11 percent Lutheran, 0.03 percent Lutheran Church-Missouri Synod, 2.42 percent Presbyterian (Cumberland), 0.72 percent Presbyterian Church in the U.S., 0.13 percent Seventh-Day Adventists, 66.46 percent Southern Baptist, 17.10 percent United Methodist, and 0.71 percent United Presbyterian. Those groups missing from the census (and thus not included in the total 56 percent of the population belonging to some organized group) include the United Baptist, General Baptist, Regular Baptist, Missionary Baptist, Holiness, Jesus Only, Negro Baptist (National and Progressive National Conventions), African Methodist Episcopal, and colored Methodist Episcopal, among others. The Protestant denominations are generally scriptural literalists, and most of them are avidly evangelical. The denominations listed in the second category are especially subject

to outbursts of emotion during religious services. They pride themselves in being practitioners of the old ways of worship and con-
ducting church business.

Caucasians living in the region are descended from various im-
migrant strains, most of their family lines tracing back to English,
Scotch-Irish, Scottish Highlander, German, or French Huguenot
ancestors. These early settlers generally came to the Eastern Pennyroyal by way of Virginia, Maryland, Pennsylvania, North Carolina,
South Carolina, and Georgia, although a few of them actually im-
migrated directly from western Europe. The English and Scotch-
Irish peoples form a solid majority, and scholars argue constantly
over the question of which group most greatly influenced the
region's cultural inheritance.

Through generations of rugged living under frontier-like conditions, these people learned to depend on each other for succor, and
family ties become especially strong. When a son or daughter got
married, it was usually to a person in the same portion of the
county—oftentimes even a distant relative. It was common for a
new couple to move in with one of the parents for a few years, or
build a cabin or small house—sometimes called a weaning house—
on the ancestral homestead. The couple never went far from home;
thus, ties with parents and brothers and sisters became progres-
sively stronger as time passed. Most of those more mobile members
of the present generation who go north of the Ohio River to find
employment in industrial cities manage to return "home" several
times a year, often every weekend. When a transplanted native
dies on distant soil in Ohio, Indiana, or Illinois, the body is brought
home to the hills to return to dust in the land of its ancestors. Just
recently, a native Monroe Countian, who had remained in California since his migration during the Bakersfield oil boom of the
1920s, was returned in death to be buried with his people.

Close family and community ties are reflected in every phase
of life, especially during the traumatic experiences felt at the time
of sickness, death, and burial. When tragedy strikes, these people
are ready to render aid, compassion, and kindness to their bereaved
neighbors. At night they sit up with the sick when death is lurking
in the shadows, and they tend to the chores and crops of the stricken

family during daylight hours. It is not at all uncommon even today for neighbors to plant the corn for the sick members of the community or harvest an entire hay crop when rain is threatening. When death occurs, neighbors no longer dress the corpse as they did in the recent past, but they do watch over the body and make the preparations for burial, even to digging the grave.

This book attempts to present the whole spectrum of beliefs, customs, and practices associated with the dead and the dying in the Kentucky foothills. Part I of the work concerns the portents which signify the impending death of a family member or a close acquaintance. These messengers of death may be recognized instantly, or they may be identified only in retrospect. A surprising number of signs have become standardized, however, to the point that they have crossed cultural and time boundaries and are recognized without hesitation when they occur. Such an example of an almost universal death omen is the bird which flies through an open window into the room of a sick person.

Part II of this volume takes up traditional beliefs and activities revolving around the trauma of death and the presence of the corpse for several hours following the demise. Nothing in the Kentucky foothills draws people as close together as a death in the community. Virtually everyone is a willing contributor to the needs of the bereaved family. Perhaps respect for the dead in general explains many of the attitudes and actions surrounding the rites of passage.

The final part of this book deals with the ultimate return of the dead in the form of ghosts. It is perhaps not strange that ghostlore should be abundantly available in the Kentucky foothills. Every activity associated with the final rites of passage seems almost to begrudge the moment when the coffin is at last placed in the open grave. It is as though folk logic demands and expects the return of the deceased, although the person may take a form which cannot be even remotely comprehended.

Other folklorists have concerned themselves with collections of death and burial lore, and with bodies of ghost narratives. Sociologists and psychologists have studied the phenomenon of death, and they have looked upon the funeral as a contemporary institution. Psychologists especially have demonstrated interest in reported instances of apparitions and other supernatural phenomena. The present work is the first to my knowledge which brings together the lore of death, burial, and ghosts in one volume. Significant also is the fact that these memorials of belief come from a fairly small area of southcentral Kentucky where the folk culture is essentially homogeneous and where traditions are stubbornly resistant. This is the Kentucky foothills, an area where traditions abound.

PART I

Omens
of Death

INTRODUCTION TO *Omens of Death*

People have believed in death warnings since the dawn of recorded history. Certain motifs still in oral circulation have been transmitted across the centuries, and literary figures, such as Chaucer and Shakespeare, have plucked death beliefs from oral tradition and recounted them in their writings. Certainly there is no paucity of recorded instances when strange occurrences were popularly interpreted as death portents, whether the focus was Ireland, England, the rest of northwestern Europe, the forbidding Orient, or the upland areas of the American South.

The people of the Kentucky foothills have been tied closely to the soil from the earliest days of settlement during the 1780s to the present time. Some of them are no longer farmers, but their memories and traditions are rooted as deeply in the land as the massive oak trees that stand as sentinels on virtually every hillside. Although many of the present generation do not really believe in the death warnings which signaled the passing of their ancestors, they do relate these occurrences as factual, for such came down to them as truth through family traditions. A few of the present occupants of the Eastern Pennyroyal still accept and cling rather tenaciously to older beliefs related to the passing of a relative or friend. Such people reflect the culture of their ancestors a century ago. In those earlier days the people of this area looked for and discovered a sign which could be interpreted as a "death token," to use the term still commonly employed in the Kentucky foothills. And apparently if a token (or omen) was not recognized in advance of death, it could be discerned in retrospect as members of the family or community searched their recollections for strange events which transpired just prior to the death. (For similar thoughts regarding ancient Icelandic traditions, consult Knut Liestøl, *The Origin of the Icelandic Family Sagas* [Oslo, 1931], 230.)

In this part of Kentucky death tokens are generally natural, casual happenings over which the human individual has no control. If, for example, one sees a cloud shaped like a coffin or if a cow bawls at night, then a death will occur. In such instances, man is powerless to change the situation and therefore submits helplessly to the decrees of the natural environment. The rather large class of prophetic signs includes physical ailments—especially during infancy and childhood—dreams, weather, common items of household furniture, domestic chores, plants, animals, and insects. Virtually all beliefs in these categories are brief and to the point, and their formula is simple: if something beyond one's control behaves in a certain manner, then death will occur. Seldom are these items documented by a belief tale to validate the incident.

Death token narratives comprise the other segment of death warnings. These belief tales, actually *memorats* because they are often firsthand experiences, contain accounts of the appearances of revenants—sometimes spectral and sometimes actual creatures—and they differ from ghost tales only in that they terminate when the narrator comments that someone died soon after, if not during, the appearance of the revenant. There are also death token stories which relate the occurrence of death to the appearance of spectral coffins, strange lights, unexplainable incidents, and ghostly cries and noises. Impending death is strangely expressed in a significantly large body of narratives which have to do with spectral persons who make an unexplained appearance (sometimes it is in the form of a revenant) just before or during their own death. The Scottish people refer to the spectral appearance of one who is about to die as a wraith, and I have borrowed the use of that term for inclusion in this book. I hasten to add that its use herein is purely for the sake of convenience, for the folk of this portion of the United States do not know the term. An additional contrast exists in the nature of the wraith's visit. In Scotland (John Brand, *Observations on Popular Antiquities* [London, 1849], 709) and other cultures of northwestern Europe, the wraith of a living person does not always indicate that he shall die soon; but death is imminent in all but one of the examples gathered from the Kentucky hillcountry.

The death belief items on the succeeding pages are collated with

The Frank C. Brown Collection of North Carolina Folklore, ed. Newman Ivey White (Durham, N. C., 1952), volumes VI and VII, when parallel accounts were found. Most of the Kentucky items in this collection do not occur in the Brown listing, however, thus perhaps indicating a prolific tradition which blossomed on the Kentucky frontier and lived on in the folk mind well past the mid-mark of the twentieth century. The ease with which the beliefs and practices can be gathered causes one to wonder whether they will ever dissipate completely.

DEATH BELIEFS

BELIEFS INVOLVING BABIES

Birthmarks

Don't ever look at anyone that's dead if you are pregnant. If you do, your baby will die; or wherever you touch yourself, it will mark the baby with a birthmark [cause a birthmark on the baby at the same place].

> *Taylor County, 1968 (BW). Informant: female, born 1903 in Taylor County.* Previously unreported, this belief is nevertheless similar to Brown 98—great fright to the pregnant woman will cause the child to be marked—which is known especially in Germany and the eastern United States.

Ailments and Remedies

If a baby doesn't get colic before it is a year old, it will die.

> *Cumberland County, 1965 (RH and SHen). Informant: female, born 1947 in Cumberland County.* Previously unreported.

You should give a newborn babe catnip herb tea to break out the hives inside the mouth. If you don't do this, the baby will die.

> *Russell County, 1968 (LP). Informant: female, born 1927 in Russell County.* Cures for hives in infants are very scarce. Brown items 312–15 reflect traditions gathered only from the American South—in North Carolina, South Carolina, and Tennessee. It is not surprising, then, that only one belief about hives in infants turned up in Kentucky's Eastern Pennyroyal. Interestingly enough, this one strikes a death note.

Care of Child

Don't cut a baby's hair until he's a year old, or he'll die.

> *Clinton County, 1963 (SW). Informant: female, born 1917 in Clin-*

ton County. Brown items 4881 and 4882 caution not to cut a baby's hair before it is eight months old (or one year old). This uncommon belief is reported only from the American South, with a possible analogy recorded in German tradition. A southern United States distribution is reinforced by two additional reports from Jefferson and Clark counties.

5   If you change the sheets or pillowcases before a certain time when the baby is born, the baby will die.

   Taylor County, 1966 (Dsh). Informant: female, born 1917 in Taylor County. Previously unreported.

Miscellaneous

6   If a child under one year old sees a dead person, it [the child] will also die.

   Cumberland County, 1965 (RH and SHen). Informant: female, born 1947 in Cumberland County. Previously unreported.

7   Never let a baby look in a mirror before it is a year old, or it will die.

   Lincoln County, 1964 (JWi). Informant: female, born 1919 in Lincoln County. Collected also from Metcalfe County (1965) and Casey County (1968), this odd belief has a rather wide distribution, having been reported from Illinois, the Ozarks, Ontario, Nova Scotia, Germany, and Spanish New Mexico. My own archives include reports from Dayton, Ohio; Charlestown, Ind.; Soddy, Tenn.; and Mercer and Clark counties, Ky., in addition to the three reports from the Kentucky foothills.

8   An exceptionally brilliant child may die before reaching adulthood.

   Taylor County, 1968 (LM). Informant: male, born 1931 in Monroe County.

9   A baby that talks before it walks will die.

   Taylor County, 1968 (LM). Informant: male, born 1931 in Monroe County.

10   If you think too much of a child it will die.

   Lincoln County, 1964 (JWi). Informant: male, born 1902 in Lincoln County. Previously unreported, this belief was collected also from Monroe County in 1950 and recently from Mercer County.

DREAMS AS DEATH WARNINGS

11   If you dream you are falling and you hit the bottom, you will die.

   Taylor County, 1965 (CC). Informant: female, born 1925 in Taylor

County. Brown 3754 notes that it is bad luck to dream of falling, but no mention has been found of the present dream belief that death comes to the falling person who hits the bottom or ground. This latter form is known also in Larue, Crittenden, Bath, and Muhlenberg counties, Ky., and in Cincinnati, Ohio. From my own childhood in Monroe County comes the memory of a community-wide belief which held that a person would die if he dreamed of falling and did not awaken on impact.

If you dream you lose one of your lower teeth, someone in the family younger than you will die.

Taylor County, 1968 (BW). Informant: female, born 1943 in Taylor County. Although Brown 4945–51 includes beliefs about what would happen should a tooth be lost, no belief therein contains the same formula and condition nor is more explicit than the present form.

If you dream of losing an upper tooth, one of your parents will die soon.

Taylor County, 1968 (BW). Informant: female, born 1943 in Taylor County. Previously unreported in this particular form.

If you dream of anything white, there is going to be a death in the near future.

Lincoln County, 1964 (BJ). Informant: female, born 1907 in Lincoln County. This belief has been reported from Norway, but its primary distribution appears to be in the United States—mainly in Florida, North Carolina, Texas, and California. See Brown 4954.

When you dream of death, it is a sign there will be marriage.

Taylor County, 1968 (RMi). Informant: male, born 1947 in Taylor County. This common folk belief enjoys a distribution almost entirely within the United States, especially in the Southeastern states. See Brown 4979. My own archives record it three times from the Kentucky foothills; also once each from Marion, Wolfe, and Breckenridge counties, Ky., and from Hamilton, Ohio.

To dream of a death is a sign of a birth.

Taylor County, 1967 (KRP). Informant: male, born 1919 in Logan County. Brown 238 is an uncommon belief, known primarily in the Upper South, Midwest, and in California.

When you dream of a marriage [variant: wedding], it is a sign of death.

Taylor County, 1968 (RMi). Informant: male, born 1947 in Taylor

County. Brown 4981. This very popular belief most likely had roots in
England before spreading to the United States, where it is remembered in several states. It was reported a second time in Taylor County
in 1968 and then twice in 1967, and once each in Adair County (1964)
and Russell County (1968). Reports were also gathered once each from
Fleming, Jefferson, Breckenridge, Hardin, and Breathitt counties and
three times from Wolfe County.

18   If you dream of a marriage there will be a death in the family.

*Russell County, 1964 (HD). Informant: male, born 1939 in Russell
County.* Brown 4982. This belief has been reported twelve times from
American tradition, including once from the Spanish-speaking Southwest. Reports also came from Green County (1964), Lincoln County
(1964), and Taylor County (1966). My own collection contains reports
from Bullitt, Logan, and Jefferson counties, Ky.; Johnson City,
Tenn.; and Dayton, Ohio.

19   If you dream of birth, it is a sign of death.

*Russell County, 1964 (RLa). Informant: male, born 1944 in Russell
County.* Brown 5138. This belief was previously collected from North
Carolina, Alabama, Indiana, Illinois, Nebraska, California, and the
Ozarks.

20   If you dream of a birth, there will be a death in the family.

*Russell County, 1964 (HD). Informant: male, born 1939 in Russell
County.* This belief is similar to item No. 19, except that it specifically
states that the person who is to die will be a member of the family.

21   If you dream of a storm, you will have a relative to die.

*Lincoln County, 1964 (JWi). Informant: female, born 1902 in Lin-
coln County.* Brown 6937 states that it is bad luck to dream of a storm.
In its present form this belief was also reported from Washington
County.

22   If you see in a dream someone who is already dead, you are near
death yourself.

*Taylor County, 1968 (RMi). Informant: male, born 1944 in Taylor
County.* To dream of the dead invokes various ill tidings. Brown 6415
states: "If you dream of the dead, there will be falling weather."
Brown 6169 claims that "To dream of the dead is a sign of bad weather," and Brown 5019, perhaps the most comparable to the present
form, notes that "To dream of seeing a coffin and seeing someone in
it is a sign of death." All forms appear to be peculiarly American.

BELIEFS ASSOCIATED WITH THE ADULT HUMAN BODY

Ears

My right ear rings real loud for awhile, then stops suddenly. Someone I know dies after this occurs.

> *Taylor County, 1966 (LB and DSk). Informant: female, born 1886
> in Taylor County.* This particular belief is related most closely to
> Brown 4910, an item which enjoys a widespread circulation through-
> out the eastern United States and into the Maritime Provinces of
> Canada. It was reported a total of four times from Taylor County in
> 1966 ("This is the sound of death," claimed an informant), once from
> an Adair County resident in 1963 ("This is called the death bell"),
> and once from a resident of Metcalfe County in 1968 ("These are
> death bells"). It was also reported from Clinton County, 1963, and
> from Russell County, 1964. My files contain reports also from Ballard
> and Kenton counties, Ky., and from Charlestown, Ind.

If a death bell rings in your ear, you will hear of a death in three
days.

> *Taylor County, 1966 (LB and DSk). Informant: female, born 1886
> in Taylor County.* Previously unreported. This form explicitly states
> the exact number of days before death occurs. Brown 4912 claims
> that the death will occur within one week.

When bells ring in your ears at night, a close friend will die.

> *Taylor County, 1966 (GN). Informant: male, born 1939 in Taylor
> County.* This form of the belief is very closely related to Brown 4910,
> in which one of the parallel references cited from New York notes that
> the death bells may be heard at night.

It is a sign of a family death if the death bell rings faintly in your
ear, then becomes real loud.

> *Taylor County, 1963 (LB and DSk). Informant: female, born 1903
> in Taylor County.* The faint sound of death bells suddenly becoming
> louder is similar to Brown 4912, which distinguishes between "ring-
> ing" noises and "a little tinkling sound." This belief was also reported
> from Taylor County in 1966.

A ringing in the ear is a sign of death, and the direction of the death
is determined by whichever ear rings.

> *Adair County, 1964 (PRA). Informant: female, born 1883 in Adair
> County.* Brown 4914. Reports previously came from North Carolina
> and Kentucky.

Sneezing

28   If the oldest one at the table sneezes during breakfast on Sunday morning, you will hear of a death before the week is over.

    Taylor County, 1966 (LB and DSk). Informant: female, born 1906 in Taylor County. This belief is somewhat parallel to Brown items 4930–32, which claim that death will occur in twenty-four hours, before the next Saturday, and before the week has passed. Although the evidence is slim, there appears to be a pattern of distribution from New England to the Middle West.

29   How ever many times you sneeze before breakfast on Sunday, you will hear of that many deaths that week.

    Clinton County, 1963 (SW). Informant: female, born 1917 in Clinton County. There is no exact recorded parallel to this belief, but it is basically similar to Brown 4924–32.

30   If the youngest child sneezes at the table, there'll be a death in the family.

    Taylor County, 1966 (GN). Informant: female, born 1925 in Taylor County. Brown 4938. This belief was reported previously only from North Carolina, Tennessee, and Alabama.

Hair

31   If you get your hair cut during the month of March, you will die before the year is out.

    Casey County, 1965 (DLM). Informant: male, age unknown, born in Casey County. Brown 4943. This was reported only in North Carolina and Tennessee tradition. I have additional reports from Washington and Mercer counties, Ky.

Sleep

32   If you sleep in the moonlight, you'll die.

    Taylor County, 1966 (DSh). Informant: female, born 1889 in Taylor County. This belief may be motivated by the folk belief that the night air is harmful to one's health.

33   If you lie with your head out the door, you will die within the year.

    Barren County, 1967 (RBB). Informant: female, born 1905 in Barren County.

34   If you step over somebody who is lying on the floor, you have to step back across them before they get up, or they will die.

Russell County, 1964 (HD). Informant: male, born 1939 in Russell County. Brown 5027. This form is found mainly in the Southern states, with one occurrence reported from Illinois. The belief was also reported from Taylor County in 1964 and 1966.

If you sing after you go to bed, there will be a death in your family.

Taylor County 1965 (CC). Informant: male, born 1913 in Taylor County. Previously unreported.

Shingles

If shingles go all around the body, the person having them will die.

Metcalfe County, 1965 (JA). Informant: male, born 1904 in Metcalfe County. Brown 4987. This is a fairly common belief throughout the South. Although my files contain only one entry of this belief, I personally have heard it uttered many times in Monroe, Taylor, and Warren counties.

Shivers or Chills

Shivers indicate that someone is walking over the spot that will be your grave.

Metcalfe County, 1968 (WLB). Informant: female, born 1928 in Metcalfe County. This belief is basically similar to Brown 4921, which has a pattern of distribution almost exclusively outside the southern region of the United States. My own files contain additional reports from Bullitt County, Ky., and Johnson City, Tenn.

When a cold chill runs up your back, someone has stepped on your burying ground.

Adair County, 1965 (GM). Informant: male, born 1941 in Adair County. Brown 4921. This same form is found in my files from Nelson and Jefferson counties, Ky., and Cincinnati, Ohio. A report also came from Monroe County in 1968.

Death Rattles

Death rattles are something that people take from twelve to twenty-four hours before they die. It is just a little rattle in their throat.

Clinton County, 1963 (SW). Informant: female, born 1917 in Clinton County. Previously unreported from the United States. It is known in England, however, especially in the northern regions. See Brand, *Popular Antiquities*, 708.

BELIEFS ASSOCIATED WITH THE HOUSE

40   If a salesman ever leaves his hat on a bed, he will die.
      Taylor County, 1966 (GN). Informant: male, born 1948 in Taylor County. Previously unreported. Perhaps this belief from the Eastern Pennyroyal may be associated with the spate of traveling salesman stories, both jokes and legends, which are so common in the Kentucky foothills. However, the belief that a hat on the bed means death has been reported from Tulsa, Okla.

41   If you sweep under anybody's bed when they're sick, they will die.
      Adair County, 1965 (CB). Informant: female, born 1880 in Adair County. Brown 4994. This uncommon item is narrowly confined to North Carolina, Tennessee, and Kentucky.

42   If a clock gongs without reason, it is a sign of death.
      Taylor County, 1966 (GN). Informant: male, born 1946 in Johnson City, Tenn. Brown 5056. This belief is widely known in Europe and North America.

43   The clock strikes when a member of the household dies.

      (a.) "There was this old Vaughn home that had at one time been an old bank—an old stone building here in Greensburg. And all the furnishings in that house were just like they had been years and years ago through two or three generations of Vaughns. And the parlor, they called it, was never opened, or the downstairs part, until some member of the Vaughn family died. And then they would have it opened and have the corpse in those rooms. And the old grandfather clock stood in the hall. And the story goes that every time one of the old Vaughns would die, this clock would strike.

      "When I was a little girl, oh, maybe a period of ten years, some of the older Vaughns died in that length of time. And it was told to me that the clock would strike when they would die."

      (b.) "There was an old man who owned a clock, and every time this clock struck, someone would die. The old clock did not run. It did strike, though, and had been striking for forty years. Robert Goodin down in Clinton County in Kentucky said the owner of this clock had come to him and told him that the clock had been striking. The man soon died."

      (a.) Green County, 1964 (JCR). Informant: female, born 1883 in Green County. (b.) Adair County, 1964 (PRA). Informant: male, born

1942 in Adair County. Previously unreported. The two versions of this belief from the Eastern Pennyroyal, described above, are similar to Brown 5056, which refers to a clock that warns of an impending death when it strikes.

To break a mirror is a sign of death.

Monroe County, 1968 (BCD). Informant: female, born 1947 in Monroe County. Brown 5065. This fairly common belief is known in England and throughout the United States, but appears to be centered north and east of the Ohio River and west of the Mississippi.

If a picture falls, someone will die.

Adair County, 1964 (PRA). Informant: female, born 1883 in Adair County. Brown 5065. This belief tends to penetrate farther into the South than item No. 44, especially with the inclusion of the sources found in my files from the Kentucky foothills and from Franklin, Jefferson, and Clark counties as well. It was also reported twice from Taylor County in 1966 and once in 1968.

If a picture falls in the house, it is a sign that someone in the family will die.

Lincoln County, 1964 (BJ). Informant: male, born 1896 in Lincoln County. Brown 5065. Note that this form explicitly states that the person who is to die is a member of the family. Reported from Taylor County (1964 and 1965), Green County (1964), and Metcalfe County (1968), my files also include reports from Boyle, Mercer, Carroll, and Hardin counties, Ky.; Murfreesboro, Tenn.; and Pittsburgh, Pa. It is listed in Samuel J. Sackett and William E. Koch, *Kansas Folklore* (Lincoln, Neb., 1961), 82.

If a picture falls face down and breaks, the person in the picture will die.

Taylor County, 1967 (MM). Informant: male, born 1888 in Taylor County. Brown 5066. This belief was recorded seven times previously from North Carolina.

When a picture falls on its face, there will be a death in the family.

Taylor County, 1966 (DSh). Informant: female, born 1889 in Taylor County. Brown 5065. I have one report of this belief from Crown Point, Ind.

If a picture fades, the person whose picture it is will die.

Adair County, 1964 (PRA). Informant: female, born 1883 in Adair County. Brown 5068. Perhaps a belief of Irish origin is the precursor of this item.

It is a sign of death to spin a chair on one leg.

Monroe County, 1968 (JCa). Informant: female, born 1946 in Wolfe County. Brown 5089. This belief is known also in Wolfe, Breckenridge, and Mercer counties.

51 If you leave a rocking chair rocking, it will cause a death in the family.

Lincoln County, 1964 (BJ). Informant: female, born 1910 in Lincoln County. Brown 5091. This item was reported once from Texas tradition. My files contain a similar belief from Jefferson County, which states that when a piece of furniture moves, its owner dies.

52 If a hoe is carried through the house, that hoe will dig your grave.

Russell County, 1968 (LP). Informant: male, born 1909 in Russell County. Brown 5395. This belief has a surprisingly narrow geographical area of acceptance. In portions of Monroe County in the 1930s, it was taboo to carry any implement into the house.

53 If you take a garden hoe through the front door, there is going to be a death in the family.

Green County, 1967 (KRP). Informant: female, born 1900 in Green County. The belief's particular form is very similar to Brown 5393 and appears to have a parallel in California tradition.

The House Itself

54 Generally, a death is forewarned by unaccountable knocking in the walls of the house.

"I lived in a house once that always had a knocking in one of the corners as if a ball were bouncing in the corner. The knocks came in 3's, and they usually came when things were quiet. We had heard that knockings were bad signs. Maybe they were warnings of something awful, perhaps death. One time a little girl became ill, and she grew no better. Once a bird lit on the child's father's shoulder while he was standing outside and then flew away toward the burying ground. When it was all over, it was realized that these were omens of death of the little girl."

Russell County, 1964 (HD). Informant: male, born 1939 in Russell County. Brown 5049 does not contain any mention of knocking noises on the walls. But that item, nonetheless, appears closely related to the present form. The story was also related in 1968 by a native of McGoffin County, who was then a resident of Taylor County.

55 A new house should not be completely finished. Some member of the family will die.

"Samuel Willis, who lives on the Lebanon Road in Taylor County, built a new house several years ago. He will not finish the house —his steps consist of concrete blocks—because his great grandfather completed a new house, and he died soon after this."

> *Taylor County, 1964 (PRA). Informant: male, born 1911 in Taylor County.* Brown 5036. This belief is known in Western Europe, Ontario, and the eastern United States.

When you build a new house, you will either gain or lose a member in your family.

> *Taylor County, 1968 (RMi). Informant: male, born 1947 in Taylor County.* This item is basically akin to Brown 5036.

If a door is cut in the house after it has been built, there will be a death in the family within a year.

> *Metcalfe County, 1965 (JA). Informant: female, born 1912 in Metcalfe County.* Brown 5043. Known primarily in the southern states and Indiana and Illinois, this belief was also reported from Taylor County (1964 and 1968). My own files contain an additional report from Jasonville, Ind.

It is the cause of death for a door to open without an apparent cause.

(a.) "This child's daddy was a drunkard, and he would beat his child. The child got sick. The people would sit up with it. In the night the door would open, and a crumpled piece of paper would blow to the bed where the child lay. It did this for three nights, then the baby died. The child was about one and a half years old. It was an unusually pretty and smart child. I don't remember if it was a boy or girl. Never told if anybody picked up the paper or not."

(b.) "There was a woman who lived near us—Dad told me before he died—who tried to nail up a door in her attic. But everytime she did and went back to check later, it was unnailed and open. She kept nailing it back for two weeks until her baby died, and then the door stayed nailed shut."

(c.) "This is a true story about my classmate and friend. He was a young man with some money and perhaps not quite fair with one of his tenants. You see, he lived on a large farm and also had tenant houses on it. He didn't believe in omens at all. As a portent of evil, one of his doors would not stay closed. No matter what he did—

lock it, bolt it, or whatever—it would open in the night with a creaking sound. This went on for a number of years. The man paid no attention to it at all, however.

"The last time the door opened, it was very quickly; and it slammed back against the wall with a loud crashing noise. On that very day, the omen was fulfilled, because the landowner, having mistreated his tenants, was shot stone dead."

> *(a.) Monroe County, 1969 (RLy). Informant: female, born 1920 in Monroe County. (b.) Taylor County, 1966 (JPi). Informant: male, born 1947 in Taylor County. (c.) Taylor County, 1969 (BS). Informant: male, born 1918 in Taylor County.* Brown 5046. Belief No. 58 appears to stem from European tradition.

59 A cracked window pane means death to someone.

> *Taylor County, 1966 (GN). Informant: female, born 1946 in Taylor County.* Previously unreported.

60 When somebody was real bad and was going to die, some kind of noise would occur in the house.

> *Taylor County, 1964 (LS). Informant: male, born 1876 in Taylor County.* Previously unreported. This superstition seems related to Brown 5048 and 5049.

61 If you hear something in the wall that sounds like the ticking of a clock, it's a sign that someone's going to die.

> *Taylor County, 1966 (GN). Informant: female, born 1911 in Taylor County.* This belief is covered in the rather amorphous listing given under Brown 5049. My files contain a report from Breckenridge County.

62 If you sit with your face to the window, you are facing your coffin.

> *Clinton County 1966 (GN). Informant: female, born 1927 in Clinton County.* Previously unreported.

BELIEFS RELATING TO THE PHYSICAL WORLD

Clouds

63 If you see a cloud shaped like a coffin, it's a sign someone will die.

> *Clinton County, 1966 (GN). Informant: female, born 1927 in Clinton County.* Previously unreported.

Stars

If you see a falling star, you will hear of a death.

> *Metcalfe County, 1968 (WLB). Informant: female, born 1913 in Bullitt County.* Brown 5143 notes that a falling star signified the death of one member of the family who lives in that direction. Brown 8555 claims that when a star falls, it means that someone is dying. None of my reports is identical to these. This belief has also been gathered from Taylor County (twice in 1966 and once in 1968), Adair County (1963 and 1964), and from Muhlenberg and Breathitt counties.

Water

To dream of muddy water is a sign of death.

> *Taylor County, 1966 (DDay). Informant: male, born 1941 in Taylor County.* This is another report of Brown 5175, a very common death belief in Europe and America. My files indicate that it is also known in Clark, Shelby, Jefferson, and Bath counties, Ky., and in Jasonville, Ind.

It is bad luck to dream of muddy water, for someone in the family will be sick or will die.

> *Metcalfe County, 1965 (JA). Informant: male, born 1914 in Metcalfe County.* Item No. 70 is a more articulate version of Brown 5175. My files contain a report from Clay County and from Taylor County (1965).

ACTIVITIES INVOLVING SPECIAL DAYS

Christmas

A green Christmas indicates the graveyard is going to be filled.

> *Lincoln County, 1965 (DP). Informant: female, born 1929 in Lincoln County.* The notion that a green Christmas means many deaths the following year (Brown 5152) is one of the most widespread of all beliefs, extending from Western Europe across the ocean waters into Canada and the United States. Although I have only one report from the Kentucky foothills, my files do include items from Logan, Mercer, and Washington counties, Ky.; Evansville, Ind.; and Hartford, Conn.

A white Christmas indicates there are not going to be many deaths.

Lincoln County, 1965 (DP). Informant: female, born 1929 in Lincoln County. This interesting item states the same philosophy contained in item No. 65, but is much less frequent in this form, occurring primarily in the southern part of the United States. A variant of this entry, "A snowy Christmas means a lean graveyard," was reported from Hartford, Conn.

69   A light Christmas stands for a good crop year and a fat graveyard.

Taylor County, 1966 (GN). Informant: female, born 1911 in Taylor County. Previously unreported. My files also include one report from adjacent Larue County.

70   If you work on Christmas, one will go out of the family in a year.

Clinton County, 1963 (SW). Informant: female, born 1917 in Clinton County. Previously unreported, but it is probably related to Brown 5098, which predicts death as the fate of the person who takes out ashes on Christmas Day.

71   If you carry ashes out of the house between Christmas and New Year's, there will be a death in the family.

Taylor County, 1964 (LS). Informant: male, born 1936 in Taylor County. This belief is closely related to Brown 5100, which is more explicit in that it predicts death before the next Christmas. In either case, this death belief is rare. Brown 5100 is known only in North Carolina, and my item was reported by one person only.

New Year's

72   A white New Year's means a fat graveyard. A lot of people will die.

Clinton County, 1966 (SW). Informant: female, born 1917 in Clinton County. Previously unreported.

73   If you sweep your floors on the first day of the year, you will sweep away one of your family.

Adair County, 1965 (CC). Informant: female, born 1937 in Adair County. Previously unreported. My files contain reports from Webster and Hardin counties.

74   If you sew on New Year's Day, you'll sew for a corpse before the year is out.

Taylor County, 1966 (GN). Informant: male, born 1940 in Taylor County. This belief is very similar to Brown 5118, which substitutes washing for sewing. I have one report of this belief from Hardin County.

Good Friday

If you wash on Good Friday, there will be a death in the family within a year.

> *Taylor County, 1968 (RMi). Informant: female, born 1900 in Taylor County.* Item No. 75 is very similar to Brown 5112, which notes that the person will wash "dead folks' clothes before the year is gone."

Friday

If you wash on the last Friday of the year, someone in the family will die the following year.

> *Taylor County, 1964 (BA and JWa). Informant: female, born 1888 in Taylor County.* Although the wording is not exactly the same as Brown 5115, this Eastern Pennyroyal belief is probably parallel.

If you start something on Friday and don't finish it, you will die before you finish it.

> *Taylor County, 1965 (GN). Informant: female, born 1932 in Taylor County.* Similar to both Brown 5021 and Brown 5126, all three forms of this belief are rare. It was also reported from Taylor County in 1966.

Don't cut out a dress on Friday unless you finish it. If it doesn't get finished, there'll be a death.

> *Metcalfe County, 1965 (JA). Informant: male, born 1904 in Metcalfe County.* Brown 5127. This belief is widespread in the United States. My files contain an additional report from Washington County.

Saturday

If you cut out a dress on Saturday, you will die before you wear it out.

> *Taylor County, 1966 (DSh). Informant: female, born 1890 in Taylor County.* Brown 5128 specifies "garment" instead of "dress"; otherwise the belief forms are identical.

BELIEFS RELATING TO PLANTS AND TREES

Flowers

If you have a rosebush that blooms twice a year, the second time is a sign of bad luck in your family or someone close to you. This is

true because this rosebush did bloom twice, and my uncle was
killed.

> *Lincoln County, 1963 (MP). Informant: female, born 1943 in Lin-
> coln County.* Closely related to Brown 5360—"A flower blooming
> out of season means death . . ."—this belief appears to have attained
> the most popularity in Canada's Maritime Provinces and in the
> American Midwest. A similar report in Sackett and Koch, *Kansas
> Folklore*, 82, bears this out. My own files include one report from
> Kenton County.

81   If you dream of flowers, it's a sign of death.

> *Taylor County, 1966 (BMS). Informant: black female, born 1918
> in Taylor County.* Previously unreported.

Trees

82   If a cedar tree is set near a grave, when it grows tall enough to shade
the grave another death will occur in the family.

> *Lincoln County, 1965 (DP). Informant: male, born 1910 in Lin-
> coln County.* This is the only known form which states that death
> will occur to a member of the planter's family when shade from the
> cedar tree covers the grave. It seems rather strange that the cedar
> tree should be used as a messenger of death, for many family ceme-
> teries are easy to spot from a distance because of the cedar tree or
> clump of cedars that hover as sentinels over the graves below.

83   When the shade of a cedar tree gets big enough to cover a grave, the
planter dies.

> *Lincoln County, 1964 (JWi). Informant: male, born 1924 in Lin-
> coln County.* This belief was reported from Taylor County in 1966.
> Additional items in my files come from Mercer, Shelby, Harlan, and
> Jefferson counties, Ky.; twice each from Kenton and Hardin counties,
> Ky.; and from Evansville, Ind.

84   Keep the cedar tree on your lawn trimmed so that its shadow will
not grow large enough to shade a grave or someone in the family
will die.

> *Russell County, 1967 (PC). Informant: female, born 1948 in Rus-
> sell County.*

85   If you plant a pine tree, you'll die when it gets big enough to shade
your grave.

> *Clinton County, 1963 (SW). Informant: female, born 1917 in Clin-
> ton County.* Brown 5382 states: "For each pine tree set out in the

yard in a line, a member of the family will die for each tree that lives."
The present form is known also in Hart and Bath counties and was
reported from Taylor County, 1966.

If you set a spruce or pine tree in your yard near the house, when it
reaches the top of the house, there will be a death in the family.

> *Lincoln County, 1965 (DP). Informant: male, born 1910 in Lincoln
> County.* Previously unreported.

If you plant a cedar tree and it dies, there will be a death in the
family.

> *Taylor County, 1964 (GN). Informant: male, born 1939 in Taylor
> County.* Brown 5373—"If a tree dies in the yard, a member of your
> family will die"—is similar to the present form, which explicitly states
> a cedar tree and implies that the tree must die in its early stage. This
> belief was also reported from Taylor County in 1966.

If you plant a willow tree, by the time it gets big enough to shade
your grave, you'll die.

> *Russell County, 1968 (LP). Informant: male, born 1917 in Russell
> County.* Another report of Brown 5386—"If one plants a weeping wil-
> low, he will die when the tree is large enough to shade his grave"—
> this belief is primarily a southern belief, as only one report from Illi-
> nois provides the exception. Item No. 88 was reported a total of four
> times from Russell County (1968) and once each from Clinton County
> (1966) and Taylor County (1965). My files contain two reports from
> Hardin County.

If you set out a weeping willow and it lives, you will be a weeping
widow.

> *Taylor County, 1966 (BMS). Informant: female, born 1921 in
> Larue County.* Previously unreported.

When dogwoods are mostly purple, it is a sign of a full graveyard.

> *Taylor County, 1966 (GN). Informant: female, born 1952 in Tay-
> lor County.* Previously unreported.

Most older people die when the sap is going up or down in trees.

> *Taylor County, 1965 (JS). Informant: female, age unknown, born
> in Taylor County.* Although this form is apparently unreported,
> Brown 1187 claims that people with consumption get worse when the
> sap goes down in the fall.

If a person has a lingering illness, he will last only until the leaves
fall.

> *Taylor County, 1966 (DSh). Informant: female, born 1890 in Tay-
> lor County.* This is an old belief that inspired a lyric song—"The

Leaves Mustn't Fall"—in the field of country music, but it has not been previously reported. The note to Brown 1187 does claim that a person with consumption will die "Either in the spring when the leaves appear on the tree, or in the fall when they drop from the trees."

93   If an ill person lives through the winter, he will die when the leaves begin to fall.

> *Taylor County, 1966 (DSh). Informant: male, born 1884 in Taylor County.* This is another belief about the sick which is related to Brown 1187 (see item No. 92).

BELIEFS RELATING TO ANIMALS AND BIRDS

Bats

94   If a bat gets into your house, there will be a death in the family.

> *Green County, 1964 (SM). Informant: female, born 1944 in Russell County.* Brown 5184. This commonly known belief has a wide geographical distribution. My files indicate that it is also known in Carroll and Bullitt counties.

Cats

95   If a cat is in the house with a sick person and the cat starts screaming, crying, and carrying on, it's a sign that the sick person is going to die.

> *Taylor County, 1966 (GN). Informant: male, born 1924 in Taylor County.* The cat as a portent of death is included in Brown items 5185–88, but none of them resembles the present belief.

Cows

96   If a cow bawls at night, someone in the family will die.

> *Taylor County, 1966 (GN). Informant: male, born 1942 in Pulaski County.* Brown 5194—"A cow bawling at night is a sign of death"— is related to the present form, but only the latter claims that the victim will be a member of the family. This form is also in my files from Logan County.

Dogs

97   When you hear dogs howling, it is a sign of death.

> *Taylor County, 1965 (CC). Informant: male, born 1909 in Murray*

County, Tenn. Brown 5208. This belief is widespread in Europe and America. It was reported from Taylor County twice in 1965 and once in 1966. My files include a report from Lincoln County in 1965 and additional reports from Hardin, Carroll, Breckenridge, Logan, and Kenton counties, Ky., and from Charlestown, Ind.

If a dog howls or bays at the moon, it is a sign of death.

Taylor County, 1965 (SHed). Informant: female, born 1920 in Harrison County, W. Va. Previously unreported. There are, however, at least seven death beliefs associated with howling dogs (see Brown 5208–14). Additional reports in my files come from Bullitt, Franklin (twice), Boyle counties, Ky.; and from Johnson City, Tenn.

If dogs howl when a person is seriously ill, that person will die in a few days.

Taylor County, 1966 (LB and DSk). Informant: female, born 1903 in Taylor County. Brown 5210 states that dogs will attempt to enter the room of a deathly ill person. The belief was reported only once from North Carolina.

When a dog rolls over on his back and stays still, you'll hear of a death.

Taylor County, 1966 (BMS). Informant: black female, born 1918 in Taylor County. Brown 5215 is the same belief but is more explicit because it states that three days will pass before death occurs.

"I had an old dog named Butch. He never ever come in the house. But one night before Bert died, he come to the door; and Bert said to let him in. That dog come into the house and walked over to Bert's bed. Bert patted the dog on the head; then Old Butch turned and walked out; and Minnie said something was going to happen. Sure 'nough, Bert died that night."

Adair County, 1965 (CB). Informant: female, born 1890 in Adair County. This narrative contains some of the ingredients mentioned in Brown 5210 (see item No. 99 above). The narrative implies that Bert was ill when the dog entered his room.

Frogs

Every frog you kill makes your life shorter.

Russell County, 1968 (LP). Informant: male, born 1909 in Russell County. This is a Southern black belief.

Poultry

103   A rooster crowing at midnight is a sign of death.

   Taylor County, 1966 (KRP). Informant: male, born 1919 in Logan County. Brown 5265 claims that death occurs to a loved one if a rooster is heard to crow at midnight. Although this belief does not have a popular distribution, it seems especially related to Western Europe. It was also reported from Adair County (1963), and three times from Taylor County (twice in 1966 and once in 1967).

104   If a rooster crows and its tail is towards the door, then someone is going to die in the family.

   Metcalfe County, 1968 (WLB). Informant: female, born 1922 in Metcalfe County. This superstition has been reported only twice before—from North Carolina and Maryland.

105   If a rooster crows facing the house, it is a sign of death.

   Taylor County, 1966 (LB and DSk). Informant: male, born 1945 in Taylor County. There is no exact parallel to this belief, but Brown 5270 refers to a report from the Ozarks stating that a rooster crowed "seven times in front of the door without turning around."

106   If a rooster comes up to your front steps and crows, there will be a death in the family.

   Taylor County, 1966 (GN). Informant: male, born 1939 in Taylor County. This belief is related to Brown 5270 (see item No. 105 above).

107   When a rooster goes around and crows all the time, some relative is going to die.

   Adair County, 1965 (GM). Informant: male, born 1941 in Adair County. Previously unreported.

108   If a rooster goes on the roost and crows an uneven number of times, there will be a death. If the rooster crows an even number of times, you will hear of a wedding.

   Metcalfe County, 1965 (JA). Informant: male, born 1895 in Metcalfe County. Previously unreported.

109   If a rooster crows at your door in the morning at least three times, it means bad news; in the afternoon, it is a sign of death.

   Taylor County, 1968 (BW). Informant: black female, born 1910 in Taylor County. This belief is related to almost all of the beliefs about roosters listed in Brown, but none is a close parallel.

110   "My great-grandmother had been sick for quite a while, and so one night she couldn't sleep at all. She got up and went into the kitchen and was looking out the window when she noticed the strangest

thing—the old rooster was perched on top of the fence. She watched for a few minutes and suddenly the rooster started crowing. She looked at the clock, and the time was only 3:00 A.M. Very disturbed about the whole ordeal, she related this event to the family the next morning. They seemed quite alarmed, too. Three days after this my great-grandmother died."

Taylor County, 1969 (BS). Informant: female, born 1947 in Taylor County.

"I always heard it was bad luck to hear a hen crow. So people would always kill the hen when it would crow. As soon as they'd hear a hen crow, they'd go kill it. And they said you'd have a death in the family if you didn't.

"So I had a little hen, and I thought so much of it. And it would go down to a panel of the fence—the same panel—every day for three days and fly upon that fence and crow. But I wouldn't kill it, 'cause I didn't believe in it. But it wasn't long until I had a death in the family."

Taylor County, 1966 (BH). Informant: female, born 1886 in Taylor County. Brown 5249. This belief has a wide but sporadic listing in the United States. It was reported once from Lincoln County (1965), twice from Taylor County (1966), and once from Metcalfe County (1968). My files also include a report from Clay County.

If a hen crows, it is a sign of death.

Adair County, 1964 (MDP). Informant: female, born 1877 in Russell County. Another report of Brown 5249 (see item No. 111 above), but in this form it is not explicitly stated that a member of the family will die if a hen crows. A report came from Taylor County in 1966, and my files include reports from Hardin, Larue, Bullitt, Logan, and Todd counties.

Birds

If a bird flutters against the window, it means death to someone inside.

Larue County, 1966 (GN). Informant: female, born 1946 in Taylor County. Brown 5279. This belief is known in Western Europe and the United States, especially east of the Mississippi. I also have a report from Clay County.

114   If a bird sits on the window sill and just stares at you, there will be a death.

> *Taylor County, 1966 (DSh). Informant: male, born 1938 in Taylor County.* This is probably most closely associated with Brown 5279 (see item No. 113 above), although the forms are not exactly alike.

115   If a bird gets into the house, it is a sign that someone is going to die.

(a.) "Mama told me this once, that Doc Evans—you remember Norma, well, her husband—said there was two strange birds come there and just flew around and around, and it wasn't but a few days until one of his boys took sick and died.

"And then in a while—maybe a year or two—they come back again, and in a few days, he took sick and died. At this time they took the gun out and killed one of the birds, but the other one got away. But they never come back, the birds didn't."

(b.) "A bird got into the house when little Tommy was very sick. The father saw the bird and said that little Tommy would be dead within three days. He died three days later."

> *(a.) Clinton County, 1963 (SW). Informant: female, born 1917 in Clinton County. (b.) Taylor County, 1964 (LS). Informant: male, born 1894 in Taylor County.* Perhaps the most widely held of any death belief, Brown 5280—"If any bird gets in your house, it's a sure sign of death"—is also one of the most common items in my own death belief files. This belief was reported from Green County (1963 and 1964), Taylor County (1965 and five times in 1966), and Russell County (1968). In addition, I have reports from Letcher, Shelby, Franklin, Kenton, Hardin, Bullitt, Clark, and Washington counties, Ky.; Dayton, Ohio; Soddy, Tenn.; Evansville, Ind.; and Charlestown, Ind. Those items containing the three-day period before death were from Metcalfe County (1965), Russell County (1968), and Wayne County (1964). Sackett and Koch, *Kansas Folklore*, 82, records it in this form, and my files contain additional reports from Larue, Mercer, Shelby, and Hardin counties, Ky.; from Pittsburg, Pa.; and from Murfreesboro, Tenn.

116   If a bird flies into your house, whomever it flies over will die.

> *Adair County, 1965 (CB). Informant: male, born 1916 in Adair County.* Brown 5283. This is a rarely reported belief.

117   If a bird flies over someone sick in bed, that person will die.

> *Taylor County, 1963 (KM). Informant: male, born 1942 in Taylor*

County. This appears to be another form of Brown 5283—"If a bird flies in the house and over the head of a person, it is a sign of death."

If a bird lights close to the bed of a sick person, it is a sign they will die before long.

> *Russell County, 1964 (HD). Informant: male, born 1935 in Russell County.* This is another report of Brown 5284, known in the British Isles, North Carolina, and Illinois. My files also contain a report from Mercer County.

If a dove is on the top of your house, it means a death in the family. "There was a little boy living near home who had just been terrible sick all summer. He just didn't seem to get any better or any worse. One day the boy's father and mother were out in the front of the house, and a turtle dove flew onto the roof of the house and started to coo. The man told his wife that this was a sign that their son would die. Sure enough, in three days the little boy was dead."

> *Russell County, 1964 (RLa). Informant: male, born 1945 in Russell County.* This belief is similar to Brown 5296—"White doves are regarded as vehicles of death"—which makes reference to similar occurrences. The belief was also gathered from Lincoln County (1965); the narrative which contains the belief was recorded in 1964 (by LS) from a male resident of Taylor County, born 1924.

If a dove lights on your shoulder, there will be a death in the family.

> *Taylor County, 1966 (MC). Informant: male, born 1914 in Taylor County.* Previously unreported.

If a dove flies in your back door, it's a sign of death in the family.

> *Taylor County, 1966 (GN). Informant: female, born 1920 in Taylor County.* This is another belief which fits into the rather amorphous Brown 5296 (see item No. 119 above), although the form is significantly different.

If an owl hoots around the house, someone in the house will die.

> *Lincoln County, 1964 (JWi). Informant: female, born 1902 in Lincoln County.* This belief probably belongs to the family of hoot owl beliefs identified as Brown 5305—"Someone dies every time an owl hoots." It is a widespread belief, both in Europe and in North America. In 1964, 1965, and 1968, reports came from Taylor County.

If a screech owl hollers three times and flies away, it is a sign of death.

> *Lincoln County, 1965 (DP). Informant: male, born 1910 in Lincoln County.* Brown 5306—"If an owl hoots three times, it means death"—

is a parallel to this belief, for an Iowa reference in Brown notes that it is a "Sure sign of death in the household if an owl hoots three consecutive nights and then leaves." This belief is rare, however, occurring otherwise only in North Carolina, Tennessee, and Ontario.

124 If a crow flies over the house, someone in the house will die.

Lincoln County, 1964 (JWi). Informant: female, born 1902 in Lincoln County. Previously unreported. My files contain a parallel belief reported from Mercer County.

125 A mockingbird singing at night is a sign of death.

Green County, 1967 (KRP). Informant: female, born 1895 in Green County. Brown 5302. This rare belief is known only in North Carolina and Tennessee. It was reported twice from Green County in 1967.

126 It is bad luck for a red bird to enter your house because it is the sign of death.

Green County, 1966 (FD). Informant: female, born 1909 in Green County. The same as Brown 5324, which adds that the death will be in the family, this was reported from North Carolina and Illinois. Two reports came from Taylor County in 1966.

127 The cry of a whippoorwill is a sign that someone is going to die.

Taylor County, 1966 (GN). Informant: male, born 1925 in Taylor County. The present belief probably belongs under Brown 5330— "If a whippoorwill alights near a house and sings, it is a token of death"—but it is not nearly as well known as the Brown entry, which makes reference to occurrences in Europe and the United States. The present belief was also reported from Adair County, 1963.

128 When a whip-o-will calls out at night, the number of times he calls will be the number of days before a death in the family.

Barren County, 1966 (GN). Informant: female, born 1946 in Barren County. This belief is not in Brown, but it, too, probably belongs under Brown 5330 (see item No. 127 above).

129 If a whippoorwill stays near your home, there will be a death within twenty-four hours.

Taylor County, 1965 (CC). Informant: female, born 1937 in Taylor County. This belief is similar to Brown 5332—"If a whippoorwill cries at your back door, you will hear of a death in less than twenty-four hours."

130 If a whippoorwill hollers close to the house, there will be a death in the family.

Taylor County, 1966 (DSh). Informant: male, born 1938 in Taylor County. This is another belief which can be classified under Brown

5330 (see item Nos. 127 and 128 above). A report was also gathered
from Metcalfe County in 1968.

If a whippoorwill lights on a sick person's bed post and sings, death
will follow.

> *Green County, 1967 (KRP). Informant: female, born 1895 in Green
> County.* Previously unreported. Compare this belief with Brown 5330
> and item Nos. 127, 128, and 130 above.

Insects

If a lightning bug got into the house, there would be a death.

> *Taylor County, 1968 (JCa). Informant: male, born 1889 in Taylor
> County.* Brown 5343—"If a lightning bug comes in the house at night,
> there will be one more or one less persons in the house the next night"
> —is the only death belief Brown recorded which involves a lightning
> bug. The present belief is not quite as articulate but, nonetheless,
> belongs in the same category. My files contain a report from Clinton
> County (1966) and from Hardin County.

If a lightning bug gets in the house and lights up, then someone will
die that year.

> *Taylor County, 1964 (GS). Informant: female, born 1924 in Taylor
> County.* Previously unreported.

If a lightning bug gets into the house, it is a sign that someone in the
family will die before the next night.

> *Adair County, 1966 (GN). Informant: female, born 1926 in Adair
> County.* Brown 5343 (see item Nos. 132 and 133 above). This belief
> was also reported from Clinton County in 1966. My files contain a
> report from Soddy, Tenn.

If you kill a lightning bug, the lightning will kill you during the
next thunderstorm.

> *Monroe County, 1967 (RBB). Informant: male, born 1902 in
> Mercer County.* Previously unreported, this Eastern Pennyroyal belief
> is interesting for its emphasis on killing the firefly and thereby induc-
> ing divine retribution.

Worms

If a measuring worm is on someone, it is measuring that person for
a coffin.

> *Russell County, 1968 (LP). Informant: female, born 1890 in Russell*

County. Brown 5347. This belief is also known in Pennsylvania, Indiana, Alabama, and among Southern Negroes. I have an additional report from Clark County.

MISCELLANEOUS OMENS OF DEATH

Suicide

137   A person who commits suicide will go to hell.

Casey County, 1964 (WRP). Informant: female, born 1897 in Casey County. Although previously unreported, I recall hearing this belief uttered during my childhood in Monroe County.

Footsteps

138   If someone walks in your tracks, you will die.

Monroe County, 1968 (BCD). Informant: female, born 1947 in Monroe County. This appears to be a borrowing from pagan beliefs and practices when magic was a part of everyday life. I have found no other report of this from oral tradition, but it is recorded in James G. Frazier's *The Golden Bough* (New York, 1951), 51–52. My records contain one report from Clark County.

News of Death

139   If you hear of a death on Monday, you will hear of another before the week is over.

Adair County, 1965 (CB). Informant: female, born 1909 in Adair County.

Lights

140   If you see a reflection of light when there is no light present, it is foretelling the death of the person it is hovering over.

Taylor County, 1968 (RMi). Informant: male, born 1944 in Taylor County. Previously unreported. The belief that such a reflection of light is an omen of death could be associated with beliefs concerning jack-o'-lanterns (Brown 5764–67).

DEATH OMEN NARRATIVES

APPEARANCE OF REVENANTS

Return of the Dead Brother

There is the Russell County story about a Duncan man who died following a brawl in which his body was lacerated with knife wounds. He came back later and motioned for his sister to follow him. Nobody could properly interpret the occurrence until she died a few years later.

Adair County, 1965 (NAB). Informant: female, born 1889 in Russell County. Appropriate here are Motifs S118, "Murder by cutting," and E226, "Dead brother's return."

The Magic Walking Cane

The night before Noah Woodbridge got shot by somebody, his mother woke up and saw this walking cane go across the room just in front of her eyes. When it got across the room, it shot off just like a gun.

Her boy, Noah, got killed the next day.

Adair County, 1965 (NAB). Informant: female, born 1903 in Russell County. This is a narrative for which there are no known parallels. Compare, however, Motifs D956, "Magic stick of wood," and D1254, "Magic staff."

Friends from the Past

Several years ago Jim Clements was working for somebody down on Caneyville Creek. They always went to work at sunup and worked until sundown or dark. Clements always had to go up the creekbed to his home.

On his way home one night, he saw two women in the creek road.

They came on toward him, and it was his aunt and a friend. Both had been dead for several years. They spoke to him; he spoke back. Said he didn't know how long he stood there, then he walked on home.

The next day another person from his family died.

Adair County, 1965 (NAB). Informant: female, born 1903 in Russell County. This belief narrative contains a motif similar to *E265, "Meeting ghost carries misfortune."

The Strange Dog

144 "I was hired out to a white woman and my sister was really bad sick. And they come after me to come home. They didn't think that she would live 'til I got there. Well, we started, and we was a-walking. The moon was a-shining as bright as day. And we had to come on to where we come across a field and then hit the main big road to come to home. And just when we got in the forks of the road—I was in front of my uncle. He come after me. And I was in front of him—and I was just a-walking along; and I happen to look down to the ground, and there was a dog—just a small dog right down—and his tail was on my feet.

"And I hollered, 'Git!'

"The dog wouldn't move, and it was just like it was pacing along. And I'd kick my feet, and I couldn't get it off my feet a-tall! And it stayed on my feet I guess a quarter of a mile. And I couldn't get that dog off my feet a-tall. I'd kick and my uncle he seen it, and he hollered at it. He went up to kick at it, but it never would get off my feet. It stayed on my feet about a quarter of a mile 'til we come to an old barn aright on the side of the road where we had to pass. And the door of the barn was right in front of the road where we had to pass. And when I got even with that old barn, that dog just went off of my feet and just went right into that door. And I never did see it no more.

"My sister died, well, before daylight that morning."

Monroe County, 1960 (LM). Informant: black female, born ca. 1884 in Monroe County. The major motif contained in this tale is *E423.1.1, "Revenant as dog," which is known in central and northwestern Europe and in the eastern part of the United States.

The Phantom Coach

"It happened here at Eighty Eight to some of my grandmother's people. It was during the Civil War, about six months before the end of the war.

"The family received word that this boy who was in the Union Army would be coming home. Not long after that, they received word that he had been injured and was admitted to the hospital. So at the end of the six months, or whenever it was, they received word that he could be expected home on such and such a date. And so the whole community, including all the family, got together to have a family reunion for the boy. And when the dinner was all set on the ground, about that time the boy was expected to arrive. But when it came time to eat, he hadn't shown up.

"All of a sudden, up the road a mile or so, they heard a wagon. They could tell it was a wagon rumbling down the road, and it got closer and closer. Soon they could see that it was a carriage and that it was drawn by six white horses. Well, the thing pulled up into the yard under the big shade tree right by the food. And they all gathered around to look at it. On the inside of the carriage was a casket. And after they all had their look at the casket and what have you, 'snap,' just like that, the whole works disappeared.

"The next day they got a telegram from the War Department saying that their boy had died in the hospital."

Monroe County, 1961 (LM). Informant: male, born 1931 in Monroe County. This story is reminiscent of the death carriage tradition known in the British Isles, primarily in Ireland. Motifs E535.1, "Phantom coach and horses," and *E538.1, "Spectral Coffin," are applicable here.

The Ghostly Hitchhiker

"This happened along about the Bray schoolhouse. I don't know whether I remember the names of these people, but I do know they were Brays.

"Bray's wife had lived there close to this Bray schoolhouse. She got sick one night, and she had a sister that lived at Cyclone—some six or seven miles maybe from there. And Mr. Bray decided that he'd go up there and get his wife's sister to come down and stay with her. But she couldn't come that night.

"It was after night when he was coming back through there and getting close to this place where we have been talking about seeing all these boogers. And said something like a girl come skipping out of the woods there and lit up behind him on his mule. And said— naturally it would scare anybody—he beat back behind him with his arm. Said it was just like hitting a featherbed. And he kept that up until he got on pretty close to home—maybe a few hundred yards—and this girl jumped down off the horse and skipped out through the woods.

"When he got home, his wife was dead."

Monroe County, 1963 (LM). Informant: male, born 1908 in Monroe County. The "Vanishing Hitchhiker" complex is evident in this early form of the legend in the Eastern Pennyroyal. Applicable here are Motifs *E272.2, "Ghost rides behind rider on horse," and *E332, "Non-malevolent road ghosts."

The Shadow of Death

147 "About the scariest hant I ebber seed in my life, was one night I was settin' up with a very dear friend's ole man, who was dyin'. We set dere expectin' his life to go out ebber minute. When his breathin' got harder and harder all de time, we knowed he couldn't live through dat night.

"About half a hour before he died, some big black thing dat looked like de shadow of a big man comes creepin' down a little at a time, and right ober the bed where the sick man lay. It keeps comin' down a little closer, jist as fast as de life goes out of the old man. When the last breath goes out of him, dis big thing like a shadow jist covers him up so we can't even see him.

"Me and his wife, we gits up and goes out in de yard to where some men are waitin'; but when we gets to the door and opens it a little, here comes in the worst lookin' thing that I have ebber seed in my life. It looked like a big black mule's head. We both jist pushed and pushed, but we could not push it out. We got out past it and told the men what we had seed. Dey all say dey see the same kind ob thing around the door. We was all scared to go in the house anymore for a long time, but when do go in, we didn't see anything around the dead man. De big shadow was ebben gone.

"After the man was buried, his wife tried to live in the house where he died, but all kinds of hants would bother her all night long. She finally moved in another house. But in this house her 'ole man would come to her ebber night and beg her to move back to her old home. She moved back and say she never see him any more but went crazy and died in the asylum anyhow."

——— *1938 (GV). Informant: black female, age and county of birth unknown, former slave of the Ingram family of Wayne County.* "The Shadow of Death" is used by permission of the Folk Music Division, Library of Congress. Applicable here are Motifs *E321, "Dead husband's friendly return"; *E421.4, "Ghosts as shadow"; and *E423, "Revenant in animal form."

The Black Creature

"This is really true, whatever it was that Uncle Benton saw. He never did know. It was back about 1900 when there was a lot of log hauling. He had to pass a place that was claimed to be hainted around the Bray schoolhouse. He was working back there on the Gilbert Maxey place or Harv Walden or someplace cutting logs. And this particular night it was dark when he come through there. Said he always felt a little skiddish coming through after night.

"He would always turn three of the mules loose and ride one. Between the Bray schoolhouse and the John Fish place was where his lead mules got scared at something and was coming back a-meeting him. And he tried to head them off. Said he couldn't head them, and they come on around by the Bray schoolhouse and out to the Aunt Mandy Harris place and around a different road and come on in home.

"He tried to make the mule that he was riding go up past the place there. He happened to look out there in front of him and could see something black laying there. And he thought probably that it was a hog or something like that. But still he couldn't get his mule by it. And said he was a little bit afraid, since he had heard so many tales about that place, to get down anyway, and investigate. And so he just turned and followed the other mules around.

"But he went right back there the next morning. Said he come to this place, and there was a mudhole there. And on this bank there— he said there couldn't anything have laid up there where he saw this—a hog, or anything. It was too rolling and he would have rolled off. And he got down and investigated and didn't see no tracks or anything.

"So he finally didn't know what it was."

Monroe County, 1963 (LM). Informant: male, born 1908 in Monroe County. Applicable motifs include E422.2.4, "Revenant in black"; *E332.2, "Person meets ghost on road"; *E520, "Animal ghosts"; and *E332, "Non-malevolent road ghosts."

Headless Woman Appears before a Death

149   Jim Jones, a man about twenty-five years of age, went upstairs to bed and dozed off to sleep. He awoke to hear someone coming up the steps. He looked toward the stairs and saw a lady without a head carrying a lamp coming up the steps. She sat down on the top of the stairs, and he covered his head with quilts. The light came closer, and he knew she was standing over his bed because of the way the light shone through the quilts. When he got enough courage to look again, she had gone away.

His mother died shortly after that. Jim felt that this was a warning to stop drinking so much.

Taylor County, 1965 (LB and DSk). Informant: female, born 1903 in Taylor County. Motif *E422.1.1, "Headless revenant," is applicable here; compare also *E425.1, "Revenant as woman."

Pappy Spreads a Sheet

150   Just before your grandpa died, he saw his pappy come one night and spread a sheet from the foot of the bed yonder to the fireplace. And in a night or two he died.

Clinton County, 1963 (SW). Informant: female, born 1872 in Clinton County. Motif *E327, "Dead father's friendly return," appears to be the only appropriate motif.

The Robed Horseman

Elp Ford lived in Larue County with his wife and his family. His father, mother, and sister lived in Taylor County at the old home place on Little Brush Creek in the Old Mac community. Late one afternoon his father and mother sent for him to come, for his sister was seriously ill. He started about night. When he got to Little Brush Creek, he rode in to let his horse drink.

There was a long, winding hill coming down to the ford of the creek from the opposite direction. Mr. Ford looked up and saw two big white horses and two men riders dressed in white robes. The time was around eleven o'clock at night. The men were singing "A Band of Angels Coming After Me." They came on down to the edge of the creek, turned around, and rode back up the hill and out of sight.

He hurried on, thinking it might be a sign that his sister was worse or dead. When he arrived his sister was better. But after he had been there about an hour, someone from Larue County came and told him that his baby had died at home with the croup about eleven that night.

> Green County, 1964 (KRP). Informant: female, born 1914 in Taylor County. Motifs appropriate here are E421, "Spectral ghosts"; *E423.1.3.4, "Revenant as white horse"; and *E575, "Ghost as omen of calamity or ill fortune."

STRANGE CASKETS

The Casket alongside the Path

There was a woman who lived in the Brush Creek community of Taylor County by the name of Mrs. Jack Steen. One day as she was walking to a spring to get drinking water for the family, she came up on a casket by the side of the path. She returned to the house and brought back some other people, but when they got there the casket was gone. A few days later, Mrs. Steen's daughter died unexpectedly.

She always believed that the casket was a sign of that death.

> Taylor County, 1965 (LB and DSk). Informant: female, born 1903 in Taylor County. This narrative contains Motif *E538.1, "Spectral coffin."

The Floating Coffin

153   This woman in Lower Burkesville said she saw this coffin come floating through the air and come to rest on her front porch. Then it left. Only she saw it, but in a few days her husband died.

> *Taylor County, 1967 (JPi). Informant: female, born 1926 in Cumberland County.* The motif included is *E538.1, "Spectral coffin"; also cf. D1641.13, "Coffin moves itself."

A Casket Blocks the Road

154   "The night before Uncle Lester's first wife died, she had got worse, and he had rode across the mountain to get Doc Bristow.

"As he was coming back across the mountain home, when he got to the foot of it, there was a casket across the road. His mule reared up and ran back up the mountain. And he couldn't get her to come back down the mountain that same way, so he had to go on home by another way.

"His wife died the next day at 12:30."

> *Clinton County, 1963 (SW). Informant: female, born 1917 in Clinton County.* This narrative contains Motif *E538.1, "Spectral coffin"; also cf. F852, "Extraordinary coffin."

The Strange Coffin

155   "Well, I lived at Russell Springs once, lived thar about seven years—lived in a little house over not fer from the Granny Combest place. One evening after working in town, I'd come in to work a-while in the garden, and the woman come a-running out toward whar I was at a-hoeing in the garden. She says, 'Tommy, run here right quick; I want to show you something!'

"I says, 'Is something a-matter with the baby?'

"She says, 'No!' she says; 'You come in a hurry!'

"I throwed my hoe up on the side of the bank, and I went jist like a racer, 'cause I was young and stout. She says, 'Come right here and look over yonder at the Old Aunt Kit Swan place.' She says, 'You've always wished to see something like a grave pop up to show you God's power and all thoses things.'

"I says, 'Yes, I wants to see.'

"She says, 'Keep a-looking between those two big apple trees thar at Aunt Kit's. It will pop up again.'

"By the time that I got a view over thar, why, it just plowed up dirt jist like you'd put in a blast. The dirt flew out, and out come the prettiest coffin as was ever looked at. Had everything to it, and was like a fish in water. It got straightened out good, then it quivvered just like something scared, then made a straight view for our house. Come as straight as an arr [arrow]. And when it got thar, it come in about, well, in about two feet of me. It come as quick as a bullet would have come, and thar it was. The woman made it to the door with the baby, and I was a-standing thar—couldn't move I was excited so. It stood thar for about five minutes, and when it did wheel, it struck back toward whar Granny lived. It cut up down thar—went all around the house and in the porch. It circled then to whar Park Litterill lived—that was another little house that was on the same place next to Granny Combest's.

"It cut over thar, then it made for a field that I had tended, and it went just like if you had shot a bullet going over that field that I had worked in. It ploughed out just like you'd a-ploughed out. That coffin going every row that I'd ploughed in thar, then made fer another little field I'd tended. It went all over, then to Jess Humbles'. Then back from that to an old fence. It got on that old fence, and then it went on it a good long ways 'til it come to a slatter-wire fence. Then it made a straight shoot back to whar it first started from to Aunt Kit's door. And it went in thar, and it cut up thar for about five minutes. And it turned thar, and from thar it went to Old Aunt Suze's. From thar out it was like picking up a big stove-wood stick and let it go on a hillside 'til it went into a chicken house.

"In about two weeks the chicken house was on fire, and I was working at about the same place a-hoeing in the garden when a big storm come up, and it began pouring down the rain. Burned up every chicken she had. And Old Aunt Suze went to wash and get lumber to build her chicken house back, and she broke something in her and just lived through the night."

Russell County, 1966 (HD). Informant: (anonymous contribution, *except that subject born 1891 in Russell County.)* This interesting belief tale from the Kentucky foothills is unique because of its extraordinary length. It contains only two motifs: *E538.1, "Spectral coffin," and D1641.13, "Coffin moves itself."

Phantom Baby and Casket

156   Before Granddaddy's first wife died he was going across this field. In a short distance, he could see a casket and a little baby in front of him. A little later his wife died of pneumonia and left a little baby. This thing he saw always disappeared before he got to it.

 Monroe County, 1968 (RLy). Informant: female, born ca. 1910 in Monroe County. Applicable here are Motifs *E421, "Spectral ghosts," and *E538.1, "Spectral coffin."

Casket Appears at Dumb Supper

157   One Halloween two girls decided they would find out who they were going to marry. If they could go through with all this, they could find out. They had to prepare supper by holding hands behind them and by not speaking and not smiling. They would carry the plates to the table, but they had to carry the plates together. They had to carry all the table linens, dishes, and food. They were supposed to have their chairs ready. If they could get this far, whoever they were going to marry would come. Then, when the two girls got the chairs placed they heard a sound like horses coming and saddles squeaking. They hitched the horses in front of the house. Then the door opened, and a casket started coming in. Then one of the girls said, "Let's speak," and they broke it.

 Later one of the girls married, and the other girl's boyfriend died. Of course, she never married. I've heard this story called "The Deaf and Dumb Supper."

 Monroe County, 1968 (RLy). Informant: female, born ca. 1920 in Monroe County. Motifs *E538.1, "Spectral coffin," and D1641.13, "Coffin moves itself," are present, along with other motifs characteristic of haint tales.

WARNING LIGHTS

Fire from the Sky

While arriving at the house of a very sick old man here in Taylor County, some friends saw a ball of fire fall from the sky to the ground near the house. Inside the house, later on, the visiting families had all their children in bed. A woman thought she heard one of the children wetting the bed, and it was going through the floor. But on arriving in the bedroom, she found all the children dry and with no sign of wetness on the floor.

That night before dawn, the old man passed away. This was always considered a death omen.

> *Taylor County, 1965 (LB and DSk). Informant: female, born 1935 in Taylor County.* This rather strange narrative from the Eastern Pennyroyal of Kentucky is related to Motifs D1812.5.0.3, "Behavior of fire as omen," and F964, "Extraordinary behavior of fire."

The Dancing Light

I was traveling alongside a creek on my way to see my father when suddenly a light appeared before me. The creek or branch is called Snake Branch. The light danced along until it was beside me, then it followed me. I ran my horse, but it still stayed by my side. I would think that it could have been the moon, but it was the darkest night I have ever seen.

The light followed me until I was almost to my father's house, then it went out, and it never appeared again. When I reached my father's house, I was told that he had died a little while before.

> *Green County, 1966 (MJM). Informant: male, born 1900 in Green County.* This tale seems associated with the jack-o'-lantern tradition; see Brown 5764–67. Motif E761.7.4, "Life-token: light goes out," is also applicable; also cf. Motif *E742, "Soul as light."

Ball of Fire Warns of Death

"Well, they's uh one night down home, we was all, uh I was setting in the door, and my husband and uh the children was out in the yard. There was a white man come up there wanting my husband to work. I tell you who it was. You know him, I guess, or heered of him. John T. Vance—I guess you heerd of him. You may know him. He come up there, asked him to work. And he was—the road's right close to the house like this road is to this house—he was standing out on the edge of the road a-talking to Wolford (my husband) wanting him to work.

"And I was a-setting in the door, and the children were out there. All at once there's a big light just shined up, and it just begin to roll over and roll over. And I guess it seemed like it was big as a hogshead in that yard—just a-rolling over going down toward him. It just rolled over and rolled over. And we all just begin to scream and holler and, and John T. jumped off his horse. And just all of we was all scared to death.

"It just kept a-rolling. It just rolled, uh, after it got into the road. It crossed the road. It went down the hill. And that just rolled over and over and over and over. You could have picked up a pin on that hill down there where we lived. It liked to have scared us all to death.

"John T. lost his little girl in just about a week."

Monroe County, 1960 (LM). Informant: black female, born 1884 in Monroe County. Appropriate here are Motifs D1812.5.0.3, "Behavior of fire as omen," and F964, "Extraordinary behavior of fire."

The Stubborn Lamp

161   Once there was a death in a family. As the old woman was dying, her son was in another part of the house. You had to go outside to get to where she was.

While trying to get her, her son tried four times to light a lamp. Each time he failed. Finally, he got to his mother's side through the darkness. After she died, he went back. And at the first try the lamp did light.

Taylor County, 1965 (LB and DSk). Informant: female, born 1935 in Taylor County. Previously unreported. Failure of a lamp to light was believed to be a sign that death was at hand. It was once fairly common to build houses in which no rooms were connected by interior doors—one had to enter the rooms from the porch.

SPIRITS

The Spirited Messenger

This man came by our house one day and told my father that a spirit was trying to communicate with him. Well, this man kept saying there was this spirit trying to talk with him. My father didn't believe in all that stuff and he wouldn't talk to the spirit. This man said that the spirit's name was Henry Jiles.

Anyhow, several days later, my father got a letter saying his nephew Henry Jiles had been killed in Cincinnati while working. This brick had fell on him and killed him.

> *Taylor County, 1964 (BAs and JWa). Informant: female, elderly, born in Taylor County.* Previously unreported. This narrative from Kentucky appears related to the seance tradition or to some other form of mysticism, but no parallels exist in oral tradition.

The Fiery-Fingered Creature

Mammy told this tale about her stepmother. Late one Sunday evening they went to the barn to milk. One or maybe both saw a person coming across field a way off. They didn't know who it was. It kept getting closer and closer and wobblier and limper. As it got real close, it just went down to the ground. Its arms flew up and fire came out to the tips of its fingers.

The next day the barn burnt.

> *Monroe County, 1968 (RLy). Informant: male, born ca. 1918 in Monroe County.* Motifs which may be related to this tale include F497, "Fire spirits," and D1812.5.0.3, "Behavior of fire as omen."

WRAITHS

The Face of the Burned Girl

"This woman had several children, and she was expecting another one. And her other children had all gotten up to a pretty good size. The youngest boy was about six years old, so one night she let him sit up a little longer than the others. All at once the little boy screamed, 'Look, mother, there's a little black girl looking in the window!'

"His mother looked, but she didn't see anything; so she told him that there wasn't anything there. He said, 'Yes there was,' and he was very scared, and he even began to cry. The mother thought he was just imagining things.

"In due course, the baby was born, and it turned out to be the prettiest child she had. It was a baby girl, and she named her Laura Mae. She was a very smart child. One day when she was about four years old, the children were out playing. It was an early fall day, and the leaves were already falling. They had raked the leaves into a pile out back, and the mother burned the leaves.

"She thought the fire was out, but actually there were a few small embers left. When the mother went back into the house, the children made a game of running back and forward through the ashes. The little girl stepped on a hot coal, and it flew up and set her dress on fire; and she was burned to death.

"The whole family was heartbroken, especially the mother. At the funeral a couple of days later, they took the boy up to see her for the last time. The little girl's face had been blackened in the fire. When he looked into the casket, he said, 'Oh, Mommy, that's not Laura Mae; it's that little black girl that I saw looking into the window!' "

Taylor County, 1966 (GS). Informant: female, middle-aged, born in Taylor County. At least two motifs are included herein: *E723.2, "Seeing one's wraith a sign that person is to die shortly," and *E723.8, "Appearance of wraith as calamity omen."

Woman's Ghost Is Seen Prior to Her Death

165   Mr. Floyd, a person in the neighborhood, once scared your Aunt Janie almost to death. He told her one night he was walking up the road just right below our house, and he met this woman. He knew her and just kept walking, but when he got even with her, she disappeared. In about two weeks this woman took sick and died.

A little later he was walking up the same road and met Janie, and she disappeared. Mr. Floyd told Janie about this, and it just like to have scared her to death. But nothing happened. I never could understand why he told her this.

Green County, 1964 (JPo). Informant: male, age unknown, born in Green County. This is the very common form of this wraith narrative. Motifs include *E723.2, "Seeing one's wraith a sign that person is to die shortly," and *E723.8, "Appearance of wraith as calamity omen."

Ghost Seen as Girl Dies

"Well now, the next time, the next vision she saw was of Little Annie. Now I remember that. That 'uz her little half-sister. [See item No. 169 below.]

"We 'uz all settin' there in the livin' room, and she looked towards the kitchen; and the door was open, and she says, 'Look! Yonder comes Little Annie!' Just like that. Just pointed and said, 'Yon.'

"And we all looked. Says, 'She's gone now, but I saw her walkin' acrost the kitchen floor in her little checkedy gingham apron.'

"And the next day we got a message that Little Annie had died that night. At the time that she saw her, she'd passed away with membrane croup. Now that was the ghost she saw, and she said it was plain to her."

Green County, 1964 (JPo). Informant: female, age unknown, born in Adair County. Included here also are Motifs *E723.2, "Seeing one's wraith a sign that person is to die shortly," and *E723.8, "Appearance of wraith as calamity omen."

Boy Is Seen in Coffin Prior to Death

"Well, you know, talking about that Williams family, I don't know whether you'd call that a ghost or not. But once they was a, I believe it was one of Mr. Williams' children, one of the boys, I think, and one of the girls went in the kitchen for sumpin' or 'nother; and she come back a-screamin' as hard as she could, and said, 'I seen my brother in a coffin in there!'

"And in a few days he died."

Adair County, 1964 (VM). Informant: male, age unknown, born in Adair County. Motifs *E538.1, "Spectral coffin," and *E723.2, "Seeing one's wraith a sign that person is to die shortly," are included in this narrative.

The Dying Man's Vision

168   "Well now, Aunt Emma Henson, Dad's own aunt, told me 'bout this, and she was there at the time. They were all sitting up with him. It was just about four hours before he died. And the family, like they used to, was all sitting around waitin' fer him to die, you might say. But anyway, they-uz with him, and he was very low sick.

"All at once he pointed, sayin', 'Look! There's Sallie! Yonder's Sallie!' Sallie was his daughter that lived at Edmonton. Said, 'Look! Yonder's Sallie! Can't you all see her?' Says, 'She just keeps a-sailin' around overhead.'

"Course, none of them didn't see her, and they thought he was just talkin' crazy, was outa his head or something. But then he went on. Said Aunt Emma said he knew all of them clear 'til he died. Says he told them that it was strange that they couldn't see her. Said, 'I saw her plain.'

"Well, the next morning—he died about four hours later—when —they didn't have telephones that day and time, you know—when a man got on his horse and started to Edmonton to tell his daughter that he was dead, 'bout halfway he met a man comin' to tell them that his daughter Sallie had died suddenly the night before. Died just the same time he saw her.

"Now that's a ghost for you!"

Adair County, 1964 (VM). Informant: female, age unknown, born in Adair County. Previously unreported. The appearance to a dying person of the wraith of the person who is about to die is perhaps a very uncommon narrative trait. Motifs include *E723.2, "Seeing one's wraith a sign that person is to die shortly."

Little Bobby Knew He Was Dying

169   "Well, this is a little story about a little playmate of mine years ago, a little boy that Uncle John White raised up until he was about fifteen years old. He was a fine little boy, and he had sent Mother word that he was a-coming to stay all night and not fix anything, only jist what she'd fix fer common. Said all he wanted was just plenty of good milk and plenty of bread, and he was satisfied; for

that was about what he had. So Mother told him to be sure to come. Me and brother Jackson were out in the yard looking for him that evening and here come Little Bobby.

"He got there, says, 'I sent you word what I wanted you to have, to fix nothing extra for me, for this will be the last trip that I will ever get to come to see the boys.'

"Mother says, 'Why, Bobby, you know you'll come again.'

" 'No!' he says, 'I'm a good boy, and I'm going up to Jesus. That's a-gonna be my home, and I'll not be turning back here again to see the boys no more. But you'll hear of it in a week that Little Bobby has gone to Jesus shore nuff.'

"And that brought tears from Mother and all of us. And, as he said, it was a true story that he had told us, and shore nuff we never seed Bobby no more."

> *Russell County, 1966 (HD). Informant: (anonymous contributor, except that subject born 1886 in Russell County.)* Several motifs are implied here: D1812.0.1, "Foreknowledge of hour of death"; M341, "Death prophesied"; and M341.1, "Prophecy: Death at certain time."

Man Is Seen One Week Before His Arrival

"That was like my father was one time in the Civil War. He was about nineteen years old then—it was about next to the last year of the Civil War.

"The last they had heard of my dad, my father was summers in the South, and my oldest half-sister—she was about like this little girl here—and my mother and her was down at the branch a-washing, and all of a sudden—they was a road went just above this spring, you know, maybe fifty yards away—she looked up and she said, 'Oh, I see Daddy coming!'

"And she really did, and she jumped up and run all the way up the road; but Daddy wasn't there. Daddy wasn't there at all. Well, they made sure he was dead, you know. But it was just a week from that time when he come.

"But it worried them; they wudn't no mail much like they are today."

Russell County, 1966 (HD). Informant: (anonymous contributor, except that subject born 1898 in Russell County.) It will be noted that although the wraith was interpreted as an omen of impending death, the wraith signified the man's arrival instead. Motif *E723, "Wraiths of persons separate from body," seems to be appropriate.

PART II

The Dead

INTRODUCTION TO THE DEAD

Death is the final rite of passage. It may come like a thief in the night in the Kentucky foothills or with painful slowness following a lingering illness. Folk beliefs and customs seem especially to surround the death and burial of an old person whose sickness was lengthy and whose passing was eventful because of excessive suffering or because of an omen presaging the death. It is recorded in folk belief of the Eastern Pennyroyal that a storm may follow the death of an old person, that a star may fall from its lofty position to signal the passing, or that a living person may know of the death because of a sudden ringing in his ear. Whatever the cause of death, whatever the portents of the impending end, the people of the Kentucky foothills accept death as an undesirable but routine event. I remember vividly the seemingly unemotional statement by the Clinton County mother of a six-year-old daughter, who sat listening with unblinking eyes: "The doctor thinks our girl has leukemia." I also recall with much admiration the young mother of six, in neighboring Pickett County, Tennessee, who actively participated in a five-hour folksinging session on a Saturday night. We were told at the close of the event that she was going to the hospital on Monday morning to undergo surgery for what was then thought to be terminal cancer. She was not outwardly bothered by her chances for survival.

Some of the beliefs associated with the dead appear to be totally incongruous. For example, one can question the rationale for believing that a mirror will break into pieces if the image of a coffin is allowed to be reflected in it, or one can logically doubt the wisdom of telling the bees of a death in the household to keep the bees from leaving. The whole point in the study of folk beliefs and customs, however, is not to put these usages through tests to determine the extent of reliability, but to bear in mind that the folk once believed and practiced all of this lore.

Many of the beliefs and customs recorded in this section on the dead remain relevant to the lives of some people of the Kentucky foothills. People here no longer lay out the corpse, for the funeral directors have assumed this delicate task. Friends still sit up with the corpse on occasion, however, whether at home or in the funeral home; they still plant and harvest crops for the family of the deceased, and, in isolated situations, the church bell still signals the time to dig the grave. Until the 1930s it was customary throughout the Eastern Pennyroyal to toll the bell on the morning of the funeral to call the neighbors in to dig the grave for the interment services that afternoon. Characteristic of the universality of folk tradition, the tolling of the bell was inherited from an English custom of the late Middle Ages.

From the moment of death until the burial, tradition in the Kentucky foothills demanded that the corpse should never be left alone and unwatched. The principal reason for this practice was respect and affection for the deceased. In some instances there was a degree of fear of supernatural intervention in earlier days, according to Kevin Danaher, *In Ireland Long Ago*, 172. In addition, up to one hundred years ago body snatchers were eager to steal an unguarded corpse and sell it to a medical school. Sean O'Súilleabhain, *Irish Wake Amusements* (Hatsboro, Pa., 1961), 166–74, disagrees that the wake was intended as a protection for the dead person against evil spirits. He contends that the living feared "that the dead person might return to take revenge on those who had succeeded to his property. Thus, the survivors did everything in their power to placate the dead. This could best be done while the dead was still with them. Hence the wake" (p. 171).

When the hour for the funeral arrived, the coffin was moved to the church—unless isolation dictated an immediate burial in the family plot—and was usually placed in front of the pulpit, where it remained until the service was over and the corpse was viewed by friends and family members for the last time. The mourners filed silently by and passed outside to await the trek to the open grave. Finally, the pallbearers carried the coffin slowly from the church toward the cemetery for final graveside services. The custom of opening the casket in church for a final view of the body generally persisted everywhere in America until around 1900. From that time on, the practice was generally restricted to the rural South.

Folk funerals in the Kentucky foothills were never elaborate before the Second World War. Burial clothes were often made at home. Coffins were generally made by the community cabinetmaker according to individual specifications. Handmade artificial flowers were used to decorate the grave when natural flowers were not in season. The corpse was transported to the church in a horse-drawn wagon when poor roads and bad weather prevented the passage of the undertaker's hearse. Even the gravestones were frequently nothing more than carefully selected handcarved field stones. All of this has changed now; the Kentucky foothills area has entered the mainstream of American funeral technology. But memories—not altogether unpleasant—of a simpler way of doing things flood the minds of many of the region's older residents.

THE DYING PERSON

171   If a person is about to die, he will die faster if his head is pointed toward the East.

> *Russell County, 1964 (RLa). Informant: male, born 1944 in Russell County.* Brown 5011.

THE HOUR OF DEATH

Weather and Cosmic Phenomena

172   A storm follows the death of a very old person. When Gordon Peeler of Rock Bridge died, there was the awfullest storm you ever saw.

> *Monroe County, 1961 (RBB). Informant: female, born 1920 in Monroe County.* This belief, not found in Brown, is also known in Mercer County.

173   If you see a star falling, this means a fairy has died.

> *Taylor County, 1964 (PRA). Informant: female, born 1944 in Adair County.* There is no parallel for this item in Brown.

174   A falling star means that someone is dying.

> *Taylor County, 1966 (GN). Informant: male, born 1924 in Taylor County.* This belief, not in Brown, is known also outside the Eastern Pennyroyal—in Larue County.

175   A falling star means someone has gone to heaven.

> *Lincoln County, 1965 (DP). Informant: male, born 1910 in Lincoln County.* Cf. Brown 1548.

176   A shooting star is actually a soul on its way to heaven.

> *Russell County, 1964 (HD). Informant: male, born 1935 in Russell County.* Brown 5148. See also Motif E741.1, "Soul in form of star."

177   When you see a shooting star, it is the sign that someone is dead [variant: dying].

Russell County, 1964 (HD). Informant: male, born 1935 in Russell County. This belief is not in Brown, but it is Motif E741.1.1, "Shooting star signifies that someone is dying."

Some people believe that the dead go to the moon, sun, or stars; and they bury them in uniform with their head turned in the direction they are to go. They believe that they come back and walk the earth haunting people.

Adair County, 1968 (NAB). Informant: female, born 1912 in Adair County. Motifs E481.8, "Land of dead in sky," and E481.8.2, "Moon as land of dead," are applicable here.

The Human Body

If you hear a ringing in your ears, there has been a death close by.

Metcalfe County, 1968 (WLB). Informant: female, born 1947 in Metcalfe County. Cf. Brown 4911.

People used to tell that after John Rivers died some boys passed by his corpse and said his eyes were like coals of fire.

Russell County, 1968 (NAB). Informant: female, born 1889 in Russell County. Cf. Motif D457.11.2, "Eyeballs transformed to torches."

Furniture

Stop the clock when someone dies.

Monroe County, 1868 (CC). Informant: male, born 1892 in Taylor County. Brown 5405. Kevin Danaher, *In Ireland Long Ago*, 173, records that at the moment of death in Ireland the clock was stopped in order that all could see the actual time of death—otherwise people would usually make inquiry. This belief has also been reported from Taylor County (1965, 1967, 1968) and Russell County (1964).

If someone dies, take a sheet and cover all the mirrors and stop all clocks in the house.

Adair County, 1964 (PRA). Informant: female, born 1893 in Russell County. Brown 5405 and 5411. This well-known belief in the Eastern Pennyroyal of Kentucky was also reported from Green County (1964), Lincoln (1964), and twice from Taylor County (1968). Outside the area, a Mercer County informant additionally stipulated that the clock was not to be started again until after the funeral.

183   Cover the mirrors in the house with a cloth when there is a dead
       body, or the whole family will have bad luck.
            *Marion County, 1967 (MM). Informant: male, born 1905 in Tay-
            lor County.* Cf. Brown 5411. No. 183 was also reported from Taylor
            County (1967) and was known in Carroll County.

184   After a death you must cover up all mirrors, or another death will
       occur.
            *Taylor County, 1966 (LB and DSk). Informant: male, born 1945 in
            Taylor County.* Brown 5411. This was reported a second time in 1966
            from Taylor County.

185   When a little neighbor boy died, soon as they brought the casket in
       the house, an old mirror that had been in the house broke all to
       pieces, as the image of the casket was in the mirror.
            *Barren County, 1959 (LM). Informant: male, born 1943 in Barren
            County.*

186   Turn the mirror to the wall when someone dies, or the first person
       to look into that mirror will be the next to die.
            *Taylor County, 1965 (CC). Informant: female, born 1922 in Taylor
            County.* Brown 5414. Reported again from Taylor County in 1966,
            this was also known in Hardin and Larue counties, Ky., and in Green
            County, Ohio.

Telling the Neighbors

187   Before telephone service was available to people in the rural areas,
       the dinner bell was used as a means of communications. Three
       rings of the bell meant "help," and everyone within hearing dis-
       tance immediately stopped whatever they were doing and rushed
       to the aid of their neighbor. Some of the neighbors stayed and sat
       with the corpse all night. The corpse wasn't left alone at any time
       until the funeral service was over.
            *Taylor County, 1967 (MM). Informant: female, born 1889 in
            Green County.* The Passing Bell, or Soul Bell, was tolled in Tudor
            England to signify the passing of a person in the community. Both
            Shakespeare and Marston referred to this custom in their writings.
            Brand, *Popular Antiquities*, 422–35, provides an extended description
            of the whole bell-ringing complex as a part of the final rites of passage.
            Additional mention is contained in Wayland D. Hand, "California
            Bells Legends," *California Folklore Quarterly* 4 (1945), 25. The prac-
            tice was also reported from Monroe County in 1970.

Bees

One must tell the bees about a death in the family to insure appease-
ment to [of] the devil, and a safe journey for the departed one.

   *Adair County, 1964 (PRA). Informant: male, born 1891 in Adair
County. Brown 7519.*

Bees will leave unless told of death.

   *Russell County, 1964 (RLa). Informant: female, born 1899 in Rus-
sell County. Brown 7519.*

Miscellaneous

When one death occurs, three will take place. Deaths occur in
threes.

   *Taylor County, 1965 (SHed). Informant: female, born 1920 in Har-
rison County, W. Va.* Cf. Brown 4903. This belief was known also in
Mercer, Shelby, and Crittenden counties, Ky.; and in Evansville and
Charlestown, Ind.

CARING FOR THE CORPSE

After the person died, the people in the neighborhood usually fixed
the dead person up for the family. The neighbors would gather
around and make the clothes for the dead, wash them [the corpse]
up, and fix their hair. A cloth was tied around the head to keep the
mouth closed, and nickels were placed on the eyes to keep them
closed.

   *Russell County, 1968 (JeC). Informant: male, born 1906 in Russell
County.* In Colonial America and in Europe of that day, "laying out"
and dressing the corpse was entrusted to female members of the family. The act had more than a symbolic value because it was thought
that those only apparently dead might be revived in the process. See
Robert W. Habenstein and William M. Lamers, *Funeral Directing*
(Milwaukee, 1955), 29–30. Bertram S. Puckle, *Funeral Customs* (London, 1926), 51–52, indicates that this custom dates from the "Dim
Ages" and later Greek and Roman practices, when it was deemed
important to make the dead appear to best advantage in the after-
life. In America, however, before the funeral undertaking evolved
into a distinct occupation, it became customary to entrust the care
of the corpse to the hands of friends and neighbors. See Habenstein,

Funeral Directing, 235–36. This practice was also reported from Rockcastle County in 1968.

192 In the 1850s a winding sheet was used occasionally as dress for burial.

> *Taylor County, 1967 (MM). Informant: female, born 1889 in Green County.*

193 In the early 1900s the dress for burial was simple clothing. Kind neighbors would come to the home of the dead person, make the burial clothes, and wash and dress the person for burial.

> *Taylor County, 1967 (MM). Informant: female, born 1883 in Green County.*

194 Up until the early 1900s shrouds were used as burial clothing. These shrouds were made of white, gray, or black material. The women's shrouds were full length, pleated in the front, with lace stitched on the pleats for decoration. The shrouds were open in the back.

> *Taylor County, 1967 (MM). Informant: female, born 1899 in Taylor County.*

195 The women were usually dressed in shoes and gloves, although some requested to be buried in their night gowns. The only ornament used was a breast pin on the front of the shroud.

> *Taylor County, 1967 (MM). Informant: female, born 1878 in Green County.*

196 A man's shroud resembled a suit of clothes. These were full length and open in the back. A regular dress shirt was used under the shroud.

> *Taylor County, 1967 (MM). Informant: male, born 1894 in Taylor County.*

197 They dressed them most usually in black or white, whichever the family chose.

> *Wayne County, 1966 (SP). Informant: male, born 1906 in Wayne County.*

198 Some of the things I remember about funerals more than fifty years ago are that if the persons who died were old, they were always buried in a black coffin. They were dressed in black. The older women were buried in black dresses, and usually had a triangular black scarf tied over their head and knotted at the throat. Young people had white clothing and white coffins.

Clinton County, 1966 (SP). Informant: female, born 1910 in Clinton County. Habenstein, *Funeral Directing,* 126, states that white coffins for young people were and still are customary among Christian groups.

Babies were buried in a white gown during the early part of the present century. The gown was elaborately trimmed with lace and several bows down the front and on the sleeves.

Taylor County, 1967 (MM). Informant: female, born 1889 in Green County.

When a death occurred, a string or handkerchief was tied around the chin to draw the mouth together. The corpse was kept in the home a very short time because there was no method for preserving the body. So the casket and body were placed in a wagon drawn by horses and taken to the family graveyard, which probably included only two or three members of the immediate family.

Russell County, 1968 (PC). Informant: male, born 1907 in Russell County.

If the corpse was kept in the home overnight, a "death watch" was conducted. In other words, two or three persons sat up with the corpse throughout the entire night. The corpse was never to be left alone until it was buried. The reason for this custom was to protect the corpse from rats which infested almost every farmstead.

Russell County, 1967 (PC). Informant: male, born 1907 in Russell County. Brand, *Popular Antiquities,* 435–38, discusses origin and practices related to the *lik-wake* in the British Isles. He cites one theory which holds that the practice of sitting up with the dead stems from ancient days when it was feared that the corpse would be carried off by some of the agents of the invisible world or exposed to the ominous liberties of brute animals. Puckle, *Funeral Customs,* 76, gives a functional interpretation to this which stems from pre-literate groups, holding that the delay between death and burial served a psychological need in gradually conditioning friends and relatives to the changed condition brought about by death and a physical need in providing an opportunity for continued close observation of the corpse, in the hope that it might return to consciousness.

I find no other reference which parallels the belief that rats might attack the corpse, although it is common to ascribe such action to cats. See the next item.

People sit up with dead bodies to keep the cats away from the corpse.

Russell County, 1968 (LP). Informant: female, born 1927 in Rus-

sell County. Brown 5427. This belief was previously reported from Clinton County in 1963.

203   They buried people just like they bury them now, but there wasn't no undertakers. They just couldn't keep them [corpses] out over one night because they didn't embalm them or nothing like that. If they kept them out over night, they would have to wet white cloths in soda water and keep on their face to keep them from turning. That's the way they kept them out then.

    Green County, 1966 (TB). Informant: female, born 1886 in Green County.

204   When a person died, the friends spread the news over the area and let all know about it. Then someone laid the body out; there was no embalming. A rag with soda water was kept on the face of the corpse at all times to keep off the outer effects of death. The body was laid out at home, and the friends and relatives came in and sat up with the corpse at night to keep the cats off the corpse.

    Marion County, 1965 (RH and SHen). Informant: male, born 1892 in Marion County.

205   Before embalming came into practice, they didn't leave the body laid out but one day. They always buried the person the next day, usually at about two o'clock in the afternoon.

    Rockcastle County, 1968 (JeC). Informant: male, born 1898 in Rockcastle County. A Larue County source noted that if the deceased had not been "diseased," the body was kept until the family arrived. But if the person had died from an incurable or contagious disease, the corpse was buried as soon as the grave could be dug.

206   Embalming wasn't practiced in Taylor County until the 1930s. Before that time, preparation for burial included bathing and dressing the corpse. Quarters were placed on the eyes, and a cloth was tied around the chin and the top of the head to prevent the mouth from opening. If a person died one day, he was buried the next.

    Taylor County, 1967 (MM). Informant: male, born 1888 in Taylor County. The practice of placing coins on the dead person's eyes was also reported from Russell County (once in 1964 and twice in 1968), Monroe County (1968), and from Taylor County (once in 1964 and twice in 1966).

A pink fluid was used to wash the face and hands as a method of embalming. Jars filled with this fluid were placed around a baby's body as a method of preservation. The practice of embalming was started to meet the needs for improved sanitation, preservation, and restoration of the body. Outside the cities prior to 1934, all embalming was done in the home. As the population grew, undertaker "parlors" were established for the benefit of the public.

Taylor County, 1967 (MM). Informant: male, born 1905 in Taylor County. One of the social effects of embalming by chemical injection was to dispel the fear of being buried alive. Many folktales told today relate the unspoken yet horrifying fear of being buried alive in earlier times. Perhaps the foundation for such a morbid thought stems from the periods in history when great plagues and epidemics may have caused sick people to be mistaken for dead and buried in the haste of disposing of the germ-ridden bodies.

The practice of embalming people in Russell County was not begun until 1931. When Mr. Pruitt, the first mortician, first started his business, he would go to the home and embalm the dead body. It was easier for the mortician to go to the home than to get the body to the funeral home because of poor roads and bad weather conditions.

Today, since the modern and convenient funeral home has come into existence, the body is usually left at the funeral home. Thus, the funeral director takes most of the responsibilities of caring for the corpse in order that the family will have less burdens after the death of a loved one.

Russell County, 1967 (MM). Informant: male, born 1906 in Russell County.

Some people claim that if you will touch a corpse, you will never again be afraid of the dead.

Cumberland County, 1965 (VB). Informant: female, born 1947 in Cumberland County. Brown 5421. This belief was also reported from Green County (1967) and Taylor County (1965) and was known in Clark, Meade, and Hardin counties, Ky.; and in Evansville, Ind.

CASKETS OR COFFINS

The old homemade caskets were made of wood and were cloth lined. Now caskets are more protective because they are made of metal. There are still places in Rockcastle County where the old wooden caskets are made. But even when wooden caskets were being made in the county, there were places in cemeteries where there were steel vaults for family burials.

> *Rockcastle County, 1968 (JeC). Informant: male, born 1898 in Rockcastle County.* The earliest known wooden coffin, according to Habenstein, *Funeral Directing*, 117, was that of Arthur, the half-mythical king of England who reigned in the fifth or sixth century. In certain burial mounds in England, coffins made from hollow logs and containing skeletons and charred bones have been occasionally unearthed.

211 The family of the one who had just died would buy lumber and get a carpenter to make the casket. Why, it didn't cost no more than ten dollars because they just bought cheap stuff. They couldn't afford too much.

> *Clinton County, 1966 (SP). Informant: male, born 1906 in Wayne County.*

212 Until good roads, churches, and funeral homes were built, the white families buried their own people and conducted their own funerals. Some relative or a neighbor who could do carpenter work constructed a plain wooden box for a casket. The carpenter or cabinetmaker selected some type of wood such as oak, chestnut, or poplar. Then, it was cut and stored in the barn loft to season out. Sometimes the person who was buried made his own casket. Until a death did occur, the casket was used for the storage of things such as potatoes or onions for the winter.

> *Russell County, 1967 (PC). Informant: female, born 1911 in Russell County.* A report also came from Green County in 1967.

213 Caskets were made in an oblong shape, small at the top, wide at the shoulders, and small at the foot. When someone died, the cabinetmaker would go to the home and get the measurements of the corpse in order to know the size that the casket was to be made. The inside of the casket was stuffed with cotton and lined with black or white silk, which was bought at the local general store.

This type casket later came to be known as the "mummy casket," and the people who made this particular type were known as the Toothpick Casket Makers of Witherspoon Manufacturing Company.

Russell County, 1967 (PC). Informant: female, born 1911 in Russell County.

Some years after the mummy coffins were made, the "bedside coffin" came into use. This was a stronger and better built casket than the mummy coffin, and was placed on a stand, or "trestle," until the corpse was hauled to the grave.

Russell County, 1967 (PC). Informant: female, born 1915 in Russell County.

The homemade coffins used during pioneer days were made of wood, usually pine, walnut, or cherry, and were perfectly rectangular.

Taylor County, 1967 (MM). Informant: male, born 1905 in Taylor County.

The coffin was covered with black material if the person were old, or white material if the person were young.

Taylor County, 1967 (MM). Informant: male, born 1888 in Taylor County.

In the early 1900s the wooden coffins were covered with a plush type of material or velvet if the family could afford the expense.

Taylor County, 1967 (MM). Informant: female, born 1899 in Taylor County.

Many different types of material were used as a lining. The most prevalent type used during the early 1900s was unbleached muslin which was purchased at a general store when needed. Hand-embroidered bleached domestic was used as a lining. These linings were padded with cotton.

Taylor County, 1967 (MM). Informant: female, born 1883 in Green County.

During the 1800s some of the coffins were made of cast iron. Crane and Breed Co. in Cincinnati made this type of coffin. These coffins were hand cast and made of molten iron. They ranged from the very ornate to a plain coffin. A glass could be inserted in the top of the coffin so the family could view their loved one. The shape of this coffin was narrow at the head, wide at the shoulders, and very narrow at the foot.

Taylor County, 1967 (MM). Informant: male, born 1905 in Taylor County.

The original wooden coffins were made in a manner that the corpse was fully revealed, meaning the entire lid was made to be removed.

Later, the pattern was changed to allow only a partial view of the corpse.

> *Taylor County, 1967 (MM). Informant: female, born 1883 in Green County.*

221   A custom in the early 1900s was the use of a silver breastplate placed on top of the coffin which stated "At Rest."

> *Taylor County, 1967 (MM). Informant: female, born 1889 in Green County.*

222   The most expensive coffin that could be purchased around 1900 was one that sold for about ninety dollars.

> *Taylor County, 1967 (MM). Informant: male, born 1905 in Taylor County.*

223   Coffins were sold by merchants at Cloyd's Landing in the early 1900s. Prices ranged upward from fifteen dollars.

> *Cumberland County, 1970 (LM). Informant: male, born 1880 in Cumberland County.*

224   Occasionally, personal items were included in the coffin. The Indians were buried in festive costumes. They would put items such as cooking vessels and tools of trade in the grave. The early settlers were buried with some of their personal effects, such as jewelry, pictures, Bibles, and gifts they cherished.

> *Taylor County, 1967 (MM). Informant: male, born 1905 in Taylor County.*

225   One mother placed the picture of her daughter's sweetheart in her daughter's coffin. A wedding band was purchased for a wife after death.

> *Taylor County, 1967 (MM). Informant: female, born 1878 in Green County.*

THE FUNERAL

The Funeral Procession

226   The corpse should always be taken from the house feet first.

> *Russell County, 1964 (RLa). Informant: female, born 1899 in Russell County.* Brown 5429.

227   Take a casket in a house head first and out feet first.

> *Clinton County, 1963 (SW). Informant: female, born 1917 in Clinton County.* Cf. Brown 5429.

The corpse was hauled to the graveyard by two mules hitched to a wagon. The driver and one or two more persons sat on the spring seat of the wagon, which was drawn over rough or rocky roads.

Clinton County, 1966 (SP). Informant: female, born 1910 in Clinton County.

Friends of the deceased usually carried the caskets if the distance to the graveyard wasn't too far. The first motor coaches or hearses entered the area in 1925. Before the funeral homes were so popular, many times the undertakers rode on mules to go embalm people.

Rockcastle County, 1968 (JeC). Informant: male, born 1898 in Rockcastle County. This information was also reported from Taylor County in 1967.

If you count the cars in a funeral procession, that will be how many years you will live.

Taylor County, 1965 (CC). Informant: female, born 1925 in Taylor County.

If a person counts the buggies in a funeral procession, it will be that many days until he will die.

Taylor County, 1966 (GN). Informant: male, age unknown, born in Taylor County.

If you count all the cars in the funeral procession, the next person you hear about dying will be in your family.

Green County, 1966 (GN). Informant: male, born 1940 in Larue County.

Count the cars in a funeral line, and it is bad luck. The next death will be in your family.

Casey County, 1968 (BW). Informant: female, born 1890 in Casey County. Cf. Brown 5453.

It is bad luck to count the cars in a funeral procession because it will be that many days until someone in your own family dies.

Taylor County, 1964 (NM). Informant: female, age unknown, born in Taylor County.

If you meet a corpse, one out of your family will die.

Green County, 1965 (EH). Informant: male, born 1900 in Green County. Brand, *Popular Antiquities*, 450, states that one should always remove his hat when meeting a funeral procession in order to appease the evil spirits attending the corpse.

Never carry a baby in a funeral procession. If you do, it will die.

Lincoln County, 1964 (JWi). Informant: female, born 1902 in Lin-

coln County. This superstition from the Eastern Pennyroyal was also known in Mercer County in the Bluegrass region.

237   It is bad luck for a wedding party to meet a funeral procession.

   Russell County, 1968 (LP). Informant: female, born 1912 in Russell County. Cf. Brown 4976.

238   The motor hearses used during the 1920s were very ornate. They were shaped like a coach, glass-enclosed, and had black fringe and tassels hanging from the inside at the top.

   Taylor County, 1967 (MM). Informant: female, born 1899 in Taylor County.

The Memorial Service

239   Sometimes in the earlier days, there was no funeral service conducted if a death occurred during harsh, winter weather. In such a case the funeral was usually set for the spring of the year or during fair weather so that the people could get to the burial site.

   The service was short. And if a preacher could not attend the funeral, some well-known relative or neighbor conducted the service. Someone usually read a passage from the Bible, and another would pray.

   People who attended the funerals, whether friends or relatives, always wore black. This custom first originated in England, and it was a tradition for the people to mourn for several days after the death of one of the family or a close relative. This was especially true of women who had to wear black clothes and enter a stage of mourning for a certain period of time. If this tradition was not practiced, neighbors and other people would accuse the woman of not paying respect to the dead. Men didn't wear black as long as women because they had the duties of making a living and couldn't remain in any lengthy state of mourning.

   Russell County, 1967 (PC). Informant: male, born 1907 in Russell County.

240   A funeral service was called a burial. It was an established custom in the middle 1800s to have the funeral service in the month of May. This custom was observed because the condition of the roads in the winter months made it almost impossible to travel.

Taylor County, 1967 (MM). Informant: female, born 1889 in Green County.

There were no definite pallbearers then. Anyone who attended the service could be assigned this task.

Taylor County, 1967 (MM). Informant: female, born 1883 in Green County.

One short funeral service was held in earlier times, either at the gravesite or in the home. If the weather permitted, the funeral service was held at the graveside. The coffin was always opened at the grave.

Taylor County, 1967 (MM). Informant: female, born 1883 in Green County.

If there were no ministers available, any outstanding citizens could officiate at the service. The service consisted of singing hymns, a prayer, and a word of advice to the friends and family of the deceased.

Taylor County, 1967 (MM). Informant: female, born 1889 in Green County.

The funerals were usually at the home. They were at a church only if it was convenient for the family. Now, there are more funerals in the funeral homes.

Rockcastle County, 1968 (JeC). Informant: male, born 1898 in Rockcastle County.

When the bodies are laid out at funeral homes now around Mt. Vernon, there are rows of chairs set up for people who come to pay their respects. They first speak to the family, then sit down and stay for awhile. This may be a practice in other places, too, but it is just the thing to do in Mt. Vernon.

Rockcastle County, 1968 (JeC). Informant: male, born 1898 in Rockcastle County.

The funeral service was an all-day meeting drug out only to eulogize the dead and actually relive the life of the deceased all over again, pointing out the good things that he had done for his neighbors, and, unless he were a Christian, skirting his moral deeds.

Now, in most places, the preacher reads who his parents were, how many children he had, their names, and so forth, and picks a

text from the Bible and says only a few things mostly for the con-
solation of the dead person's family.

> *Rockcastle County, 1968 (JeC). Informant: male, born 1898 in*
> *Rockcastle County.*

247   In the late 1800s and early 1900s in Taylor County, it was considered proper to wear mourning clothes for a period of twelve
months. The women wore black clothing for a period of six months
and black and white clothing for the next six months.

> *Taylor County, 1967 (MM). Informant: female, born 1878 in*
> *Green County.* Brand, *Popular Antiquities,* 467–70, discusses the his-
> tory of colors used in mourning at funerals. The Romans generally
> used white as the mourning color, and this custom prevailed through-
> out Western Europe through the Middle Ages. The vogue of black
> was given a powerful impetus in 1498 when black was substituted for
> white by Anne, the widow of Charles VIII of France. See Habenstein,
> *Funeral Directing,* 126.

248   The people wore black while in mourning for the dead. The minister wore a Prince Albert coat with a pocket in the split of the tail in
which to carry his Bible and song book.

> *Rockcastle County, 1968 (JeC). Informant: male, born 1898 in*
> *Rockcastle County.*

249   Now, in Mt. Vernon, the body is taken to the back of the church,
and all of the people pass by one at a time to have a last look at the
deceased. And everyone goes outside, stands, and waits until the
the family passes to have their last look at the deceased. They do not
get into their cars until the family does.

> *Rockcastle County, 1968 (JeC). Informant: male, born 1898 in*
> *Rockcastle County.* The undertaker, if present, directed the pace of
> the pallbearers from the church to the cemetery. He was accompanied
> by the minister. The pallbearers deposited the casket over the grave
> and took their places facing the family. The minister then began the
> service to commit the body to the grave. Sometimes the casket was
> reopened, but generally not. Under the direction of the undertaker,
> or by a skilled pallbearer, the casket was lowered into the grave by
> means of heavy fiber belts. Filling the grave with dirt came next. In
> some places the family stayed to watch; in other places they were led
> away to prevent still another cry of anguish. A note in Habenstein's
> *Funeral Directing,* 412, claims that in Parris, Missouri, around 1900
> and before, the filling of the grave took the form of a contest with the

Cracked and broken window panes often signal a deserted dwelling, a common site for ghosts in folklore of the Pennyroyal.

Lore of death and ghosts endures in the folk tradition because of the persist-
ence of storytellers such as Sam Moore *(above)*, a history buff and wood
whittler of Green County. *Right*: Country lanes, such as this haunted spot
in Monroe County, figure prominently in death-related tales and beliefs
of the Eastern Pennyroyal.

The abandoned Montgomery mill (*above*) on Pitman Creek in Green County provides a typical setting for one of the hillcountry's ghost tales. *Right*: The grave represents finality for the body but, frequently in oral tradition, is merely the beginning for a supernatural appearance. Marvin Moody and Clutie Bailey prepare this grave in the Sulphur Lick community.

Above: A belief from Taylor County warns that "if a rooster crows facing the house, it is a sign of death." *Right*: Opal Howard, storyteller, peers inside an old haunted house near her home in northern Monroe County.

Standing in the haunted Hiestand graveyard near Campbellsville, its owner Harley L. Gilmore recounts one of the ghost tales associated with this former burial ground.

masculine friends vying with each other in their ability to manipulate a shovel. Nobody thought of leaving until the grave was filled.

Use of Flowers

Very few flowers were used at funerals, and those that were brought by a relative or some kind neighbor had all the foliage picked off and were tied in round bundles, sometimes with a scrap of ribbon, but more often with a string.

> *Clinton County, 1966 (SP). Informant: female, born 1910 in Clinton County.* The practice of placing flowers upon the grave-sites of departed friends and of planting sweet-scented flowers and evergreens over the graves stems from ancient church practices. See Brand, *Popular Antiquities*, 485–86.
>
> "Funeral flowers, today the major symbol and a huge item of national expenditure, did not make their appearance in England or America until after the middle of the nineteenth century, and only then over the opposition of church leaders." Jessica Mitford, *The American Way of Death* (New York, 1963), 198–99.

"Everytime someone died, and when there were flowers at all in season, my mother would send a huge bouquet to the grave. They'd take the shovel handle and stick it down in the grave mound and then pour water in the hole. Then they would stick the bouquet in there and it would keep for two or three days."

> *Taylor County, 1967 (MM). Informant: female, born 1899 in Monroe County.* This information was also obtained from Cumberland County in 1970.

They didn't have flowers unless the relatives stopped to pick a few wild ones.

> *Clinton County, 1966 (SP). Informant: male, born 1906 in Wayne County.*

It is bad luck to count the bunches of flowers at a funeral.

> *Green County, 1967 (KRP). Informant: male, born 1917 in Green County.*

Fresh imported flowers could be purchased from floral shops by the mid-1930s.

> *Cumberland County, 1970 (LM). Informant: female, born 1899 in Cumberland County.*

255   If there was any singing at some of the funerals, the minister usually
       did the singing.
         *Rockcastle County, 1968 (JeC). Informant: male, born 1898 in
         Rockcastle County.*

256   The congregation sang such songs as "Love Lifted Me," "O, How
       Precious is the Promise," and "When the Evening Shadows Gather."
         *Clinton County, 1966 (SP). Informant: female, born 1910 in Clin-
         ton County.*

Burial

257   People are buried facing the east so they can face the rising sun.
         *Monroe County, 1968 (BD). Informant: female, born 1947 in Mon-
         roe County.* Brown 5482. A report also came from Monroe County
         in 1967.

258   People are buried facing the east so that they will meet the Savior
       face to face on resurrection morning.
         *Monroe County, 1967 (NL). Informant: male, born ca. 1909 in
         Monroe County.* Brown 5482. This was also reported a second time
         that same year from Monroe County.

259   Negroes never leave a grave open overnight. This means it is neces-
       sary to dig the grave on the day of the funeral.
         *Green County, 1967 (MM). Informant: male, born 1926 in Green
         County.*

260   If it rains in an open grave, another member of the family will go
       out in a year.
         *Metcalfe County, 1968 (SW). Informant: female, born 1925 in
         Metcalfe County.* Cf. Brown 5514. This belief was also reported from
         Clinton County (1963) and known in Shelby, Fleming, and Hardin
         counties.

261   If it rains on the day a dead person is buried, that person will go to
       heaven.
         *Taylor County, 1966 (DSh). Informant: male, born 1947 in Taylor
         County.* Brown 5516. This superstition was also known outside the
         Eastern Pennyroyal—in Kenton County.

262   Funerals were horrible in those days, especially to children. I re-
       member distinctly being at the funeral of an old man who had
       passed away in our neighborhood. His coffin was set on planks, laid
       beside his grave. He had long black hair and a black beard. His

eyes were partly open and his mouth was open. When the relatives gathered to view the remains, some went into hysteria. Others pushed one another aside to get a closer view.

Clinton County, 1966 (SP). Informant: female, born 1910 in Clinton County.

They set the casket down on two rails on the side of the grave. They would sing a song, have a prayer, and that was all. Most of them had the service by the grave.

Clinton County, 1966 (SP). Informant: male, born 1906 in Wayne County.

After the services, the men lowered the casket into the grave by check lines. It took about four men on each side of the grave. After the casket was put on the bottom, they pulled the check lines up. Then they put dirt in on top of the casket.

Clinton County, 1966 (SP). Informant: male, born 1906 in Wayne County.

The grave was dug by hand. The bottom of the grave pit was the size of the coffin, but the top of the pit extended six inches. This practice prevented dirt from falling in on the coffin.

The graves were dynamited when rock was present. One person requested that no water be allowed to touch his coffin. The family made arrangements to have concrete poured over the bottom of the grave. After the coffin was lowered into the grave, concrete was poured in, thus completely enclosing the coffin in cement.

Taylor County, 1967 (MM). Informant: female, born 1894 in Taylor County.

Graves were dug a certain width and length. In the center of the grave was a niche the same size as the casket. After the casket was placed in this niche, oak planks were laid on top of it. Then all of the space above the planks was filled in with dirt.

Graves of people buried in this manner have a great tendency to sink almost a foot within a year or so after the person is buried. The reason for this is because the acid in the oak causes the wood to decay and, also, the bones of the body to decay. This seems to be the reason that the skeletons of very few white people are found, while skeletons of Indians that are found are well preserved.

Russell County, 1967 (PC). Informant: male, born 1907 in Russell County.

267   Nowdays, people sometimes refer to certain farmland as "poor as a graveyard." This saying was supposed to have originated from the Indian custom of burying their dead on very poor spots of ground, especially unsuitable for cultivation.

    Russell County, 1967 (PC). Informant: male, born 1907 in Russell County.

268   The person who leaves the grave first will be the next person to die.

    Russell County, 1964 (RLa). Informant: female, born 1899 in Russell County. Brown 5523.

269   The tool for digging a grave should be left at the grave for several days.

    Russell County, 1964 (RLa). Informant: female, born 1899 in Russell County. Cf. Brown 5484.

270   Put conch shells on graves because they will make mournful notes when blown. In this way the death of a friend can be mourned.

    Adair County, 1964 (PRA). Informant: male, born 1891 in Adair County. Cf. Brown 5502.

271   Some people don't believe in having any grass on their grave. They just want the dirt mounded up.

    Monroe County, 1967 (NL). Informant: male, born 1928 in Monroe County.

272   When a grave sinks early, another will follow soon.

    Taylor County, 1967 (MM). Informant: female, born 1889 in Green County.

273   If you play on graves, you'll be dead before you are twenty.

    Taylor County, 1966 (BMS). Informant: female, born 1918 in Taylor County.

274   If you step over a grave, you'll die soon.

    Russell County, 1968 (LP). Informant: female, born 1903 in Russell County. Brown 5499. A report of this also came from Taylor County in 1966.

275   Old Man Jones at Broughtown wanted to be buried in a cedar coffin and under a cedar tree so he could go through hell a-poppin' and a-crackin'. He was buried this way, too.

    Lincoln County, 1965 (BJ). Informant: male, born 1943 in Lincoln County.

PART III

The Return of the Dead

INTRODUCTION TO GHOSTLORE

CULTURAL MILIEUX

Ghost tale is perhaps the term most generally applied by the folk of the Kentucky foothills to denote any of the massive corpus of legends dealing with the supernatural which are inextricably tied up with certain haunted houses, bridges, and secluded spots along the road. Some people in the Eastern Pennyroyal use the expression *scary story* when they refer to such a narrative, and others use *haint tale* in the same sense. The more sophisticated term *haunt tale*, however, is never employed by the folk in genuine storytelling situations. An Adair County family refers to the whole body of supernatural legends as *tramp tales*, and most of the members of my own childhood community in Monroe County used the expression *bear tales* to describe ghost and other scary stories. Interestingly enough, a bear-tale session never produced stories about bears. I recall very well how, during my early years, several men of the community would gather at my father's house on Sunday afternoons. He was the local barber—not a licensed one, mind you, for rarely was he offered more than ten cents a head for haircuts—and the "barber shop" was located in our kitchen at the side of the fireplace hearth where a small window permitted natural light to enter the room. Once the men had congregated it was not long until one of them— or perhaps one of us boys—would suggest, "Let's tell bear tales." Tale swapping went on until bedtime that night. The same old stories? Yes, but it seemed that each telling made them more alive, more realistic, and more dramatic to the members of the group.

Perhaps the most natural setting for a story recounting a supernatural situation was the home, especially the home of grandparents who seemed to derive a great degree of satisfaction from telling the old family legends to their grandchildren. Such stories were always told for the truth, and none of the gruesome and hoary details were spared. In the words of one informant, "Why, Aunt Randy has told me old scary tales! She used to stay with us, and that's what she'd do of a night. Would tell me old tales of things that happened back when she was a young girl. That's what she would sit and tell me! Then I'd be so scared of a night, I couldn't go to sleep. I'd lay there and study about what all Aunt Randy had told me. I'd get so nervous I couldn't stand it!" Grandparents and grandchildren seem to form a vital axis in the transmission of oral traditions. This is probably because grandparents in the Eastern Pennyroyal of Kentucky—and likely elsewhere—assume some sort of ancestral hue to the later generations, especially the young people, who revere them and willingly accord them a special position of respect and dignity. In this capacity, the grandchildren and great-grandchildren look to them for recreation, companionship, and leadership. Parents are busy making a living. Even during their off hours, Kentucky hillcountry parents do not feel at liberty to fraternize too freely with their children. It is a matter of sustaining discipline, among other reasons. In more than a few instances, I have recovered stories and songs from informants who had learned the items from grandparents. Strangely enough, these bits of folklore were not known by the second generation, thus indicating a generation gap in the process of oral transmittal.

Country stores serve as the second major place where tales are exchanged. But unlike the family situations which call for a vertical or downward type of transmission from one generation to another, the country store society, comprised mainly of middle-aged to old males, engages in a horizontal exchange of traditions from one person to another within the same generation. Supernatural legends are only one small segment of the stories told at the country stores. For this reason they are not usually termed haint tales or bear tales or ghost stories; instead they are grouped with local historical legends and other folktales under the generic umbrella of *old tales*.

Tale swapping is a dynamic process in family and other intimate small groups. There is constant give-and-take, even by those who do not actually engage in the verbalizing action. Eyes make constant contact with all those present. It is these glances, coupled with occasional uneasy shifts in sitting position, that reaffirm belief and intensify the group communicative process. Individual narrative art is rewarded by the oohs and aahs and the occasional groans, shudders, and perhaps shrieks from the audience when a performer completes the legend.

In circumstances such as this, the narrator may be an old grandmother or grandfather in solo performance. Generally, however, two or three persons in the group exchange tales. Such being the case, allowances are made for the contributions of each participant in round-robin fashion. And although they all believe the tales told by the others, each contributor will often begin the next narrative by validating its authenticity. "Now, this one really happened," or "Now, Uncle George swore that he saw this thing . . . ," and so on.

THE ELEMENT OF BELIEF

A Negro resident of Tompkinsville sat close to the flimsy sheet metal stove in the only front room her shotgun house afforded. After almost an hour of narrating witch tales, death omen narratives, and ghost stories into my tape recorder, she stopped suddenly in the middle of a ghost story, looked me squarely in the eyes and inquired, "Mister, do you believe in ghostes?" I was on the spot! If I said, "Yes, I believe in them," then I would have been guilty of uttering a false statement for the sake of perhaps pleasing my informant. If, on the other hand, I had said, "No, I cannot accept them as truth," then she would have stopped the recording session abruptly. Fate was with me, for when I responded, "Well, they certainly tell some interesting stories about ghosts," she resumed the story she was telling and after that never touched on the question of belief in the stories contained in her repertory.

It is not my purpose to include or exclude stories here on the basis of the informants' beliefs in the contents of the narratives, but a few comments should be made on this point. People do believe in ghosts. Eighteen of these stories were told as personal experiences of encounters with a supernatural being or some form of the supernatural. Belief is paramount and unquestioned in such cases. Of the approximately 175 narratives which call for a belief conviction on the part of the narrator, only three were told by persons who made a fairly definite statement of disbelief in ghosts. All of the other narratives were recounted by persons who either believed in the supernatural creatures or manifestations, or told them as family episodes experienced by the person or persons described in the happenings. Any incongruity between total belief and hesitant belief is explained away in the folk rationale on the basis made articulate by one informant: "Things just aren't the same now as they were back in those days. Even if we don't see things today, I believe they did see them in olden times."

One reason certain hillcountry people believe in ghosts is that for the most part such persons are products of their cultural matrix; that is, the milieu in which they were reared was one in which ghost stories were a part of the culture trait. If parents or grandparents told ghost stories to frighten children into submission, or if ghost stories were a part of the folk process of entertainment and were told often, the active participants in these traditions would believe in ghosts more than those persons who were brought up in an environment to which ghost narratives were alien. One informant stated emphatically, "I'm afraid of ghosts and refuse to have anything to do with them." Another commented, "I didn't like to hear them. That's the reason I don't know any."

THE PHYSICAL AND CULTURAL SETTING

Unlike märchen and mythical tales which are set within an indefinite framework of time and which unfold within unrealistic worlds, these supernatural legends took place almost exclusively at a precise or definable time in the past and are studded with routine mention—but seldom contain a full description—of natural environmental elements and items of material or human culture. A cursory inventory of the frequency of occurrences of terms which are concerned with those elements over which man exercises little or no control reveals that the terms *night, dark,* or *darkness* are used a total of eighty-one times in the tales presented in this book, while the terms *day*, *morning*, and *afternoon* appear only nine times. There is little question, then, but that ghosts do indeed prowl at night in the Eastern Pennyroyal. Interestingly enough, however, these nocturnal phenomena do not appear when the heavens are being ripped apart by storms, winds, and bolts of lightning—features which are common in ghost literature written for the popular market. Of the 216 ghost narratives in this collection, only fifteen mention any turbulence in the elements—most of the fifteen simply state that it was raining; two note that "it was coming up a storm."

Among the physical features commonly mentioned are hills (catalogued 22 times) and creeks and trees (listed 13 times each). Front yards, which are fairly popular haunts of ghosts, came in for 12 mentions, with hollows, fields, woods, and grounds completing the list of features of the physical landscape more often employed in ghost narratives. Ghosts did not always occur in connection with each mention of these topographic features, but apparitions did appear much of the time.

More popular than any of the foregoing was the word *road* (or occasionally its synonyms *lane* and *trail*) which was employed 35 times, usually in connection with an encounter with supernatural phenomena. A road is really the product of human culture, however, and therefore could just as easily be classified under that category rather than physical.

The tales in this collection were also inventoried for the total number of occurrences of words related to the human cultural aspects of the environment. This count revealed that the term *house* was employed in 98 narratives—almost 50 percent of the total. There is little wonder, then, that any mention of the word *ghost* conjures up in our minds a dilapidated structure with banging shutters and creaking doors. That *graveyard* or *cemetery* should place second with 53 mentions is also no surprise. Along with the house, the graveyard thus appears as a rather constant factor in the site and action of many ghost narratives. Virtually all of the remaining items on the inventory related to the environment are associated with some specific part of houses—doors were mentioned 43 times, thus outdistancing the 42 times that floors, bedrooms, living rooms, kitchens, unspecified rooms, closets, and halls were collectively mentioned. Stairways were cited in 18 instances, almost always in connection with the appearance of a ghost; the upstairs area came in for 23 listings; and windows were counted 16 times. Beds occurred in 21 narratives, and all other types of furniture appeared in 22. Items of clothing and bed clothing together counted for 43 occurrences in the tales.

These statistics certainly demonstrate that the appearances of most of the ghosts are associated with the house, and more specifically with certain parts of the house. In some instances the ghost may even be emerging from a fireplace, playing a piano in a particular room, or coming down a fireplace chimney.

Where do ghosts appear outside the house at the time they are seen or heard? In addition to their fondness for the graveyard as a locale, ghosts may decide to invade a yard to pick roses or to lurk in a thicket of bushes, in a haunted tree, or along a rainswept roadway. A specter could appear in such places as a schoolhouse doorway, a pond, a cave, or a funeral home. The ghost may be seen as blood in the spring water, or may be seen walking down a hill or riding on the hood of an automobile.

Such precise locations given by narrators of ghost tales are understandable because their stories are very personal to them; the accounts deal with the deaths of specific persons—usually relatives or close associates of the family. It is this close family tie to the deceased that causes a narrator to be fairly definite in placing the location of the reappearance of the deceased in the form of a ghost.

Another familiarity of the narrators emerged in the inventory of the tales in this collection. Fifty-seven of the 216 tales mentioned animals. Included were dogs (15), cats (4), sheep (6), cattle (7), and the horse alone accounted for 26 of the animal occurrences. The first four animal types were ghosts themselves in a sizeable number of tales, but never was this true for the horse. The horse was never portrayed as a ghost (one unique story tells about a fire-breathing horse, however), but instead is pictured as an animal which is sensitive to the supernatural and can even sense the presence of death and of ghosts. If all the stories containing the mention of horses were grouped and studied, perhaps it would be seen that a whole body of legends and legend complexes utilizes the horse as a stock character.

CHARACTERISTICS OF THE GHOSTS

Despite popular belief, ghosts robed in white do not wait in hiding and then jump in front of some unsuspecting person and yell, "boo!" To the contrary, ghosts go about their business in a very unpretentious manner and appear to be little desirous of any fanfare. They have a role to perform. If this can be accomplished without contact with living humans, then they are quite content to remain unseen. Their missions do frequently dictate contact with the living, however. Louis C. Jones has sufficiently explained the reasons why ghosts in upstate New York return to their old haunts (*Things That Go Bump in the Night* [New York, 1959], 19–55). Those reasons fall roughly into the following categories: "They come back to re-enact their own deaths; to complete unfinished business; to re-engage in what were their normal pursuits when they were alive; to protest or punish; or, finally, to warn, console, inform, guard, or reward the living" (*Ibid.*, 19).

There is no real difference in these motifs and the motifs of the ghosts of the Kentucky foothills, except that the first two categories are not common in this geographical area. In addition to accepting for southcentral Kentucky the other categories espoused by Jones, I would propose a new category to embrace the ghosts who come back for no apparent reason. In truth, this category would constitute the largest block of stories from the Eastern Pennyroyal. These are stories in which a ghost may be seen, but with no resultant action, or may not be seen—but noises from a specter are heard. It is interesting to note further that no reason is ever stated for these noises.

On the other hand, some stories give a definite reason for the return of a spirit. Specifically, in the order of appearance in this book, the explicit reasons for the return of ghosts are as follows:

tombstone for a dead man not yet erected over his grave; person had died of starvation and his ghost had returned to eat food; fireplace hearth had been built over the grave; body was restless in the grave; a workbench had been erected over the family burial plot; ghost returned to finish playing a tune on the piano; and mother returned to inquire about her baby's whereabouts. Other reasons for the return of ghosts were: to retaliate because a woman's husband had re-married at her death; to seek vengeance; to determine who had picked pins from the dead person's shroud; to look at former students; to re-enact death; to haunt husband; to identify murderer; to punish for theft of part of corpse; to haunt man who pocketed money; to punish man for drinking; to search for money; to torment the killer into admitting guilt; to reveal hidden money; to haunt spot where murder occurred; to get occupants to give up their claim to house; and to play a prank.

Ghosts are generally seen by the living. As a matter of fact, supernatural phenomena were witnessed in 119 of the narratives relevant to this point, but in the other stories the ghosts were only heard as noises or only surmised to be ghosts. The unseen category is rather amorphous and is comprised of ghostly lights, eerie noises, and unnatural sounds. Such manifestations allow the human mind to conjure up thoughts of ghosts and other supernatural creatures when the cultural matrix of the people makes allowances for such phenomena.

A final comment might be made regarding the sex of ghosts. There are more ghosts of men than women, at a four to three ratio. Interestingly enough, while male ghosts are most numerous in ghostlore, in witch narratives—that large body of legends at the other end of the supernatural spectrum—women are the key figures.

GHOST NARRATIVES

THE UNSATISFIED DEAD

Will Jackman Fiddles Again

Old Man Will Jackman built that old house down on the creek over a hundred years ago. He was a rich man, and he had all sorts of fine furniture and stuff in it. You know the house; it was the one you was born in.

Now one time Old Will got sick and died, and two or three of his family died, too. They buried them in the graveyard up on the hill across the creek.

Will's boy, Bruce, come into a lot of money. He give most of it to Myrtle Cagle, and she had a young'un by him. And he got in some more trouble, and he went out to Oklahoma and, I think, died there not long after.

But, now, when Arlo Rippetoe was living down there after all them Pettys died, he got to hearing strange things at night. Chains would sound like they was dropped from the top of the house and would make a terrible racket. Arlo had an old pistol. One night he heard somebody walking around the house. He got up and went out and couldn't see, but down in the road in front of the house was this fine black carriage with a fine span of black horses pulling it. Arlo said it looked just like a hearse to him.

Well, he went out and it disappeared! He went back in the house. This went on for some time, and Arlo said that he would be woke up by fiddle music. Old Man Will Jackman was a good fiddler, and Arlo heard him so he knew that it was Old Man Will playing.

One day Arlo said he was poking around in a closet and found Old Man Will's and his kin's tombstones. They had been bought but not put up. Arlo was good at that sort of thing, and he went and put up the stones. And forever after that, he said, he had not heard anything there.

Adair County, 1966 (RSu). Informant: female, age unknown, born in Adair County. This gripping narrative reads like a dictionary of legend motifs. The very common *E281, "Ghosts haunt house," is present, along with the amorphous Motif *E402, "Mysterious ghost-like noises heard." Other motifs in this sequence, mainly of English-American origin, include *E402.1.2, "Footsteps of invisible ghost heard"; *E402.1.3(a), "Ghost plays violin"; and *E402.1.4, "Invisible ghost jingles chains."

The laying of the ghost by erecting the neglected gravestones had not been reported previously from oral tradition but is related to Motif *E451, "Ghost finds rest when certain things happen." The "Phantom coach and horses" is classified under Motif *E535.1. Baughman lists additional sources for Motif *E535.2(a), "Ghostly wagon drawn by two black horses," reported only from Illinois tradition previously.

The Starving Woman

277   There is an old haunted house in the southern portion of Barren County near the Austin community. It is said that an old woman whose name was Stephens starved to death while living alone there. When she was dying someone gave her a piece of cornbread. She grabbed it and ate it like she was starving. The old lady was laid to rest in a nearby graveyard, but her haint continued to plague the old house as rattling dishes and strange noises.

The hungry supernatural creature was finally quieted by a subsequent family of residents who moved in after others had been frightened away. "Go ahead and eat all you want, Miz Stephens," they would say to her, as she moved about the kitchen foraging through the dishes and utensils. Eventually, the noises ceased as the appeased spirit returned to the graveyard.

Barren County, 1966 (TT). Informant: female, born 1927 in Barren County. The informant learned this narrative from her mother. Motif *E281, "Ghosts haunt house," is applicable here, as well as *E402, "Mysterious ghost-like noises heard," and *E402.1.8, "Miscellaneous sounds made by ghost of human being."

The Lady of the Hearth

The massive stone fireplace was the center of family life in pioneer Kentucky. In Lincoln County, in many respects the gateway to the West, a well-to-do family built a new house containing such a chimney, a large hand-hewn stone affair. When the family occupied their new home, they began to notice something odd about the fireplace. It seems that when the fire would die down at night and the embers had been banked for the night, a strange light would appear and shine in the darkness. Investigations revealed that it was not something in or on any of the stones.

The family became terribly frightened as time went on but had not been willing to stay in the room with the light. They employed a man to come and watch the light and attempt to figure out what was causing it. The man became frightened and ran away without getting to the source of the ghostly light.

Two other men were brought in to sit as a pair and study the light when it appeared. That night, the light came forth and soon afterwards the form of a woman materialized on the hearth before their very eyes. They talked with the troubled creature and learned that the fireplace had been over two graves.

The people who owned the house tore away the fireplace and removed the skeletal remains from the graves and buried them nearby in an undisturbed spot. From that time forward the light has not been seen in the big fireplace.

Taylor County, 1965 (DP). Informant: male, born 1904 in Lincoln County. This belief narrative contains motifs which are tied strongly to British and American tradition: *E334.2, "Ghost haunts burial spot"; *E338(b), "Female ghost seen in house"; and *E530.1.3, "Ghost light haunts burial spot."

The Tinkling Bell

North of Glasgow, the county seat of Barren County, some eighty years ago two brothers had a quarrel in a ridge cemetery and killed each other. Local legend now has it that when a person walks near the cemetery at night during the full of the moon, he can hear a bell ringing. It is the ghosts of the two brothers, so they say. They are restless and the grave will not contain their spirits.

One night when the moon was full a resident of the community went coon hunting, and during the course of the evening, the hounds led him by the cemetery. He reported that he most assuredly heard a tinkling bell coming from the burial area.

Others from the community have made similar reports within recent years.

> *Bradenton, Fla., 1967 (BAk). Informant: male, middle-aged, born in Barren County.* Motif *E334.2.1, "Ghost of murdered person haunts burial spot," is known widely in European tradition. Motifs *E413, "Murdered person cannot rest in grave," and *E533, "Ghostly bell," are reported only from the British Isles and the United States.

The Ghost Hand

280   There was a man went walking through the woods, and he noticed that his dog had something in its mouth. When he made the dog drop it, he saw that it was the bones of a human hand.

He wrapped them up in his handkerchief to take them home. The hand pinched him several times on his way home.

He put it in an old cupboard, and every night a knocking on the door caused him to get up and open the cupboard, and the hand would fall out and pinch his naked toes.

> *Adair County, 1968 (NAB). Informant: female, born 1908 in Russell County.* This story is often told as a "Boo!" story in a vein similar to "The Big Toe" or "The Golden Arm." If disassociated from their function, however, the stories containing Motif *E422.1.11.3, "Ghost as hand or hands," appear to be related to the legend complex associated with the unsatisfied dead.

Revenant of the Antebellum Homeowner

281   "If I tell you this one, you will really think my grandmother is cracked; but she says it is the truth. She was ten years old at the time. Wiley was the male Negro slave of whom the family thought a lot. He had been with the family for a long time. My grandmother said that she was walking down the hall and saw this real good-looking gentleman standing in the hallway.

"They spoke, and she went on outside to the backyard where Wiley was. She said the gentleman was dressed in a cape and top hat. She asked Wiley who the man was who was in the hallway of the house. He remarked that he didn't know, but that he would go see who it was.

"She said Wiley turned around and ran out the door as soon as he saw the figure of the man. When they got outside and Wiley regained his composure, he said that that man was the person who had owned the house before the family bought it. He was supposed to have been killed in the Civil War."

Taylor County, 1964 (PB). Informant: female, born 1946 in Taylor County. This is an unusual report of Motif *E425.2, "Revenant as man," known primarily in Ireland.

The Unidentified Footsteps

One night these two men had been sitting up with a sick man in the community. One of the men had to walk home alone quite a distance in the deep of night. Something on the other side of the fence walked along beside him as he walked. If he ran, it ran too. If he walked, it walked.

It is supposed to have been a dead man who was buried in the nearby field.

Adair County, 1968 (NAB). Informant: female, born 1912 in Adair County. Common indeed are the ghost narratives in this extensive legend complex dealing with haunted burial spots. Such legends all appear related generically, despite the fact that the motifs may differ dramatically and present a profile of individuality. Motifs *E334.2, "Ghost haunts burial spot," and *E402.1.2, "Footsteps of invisible ghost heard," are both included in this traditional narrative known in England and the United States.

Female Ghost Haunts Burial Spot

Over in the hillcountry of Casey County, there was a man who had a work bench in a cave near his home.

He felt something strange, like someone was looking at him—watching him at work. He could see this woman standing in the darkness of the cave. He moved in toward where she was but found no one there.

He returned to his work only to see the specter staring at him again. He worried and worried until he got the notion to move the work bench and dig beneath it. There he found a whole family buried.

> *Russell County, 1968 (DDab). Informant: (anonymous contributor, except that subject born in Russell County).* Motif *E334.2, "Ghost haunts burial spot," is known only in English and American tradition. Motif *E425.1, "Revenant as woman," is also present in this fragmented narrative. See also comments for story No. 282.

Suicide Cannot Rest in Grave

284   "There was this house in Taylor County where a boy killed himself. A lady went down there to see the old house. She was told that people would not stay in the structure, that they would see something in there and come running out frightened half to death.

"They showed this lady the upstairs area of the house, and when they opened the door to one of the rooms, something ran out on her. Something could be seen there, but she never could say what it was. But she come running out of the house, too!"

> *Bradenton, Fla., 1964 (BAk). Informant: (anonymous contributor, except that subject born in Taylor County).* This narrative contains the oft-reported Motif *E411.1.1, "Suicide cannot rest in grave," known in County York (England) and in Pennsylvania, and the similar *E334.4, "Ghost of suicide seen at death spot or near by," reported only from the British Isles and the United States.

RETURN TO COMPLETE UNFINISHED BUSINESS

The Piano Still Plays

285   The old house across the road from my place is said to be hainted. No one has lived in that old house since Jimmy Gray's daughter was killed there several years ago. She was found stone dead sitting at her piano, by one of the neighbors.

Jimmy Gray was never found or heard from around here after

her death. It is said that he killed her while she was playing the piano. The neighbors buried her behind the Old Gray house.

Now, every night at 12 o'clock the old piano can be heard playing in the night. People reckon it is her ghost coming back to finish the song she was playing. Too, people say the house is hainted because one night some people were traveling from Liberty to McKinney, and they saw two figures leaving the old house. The ghosts darted across the road in front of the travelers and disappeared on the other side.

> *Lincoln County, 1964 (JWi). Informant: male, middle-aged, born in Lincoln County.* Although this narrative is unique in the story it tells, there is nothing about its motif components which sets it apart from several other stories found in the Eastern Pennyroyal of Kentucky. Fairly standard motifs include *E281, "Ghosts haunt house"; *E334.2.1, "Ghost of murdered person haunts burial spot"; and *E402.1.3, "Invisible ghost plays musical instrument."

Ghost of Buried Man

Once there was a fellow named Gwinn Gaulden who married a Wilson girl. Like a lot of people, she was afraid of funerals. Well, she wouldn't go to some neighbor man's funeral.

After the fellow was dead and had been buried, Gaulden's wife come along by the graveyard. And she come on home and told 'em that she had seen him standing at the grave, and she even told 'em what kind of clothes he had on. The people told her that they were the clothes he had been buried in.

> *Adair County, 1968 (NAB). Informant: female, born 1889 in Russell County.* Applicable motifs include *E334.2, "Ghost haunts burial spot," and *E425.2, "Revenant as man."

Ghost Mother Inquires about Baby

This is a story about my Aunt Betty and Sam Barnett. I can't remember too awful much about it, but I'll tell you what I can.

My Aunt Betty died and left some little children without a mama. And Sam said that he saw a woman coming across the field all dressed in white. And it was Aunt Betty. She had been dead for quite awhile at that time. She asked him where her baby was, and he told her Bart had it—that was her brother.

That must have satisfied her for she just kept right on walking.

*Adair County, 1968 (NAB). Informant: female, born 1889 in Russell County. This is another of the many ghost narratives containing a woman dressed in white as the chief actor. For a fuller consideration of the woman in white complex, consult Jones, Things That Go Bump in the Night, Ch. 4. Applicable motifs are *E323, "Dead mother's friendly return"; *E323.1, "Dead mother returns to see baby," known in Minnesota and Utah; and *E422.4.4(a), "Female revenant in white clothing."*

The Visitor in My Room

288   In passing through a village not many years ago, I stopped to spend the night with a very dear friend whose husband had recently died. This family had once lived very close neighbor to me, and I had known the husband very well when he was living. I had supper and spent a very pleasant evening with the family, which consisted of the mother and three daughters. When it came time to retire for the night, the mother asked me if I were afraid to sleep upstairs.

After assuring her that I was not afraid to sleep any place in the house, I was shown to my bedroom, which was a small upstairs room with a wall which seemed to separate it from another room, but there was no door leading into it. Everything seemed very quiet, and I turned out my light and was soon asleep.

I did not know how long I had been asleep, but I was suddenly awakened by a noise which seemed to be in the room or in the room just behind the wall. It seemed to be a carpenter at work, such sawing and hammering as I have never heard before. I listened for a few minutes, thinking perhaps it was morning and that someone was up and at work, but I finally decided to turn on the light and see what time it was.

When I turned on the light, the sawing and hammering stopped; but I could see someone standing in the corner of the room—the husband of the friend with whom I was spending the night. He had on a dark hat which was slightly drawn over his face, but I at once recognized him. I kept the light on for some time, but I did not speak and he did not make a move but stood perfectly still with his hammer and saw in his hand.

I finally decided that there was no use in alarming the family or to continue staring at him, so I again turned out the light. Immediately, the sawing and hammering began as loud as ever.

Several times during the night, I would again turn on the light. Each time the noise would stop, and the form of the man would stand perfectly still until the light was out again.

The next morning the family asked me if I slept. I replied that something made a lot of noise, but that it might have been rats. They looked at me in perfect horror, and the mother said, "It might have been."

Wayne County, 1938 (GV). Informant: female, age unknown, probably born in Wayne County. "The Visitor in My Room" is used by permission of the Folk Music Division, Library of Congress. I consider this story to be one of the most interesting and complete narratives to be collected by the Federal Writer's Project during the 1930s. Several motifs are present, but the prominent ones are *E279.2, "Ghost disturbs sleeping person," found in New York previously; *E402, "Mysterious ghost-like noises heard"; *E422.4.5, "Revenant in male dress"; and *E425.2, "Revenant as man."

Dead Man Whittles on the Porch

"There was a man and a woman over around Sulphur Lick, and the man was crazy. He went out to the barn and shot hisself—took his own life.

"They buried him on a hill not far from the house. And the woman said that one night she saw him coming over the hill. He come on to the house and walked up and down the porch wanting in.

"She said when he was alive, about one o'clock he went out on the porch each day and whittled. She said about that time now she could still hear him whittling."

Monroe County, 1958 (RMo). Informant: female, born 1943 in Monroe County. This story includes Motif *E425.2, "Revenant as man."

RETURN TO SEEK VENGEANCE

The Ghost of His First Wife

290   There was a man who married again because his wife had died. His first wife had said that if he married after she died, she would come back and haunt them. Well, the first night of their marriage in the first wife's house, they were awakened by something that sounded like chains being rattled upstairs. The first thing he thought of was his wife's threat.

They never spent another night in that house.

> *Adair County, 1966 (RSu). Informant: female, middle-aged, born in Adair County.* "The Ghost of His First Wife" contains two basic motifs, known primarily in Anglo-American tradition: Motif *E221.1, "Dead wife haunts husband on second marriage," and *E402.1.4, "Invisible ghost jingles chains."

Wife Returns to Seek Vengeance

291   Once there was a man by the name of Ancle Biggerstaff who was very mean to his wife. After she died, one night as he was coming home, his horse suddenly balked in the road. There in front of them was his wife in her coffin. He tried every way to get the horse to go around the coffin, but it wouldn't go. Finally he got off and tried to lead the horse, but he still couldn't get it to budge. In the end he had to turn in another direction.

> *Monroe County, 1959 (LM). Informant: female, born 1944 in Barren County.* Applicable here are Motifs *E411.1, "Murderer cannot rest in grave," found in Cornwall (England) and New York; and *E421.1.2, "Ghost visible to horses alone." The notion that the lead horse balks at the sight of death and refuses to continue on course is a fairly common concept and has been recovered in southern Kentucky on numerous occasions, including one report from the editor's family.

Aunt Returns to Get Even

292   My aunt and I had trouble over putting shingles on a barn once. The night she died something landed on my house top; sounded

like it was going to tear the roof off. I know it was her trying to get even with me.

Taylor County, 1966 (LM). Informant: female, age unknown, born in Barren County. The informant remembered this extremely brief narrative from her childhood during the 1930s. (The brevity of "Aunt Returns to Get Even" is not unusual—many ghost legends are of this length and structure.) The story is nothing more than an utterance of a motif and that is the only element which gives this story type its cohesion. The motif is *E220, "Dead relative's malevolent return."

DISAPPEARING GHOSTS

Man Watches His Dead Aunt Pick Roses

This woman said that her first cousin's mother had been dead for several years when one day her cousin walked out of the door and saw his mother standing picking roses from the rosebush. She was all dressed up with her bonnet on like she used to wear, and she motioned for him to come to her. He went back in the house to get his hat and told the other members of the family what he saw and that she motioned for him, and he was going to her.

When he went back outside, she had disappeared and was never seen again.

Adair County, 1964 (KB). Informant: (anonymous contributor, except that subject is female resident of Adair County). Ghosts commonly return to relatives fully clothed and readily recognizable by those persons who see them. The only identifiable motif in this story is *E422.4.4, "Revenant in female dress," since the color of the clothing is not actually stated in this instance.

The Ghost Woman

"A long time ago my mother lived on a farm in Taylor County. And one day she looked out of the window, and she saw a woman standing in a field near their home. There wasn't another house very close, and all the land was level and flat and you could see a good distance. This woman stooped down as if to pick something up and then slowly stood up and held her hands out. My mother thought it was a visitor who was coming to see her, and she thought she would go and do some little task before the guest got there. It was only a moment until she glanced up again, but the woman was gone.

"My mother never knew who or what it was, and she never saw it again."

Taylor County, 1964 (GS). Informant: female, middle-aged, born in Taylor County. The only discernible element in this disappearing ghostwoman narrative is Motif *E425.1, "Revenant as woman."

"Look, There's Cousin Jimmy"

295   "The last vision she saw was Cousin Jimmy Thompson. He had killed himself. About two weeks after he killed himself, she'uz sittin' by the window an' looked out an' saw him ride up, said just like he always did, an' throw his bridle reins over the palin' fence an' jump off his horse. An' she hollered, said, 'Look, children! There's Cousin Jimmy.' An' said when she hollered an' told 'em to look—there was Cousin Jimmy—why, he commenced fadin' an' was gone!"

Adair County, 1964 (VM). Informant: female, elderly, born in Adair County. Motif *E334.4, "Ghost of suicide seen at death spot or near by," is relevant here. Implied is Motif *E411.1.1, "Suicide cannot rest in grave," reported previously from County York (England) and Pennsylvania.

The Little Girl Dressed in White

296   "Granny Harris lived on the Ben Baxter Place. And every day when she went to the spring, she saw a little girl dressed in white sitting on the fence. As long as she looked directly at the little girl she could see her, but just as soon as she took her eyes away, even for a moment, the little girl would disappear."

Taylor County, 1964 (GS). Informant: female, middle-aged, born in Taylor County. Applicable here is Motif *E422.4.4(a), "Female revenant in white clothing." Cf. *E425.1.1, "Revenant as lady in white."

Little Joseph in His Coffin

297   "Well, your Uncle Ben saw Little Joseph the day he came back from the funeral. Now, he says as to whether he really saw anything,

or whether it was just a figment of his mind, he don't know. But it'uz comin' up a storm an' they—just a few hours after they had buried him, and he was standin' lookin' out an' said just all at oncet there stood somebody dressed in white holdin' Little Joseph in their arms, an' said 'twas Little Joseph just as plain as he was when he saw him in the coffin. But now he says it didn't last very long, but said it frightened him at first, but said it was just so plain. Said it looked like just a woman dressed in white with Little Joseph in her arms, an' said then it was gone."

Adair County, 1964 (VM). Informant: female, elderly, born in Adair County. This intriguing story is studded with motifs and has all the earmarks of a complex legend, one which may be related to the "Weeping Woman" tradition in Mexico and the southwestern United States. Important motifs include *E324, "Dead child's friendly return to parents"; *E422.4.4(a), "Female revenant in white clothing"; and *E425.1.4, "Revenant as woman carrying baby," found only in Maine. Cf. *E425.1.1, "Revenant as lady in white."

The Ghost in the Striped Coveralls

"Uncle Jimmy was never afraid of anything and never believed in ghosts. He would go fox hunting at night by himself. Down below his house people had talked of seeing things before, but he never believed them. Late one night Uncle Jimmy and Roscoe's brother were going home from fox hunting in an old car, and Roscoe's brother was driving.

"They saw a man walking in the road up ahead of them who was wearing striped coveralls. He was walking near a cemetery. Neither one of the men said anything, but Roscoe's brother slowed down to pick up the man. They stopped, and the man suddenly walked in front of the car and just rised and floated up in the air. Neither one of the men said anything, but Roscoe's brother wasn't going to because he knew how Uncle Jimmy felt about this sort of thing, and he also thought that he could have imagined it. After they had gone down the road a little ways, Uncle Jimmy said, 'Did you see what I saw back there a minute ago?' And Roscoe's brother said, 'Yes, but I didn't say anything because I thought maybe I imagined it.'

"Both men had seen it, but neither one knew how to explain it. Uncle Jimmy said that in all of his years of hunting and rambling that that was the first such thing as that he had ever seen."

Adair County, 1964 (KB). Informant: (anonymous contributor, except that subject is male resident of Adair County). This story contains Motifs *E334.2, "Ghost haunts burial spot"; E421.5, "Ghost seen by two or more persons; they corroborate the appearance"; and *E422.4.5, "Revenant in male dress."

A Headless Woman

299   There was a case of typhoid in the house on the hill up above the Old Ike Boyles house. And they were setting up there. Two of the men wanted a drink. They were afraid to drink there so they went down to the Ike Boyles house after a drink. When they started in the gate, a woman without a head walked out and went toward the garden where the graveyard was. They just turned and walked away and never said a word to each other about it.

Clinton County, 1966 (——). Informant: female, born during 1930s in Barren County. The collector of this narrative was also the informant. Motifs in this headless person legend include *E334.2, "Ghost haunts burial spot"; *E421.5, "Ghost seen by two or more persons; they corroborate the appearance"; and *E422.1.1(b), "Headless woman, appearance only."

Woman Dressed in Black

300   "Me and my sister was in a house that a woman had just died in, and they had moved out all the furniture. (The house belonged to my father.) It was in the spring of the year, and we had two plant beds pretty close to this house. My dad and mother had left us in the house, and they had walked down to the plant bed. It was a one-room building with an upstairs and just more-so a step-ladder made, you know, to go upstairs. Well, me and my sister was picking up pins right in front of the door. (The door was open—warm.) They wudn't anything or nobody in the house at the time we went in there. I turned around and looked towards one corner of the house. There stood a woman dressed in black. Her dress looked like it touched the floor. And she stood there about a second, I'd say. She

walked catercorned across the house to the step-ladder. It looked more like she just floated to me. You couldn't hear her footsteps or anything. And she got to this step-ladder, she stopped, turned around, stood there for, looked like about a minute, and she went up the steps—up to the upstairs.

"Of course, we just froze, that's all. Then we went out in the yard and called our daddy and mother. My daddy come to the house, and we told him what had happened. He went upstairs, looked around, said there wasn't anything up there at all.

"Pickin' up pins out of a dead woman's clothes. But don't think this is why it happened."

Green County, 1963 (MP). Informant: male, born 1898 in Green County. This graphic personal account of a ghost woman in black contains Motif *E422.4.4(e), "Female revenant in black dress," reported from Yorkshire and Lincolnshire (England), and from Illinois and Texas.

The Woman in White

There was Uncle Lige Clemons and Frank Baxter. Frank's wife hadn't been dead maybe more than one or two months. They'd been out somewhere together that night. Went to bed. Bliss Bowman was sleeping with his face away from the door. He heard this noise and turned his face toward the door. He said he saw a woman dressed in white. Said he didn't sleep anymore that night.

Monroe County, 1969 (RLy). Informant: male, born ca. 1915 in Monroe County. This virtually amorphous legend contains Motif *E422.4.4(a), "Female revenant in white clothing." Cf. Motif *E425.1.1, "Revenant as lady in white." A very similar story was collected in Adair County in 1965 from a former resident of Green County: "I lived in a large house in Green County with my parents that was said to be haunted. It was told that a woman dressed in white would come in the back door and go through a hall and out the front door. . . . They also said she would appear in the parlor from behind the organ when the girls would go in there to play and sing."

A Girl Dressed in White

There was two houses at the end of a dead-end street. One person looked out and saw a girl dressed in white with long white hair come up the street and go up to the other house, knock on the door, and go in. The next day when asked who her visitor was, the lady said she had had no visitor. The other lady swears she saw someone enter the house.

> *Taylor County, 1963 (KM) Informant: female, middle-aged, born in Taylor County.* Motif *E422.4.4(a), "Female revenant in white clothing," is applicable here. Cf. also *E425.1.1, "Revenant as lady in white."

The White Thing

303   One night this little girl went out to the chicken house to close up the chickens. As she went back to the house, she heard something behind her. Looking back, she saw something all white following her. She was so frightened that she just fell in the door, and someone helped her in. The white thing disappeared.

> *Adair County, 1968 (NAB). Informant: female, middle-aged, born in Adair County.* Many motifs are implied here, but no meaningful ones can be cited.

The Unobtrusive Ghost

304   My Grandma Furkin used to tell us about a female ghost coming to their house. She said her voice was sweet, but that she seldom laughed. She never seemed to hear or see, and she moved like a phantom through the house, closing doors noiselessly. She appeared suddenly when least expected, and she disappeared as suddenly as she came. No one ever knew what became of her, or who she was.

> *Adair County, 1968 (NAB). Informant: female, middle-aged, born in Adair County.* The only recognizable motif in this story of a ghost's phantom-like actions is *E425.1, "Revenant as woman."

The Return of the Schoolteacher

305   There was this teacher who had died, and the children had loved her very much. She loved the children and her work very much, too. She was said to have come back to the schoolhouse two or three different times, and one time she came when all the children were there and everybody saw her. She stood in the doorway and looked

at her former students and then she disappeared and never came
back again.

Taylor County, 1964 (LS). Informant: (anonymous contributor, except that subject is male resident of Taylor County). The motif in this story is similar to *E338.7, "Ghost haunts educational institution," found in New York only.

The Ghostly Dancers

"Now, here's a story that come through my dad and Uncle Joe Simms, Ed Simms' daddy. Way years ago, they was just young men— my father wasn't married. Joe was married—but they had been out a-Christmasing, like say this Christmas; and they were a-goin', started home. (At them days they had big dances.) And they had heerd music and dancing, and they decided to go by that old place, which they said that they had had a dance thar at one time; and the old man beggin' them not to dance, but they went ahead with their dancing.

"And after they got in reach of the house, they went up and knocked at the door; but nobody opened the door on them. One replied that if they didn't let them in, 'If you don't, we'll push the door down and come in. We want to see the people and want to hear the music.' So they went ahead with their dancing. So they went to an old time high winder where there was an old time stone chimney stood by the winder. And my father lifted Joe up till he could get up into the winder, and the lights went out. They could see them dancing with their white handkerchiefs, calling the set, fine music; and when the light would go out, why, they couldn't see. But Joe said to Father, 'While I'm up here, I'm a-gonna go from one corner to the other to see if they han't people in here.' He got scared to death nearly, and Dad had to help him get back out. When he hit the ground, the music started again; and they went to trompin' and dancing and going right ahead with it. Well, they seed they wasn't nobody there, and they started runnin' and they was nobody at all. Just ended up that way. Just something there to be seen and heard."

Russell County, 1964 (HD). Informant: (anonymous contributor, *except that subject born 1886 in Russell County).* Three recognizable motifs are included in this somewhat lengthy account about strange lights and ghostly dancers: *E281, "Ghosts haunt house"; *E402, "Mysterious ghost-like noises heard"; and *E337.1.3(b), "Sounds of dance in haunted house," known only in Pennsylvania.

The Black Coffin

307   There is an old house located just off Highway 61 in the Happy Hollow Community about one mile from Greensburg that seemed haunted on one occasion. This incident occurred in 1932, and J. W. Thomas was the sheriff of Green County. A Mr. Ragland, his wife, and three children came to the sheriff's office in a state of almost shock. They had gotten up after daylight late in August and gone into the kitchen to fix breakfast. They fixed the usual country breakfast consisting of bacon, eggs, cornbread, and coffee. As they were eating, they heard footsteps in the hallway. They were not expecting anyone, but they thought it was some of the neighbors. They listened to the footsteps more carefully, and one of the family opened the door. There were four men dressed in black, carrying a black coffin. And on top of the black coffin was a small white lamb. The sheriff found nothing in his investigation of the house.

   Green County, 1967 (KP). Informant: male, born ca. 1908 in Green County. This ghost narrative, which is set in the recent past, contains Motifs *E281, "Ghosts haunt house"; *E402.1.2, "Footsteps of invisible ghost heard"; *E423.1.6, "Revenant as lamb"; and *E491.1, "Phantom funeral procession." See the three similar narratives given in the annotations accompanying story No. 309.

The Bleeding Sheep on the Coffin

308   "It's only hearsay, but most ghost stories are. Out in the country—I can't say where—there was an old house. I think it's been torn down now, but the house was there when my father was sheriff. Sam Thomas, he was deputy sheriff, and there was a house, five or six people lived in it. And one night they were sitting at the breakfast table, sit up rather late. It was midnight, and they heard something at the door.

   "All of a sudden the door flew open, and in came six men carrying a casket with a sheep standing on top of the casket without a head. The sheep had no head; the sheep was bleeding at the neck. These six men carried the casket with the sheep in the front door, went through the house, and went out the back door. They did this every night at midnight for ages until the family died. And it is said that people in Green County went out there to see it. And this is supposed to be a true story."

> *Green County, 1964 (JR). Informant: male, born ca. 1908 in Green County.* This haunted house legend contains the same motifs as No. 307, but in addition includes a description of a bleeding, headless sheep for which no motif was found. The same informant provided both stories. See the three similar stories printed in the annotations following the regular documentation to story No. 309.

Ghosts Enter House Carrying Casket

"Well, it has been something like thirty years ago, I guess, here in Green County about two or three miles from Greensburg, in an old house that was known as the Old Blakeman Place. A family by the name of Edwards, so it happens, were living there as tenants of this place. And one night as they were eating supper, the best I remember it, they were at the table; and they all ran out of the house frightened to death and went to a neighbor's and wouldn't go back home. And they said that in the midst of sitting there—in the Edwards Place—that people came in (I don't remember how many people—whether there were one or two—but they evidently appeared to them like a ghostly apparition of some kind) came into the house carrying a casket.

"So they just left home, and of course the story spread like wildfire all over town, and it became the chief pastime of all the residents around here to go out to the Old Edwards Place and see if they could see the ghosts. Everybody in town just took it time about in going out there, and I remember going in a car with some people, and we went all over the house. And there was the table with the dishes on it just like they got up and left, with the remains of food and everything else. Of course, we didn't find any ghosts, but at night even a bunch of the high school kids would get in cars. That was real fun, you know, to drive out to that Old Edwards house, and we'd park the car around there by the side of the house and watch to see if we could see anything. And, of course, we could imagine nearly everything—the moon shining, the trees moving and shining on the windows. So at various times someone would say, 'Oh, look, look, look, I see something!' And a number of people claim that they did see things. I never did see anything, anywhere; nothing except just movements of the trees. It was just fun to scare yourself half to death."

> *Green County, 1964 (JR). Informant: female, very elderly, born in Green County.* This appears to be a parallel account of the events described in story No. 307 and contains two of the same motifs (*E281 and *E491.1).

[307–309]   Three additional fragmented legends, told by an informant born in 1944, are distinctly related in both theme and structure to the accounts given in Nos. 307, 308, and 309:

"Once upon a time a young girl was sitting on the stairsteps of her home. Suddenly she looked up, and two men with no heads were carrying a coffin down the steps. They went on past her without saying a word. She followed them on out the door and went as far as the gate. But when they got to the gate, they vanished into thin air." (Motifs are related to *E422.1.1, "Headless revenant"; *E538.1, "Spectral coffin"; and F511.0.1, "Headless person.")

"One night as everyone was sitting around the fire, they heard someone coming down the stairs. They all got up, and there were four men with no heads carrying a casket. They followed the men to the gate where they disappeared." (Motifs *E422.1.1, *E538.1, and F511.01.)

"One day some boys got together and decided that they would spend the night in this haunted house. That night after they were asleep, something woke them. So they got up and went to the door, and out in the yard were six men without no heads. Then they came through the door and vanished into thin air." (Motif F511.0.1, "Headless person"; cf. *E422.1.1, "Headless revenant.")

> *Monroe County, 1958 (LM). Informant: female, born 1944 in Barren County.*

The Topless Man

310   I can remember my grandmother, who would be about ninety years old now if she were living, telling me that when she was a

young woman, she heard someone going up the steps in the house. She didn't know there was anyone in the house, so she went and looked; and she saw a man's legs going up the steps, but there was no body attached.

I was only a little girl when I can remember her telling me this.

Taylor County, 1968 (LM). Informant: female, born 1946 in Adair County. The only identifiable element in this rare story is Motif *E422.1.11, "Revenant as part of body."

Uncle Lattimore's Ghost

"They's a man by the name of Lattimore. Uncle Bill Zeke Coe said he didn't believe in no such things as a haint. You know, people called them, you know, haints. Said he didn't believe they was nobody could come back! And said one day he was working over at Short Chappell's. And this was so! And said he went down on the creek one evening, and come in. Said it was almost dark. Said he looked (they'd buried Uncle Bill Lattimore that evening; that was so! Uncle Bill Zeke), said he looked and seed Uncle Bill Lattimore coming down the hill, and they had just buried him that evening. And it was almost dark. And said he was aiming to speak to him. Said he was coming up the hill, and he looked up. He just bowed his head down, stepping over in a little gully. And said when he looked up, he was aiming to speak to him. And said Uncle Lattimore just went right around behind the tree, and he disappeared. He never did see him no more."

Monroe County, 1961 (LM). Informant: black female, born 1912 in Cumberland County. Motif *E425.2, "Revenant as man," is probably applicable here.

The White Dog-like Thing

Me and Hugh and Wallace and Jack and Billy Jones were sitting on the porch about middle ways down. It was just about good dark. And then there was a little low place in the yard (it's still here). We had an old spotted dog. In the fall of the year when the leaves were beginning to fall, the dog was lying in that low place. Suddenly, there was a rustling in the leaves, and I looked up and saw

something white in the low place. It moved around, then vanished.
I thought it was the old dog, but in a moment he raised up and
barked. I still don't know what it was.

> *Monroe County, 1969 (RLy). Informant: male, born ca. 1915 in
> Monroe County.* There are not enough characteristics of the dog-like
> creature given in this account to enable motif identification.

Shadowy Figures

313   I used to live in this old log-cabin-type house that was just up a
creek. It was wintertime, and the fire was crackling while the inmates had been talking of the past, other members of the family,
and about death, births, and marriages. Outside the wind whined
through the old pine trees; and every now and then, a loose board
would slap against the side of the house.

The noise from another room caused all the inmates, including
myself, to look in that direction. Profound horror paralyzed each
one of us as we all saw moving figures moving in crouched positions
in single file like shadows on the wall—moving from left to right.
These figures were dressed in gray.

> *Taylor County, 1969 (BS). Informant: male, age unknown, born in
> Magoffin County.* Although several motifs deal with phantom-like
> figures, the major element from the viewpoint of the narrator is Motif
> *E421.5, "Ghost seen by two or more persons; they corroborate the
> appearance."

Mother's Return

314   When your grandmother's aunt that was stayin' with her—she felt
like somethin' was a-pressin' on her. She called her aunt an' told
her, said to her aunt, "Don't mash me so." She'uz just wakin' up an'
—but when she opened—the aunt answered her from the kitchen
(she was in the kitchen). And when she opened her eyes why 'twas
her mother! "Ooo," she says, "Aunt Ann, it's Mother!" And said
just when she said that, why, she just floated away. By the time she
got to the ceilin', she was gone. But said 'twas very plain. She saw
it as plain as ever she saw her mother when she was alive.

> *Adair County, 1964 (VM). Informant: female, elderly, born in*

Adair County. This interesting account of a dead mother's return contains Motif *E323.6, "Mother returns to encourage daughter in great difficulties," found only in England.

REENACTMENT OF MURDERS

The Cruel Slaveowner

There is a legend about a house in Lincoln County. It is a huge house containing about fifteen rooms, a big hall, and all. It was built around the last part of the 1700s or during the early 1800s.

The owner had the slaves, and he was real mean to some of them. He would rape the young Negro girls and beat the men to death if they didn't do as they were told. It is said that he beat several men to death because they didn't do as they were told. They told that he beat several men to death in the huge basement in which they would be tied up, and a whip would be used on them by the master.

The most important part of this story is that in a certain time of the year, all these dead people that had been murdered would come back to life again; and all would be re-murdered. If a person went to this house on a certain night, he could see and talk to these people, but they would kill him before he left. No one has ever got out in time to tell the real story; and many people were paid to do this, but they were always found dead the next morning.

Lincoln County, 1964 (BJ). Informant: (anonymous contributor, except that subject is male resident of Lincoln County). This story is a fine example of the historicity claimed for many ghost narratives. It begins with a description of totally congruous events and then concludes with an episode which brings the supernatural into focus. This rare story contains Motif *E233, "Return from the dead to avenge murder," and concludes by alluding to Motif *H1411, "Fear test: staying in haunted house," and Type 326, *The Youth Who Wanted to Learn What Fear Is.*

Body of Hanged Man Seen after Burial

On the Winn Place over here in Barren County, a man was hanged several years ago. The place of the hanging was on a high hill which overlooked the countryside.

The night after he had been hung that day, his body could be seen hanging there, although he had been buried.

Monroe County, 1958 (LM). Informant: male, born 1936 in Barren County. This fragmented narrative contains Motif *E425.2, "Revenant as man."

THE VANISHING HITCHHIKER

Unseen Ghost Follows Man alongside the Road

317   When this man went to see his girlfriend, he had to walk through a swamp to get to her house. One night he stayed rather late, and when he came back through the swamp, he heard something following him along the edge of the road. When he looked he could see nothing, and when he walked it walked, and when he ran it ran. He said that when he got to the edge of the swamp, the sound stopped in some weeds at the edge of the road. He picked up a rock and threw it into the weeds, but no sound came from the side of the road.

Unto this day he doesn't know what he heard.

Taylor County, 1964 (LM). Informant: female, born 1944 in Green County. This unseen road ghost narrative is likely related to Motif *E332, "Non-malevolent road ghosts."

Ghost Rides Horse behind Man (a)

318   "I heard tell of this thing that hovered there at the Gregory Graveyard. Lots of people have told me that if you'd pass by there on a horse at night, something would hop on the horse behind them. They never did see anything. At least this fellow who told me this didn't see anything. But the horse would cut up and act funny."

Monroe County, 1961 (LM). Informant: male, born 1915 in Monroe County. Motif *E272.2, "Ghost rides behind rider on horse," is previously indexed from British tradition with a single exception from Alabama Negro tradition. However, recent Kentucky collections contain stories with this motif. See Elizabeth B. Cornett, "Belief Tales of Knott and Perry Counties," *Kentucky Folklore Record* 2:3 (July–Sept. 1956), 69–75; Ethel Owens, "Ghost Tales from Breathitt County," *Kentucky Folklore Record* 5:3 (July–Sept. 1959), 81–86; Lynwood Montell, "Belief Tales from Barren County," *Kentucky Folklore Record* 8:1 (Jan.–March 1962), 11–17. Louis C. Jones, *Things That Go Bump in the Night*, 167, says this story may be a variant of the vanishing hitchhiker legend complex.

An almost identical version of this story was collected from Monroe County in 1958, and an intriguing variant was also gathered from Barren County tradition the same year. That brief account claims: "There is a place around Tracy where something would jump on your horse and would tear the horse all to pieces."

Ghost Rides Horse behind Man (b)

"Down at Muldraughs Hill, down here on Muldraughs Hill, there was a man killed there at the foot of Little Muldraughs Hill, and they said that every time anybody would pass that place where this man was killed . . . . They used to ride horses, you know, more so than they did any other way. So, said when he would start to pass by that place, somebody would jump up behind him on his horse. And said he would look around to see if he would see him, and the man would dodge on the other side. And he would look on the other side, and he'd dodge on this side. And when he'd pass that place where he was killed, he would disappear. Some men would pass there, and they'd run their horses as fast as they could run. But whatever that was, would jump on behind them—make no difference how fast the horses would run."

Taylor County, 1964 (BH). Informant: female, born 1888 in Taylor County. Several motifs are present in this narrative: *E272.2, "Ghost rides behind rider on horse"; *E332.3.1, "Ghost rides on horseback with rider"; *E334.2.2, "Ghost of person killed in accident seen at death or burial spot"; and *E422.1.1.3.1, "Headless ghost rides horse."

Ghost Rides Horse behind Man (c)

There was this man who was mean to his wife, and finally she died. He loved to ride his mule along this certain spot. But when he did, his wife's ghost would jump on the back of his horse behind him.

And he would run his mule nearly to death trying to get away from her. And when he passed a certain spot in the trail, she would jump off the mule's back and disappear into the woods.

> *Russell County, 1965 (SS). Informant: female, born ca. 1932 in Russell County.* Present are Motifs *E272.2, "Ghost rides behind rider on horse"; *E332.1, "Ghost appears at road and stream"; and *E332.3.1, "Ghost rides on horseback with rider."

Ghost Rides Horse behind Man (d)

321   One time a man was riding his horse home late one time, and he had to ride past this old abandoned house which was supposed to be hainted. There was a high bank on one side of the road near the house, and the horse began to jump around and act scared as it came closer to the bank. The horse wouldn't go any farther. Suddenly, the ghost of a woman jumped from the bank onto the horse, back of the man, and the horse took off running. As the horse and rider passed the house, the ghost jumped off and disappeared.

> *Adair County, 1964 (KB). Informant: male, middle-aged, born in Adair County.* The same motifs found in story No. 320 are again present, plus *E421.1.2(b), "Horse sees ghost and is unable to proceed on way."

Ghost Rides Horse behind Man (e)

322   "My brother had been to Tompkinsville and was coming down Meshack Road. And they's a big old sycamore tree stood there on the road. And people said that they'd been passing there, and this thing would jump out of a tree and just get you around the waist and hold you. It would hold you about a mile down that creek. It wouldn't get off. You couldn't push it off, nor you couldn't feel it with your hands. But it would hold you tight.

"And my brother, he didn't believe it. He said, 'Ah, that's not so! It couldn't be!'

"Well, one night he went to town. And he got delayed up there, and he was coming on down the road a-riding a horse. He got nearly to that tree. Said he happened to think about it. Said he said, 'I'll see tonight whether anything jumps on the horse behind me.' Said,

'That's not so no-how.' Said he hit his horse and spurred him right down by that tree. Said just about the time he got under the tree, something just leaped on it behind him, just gathered him. Said he twisted, and he turned, and he spurred his horse; and that horse come down that creek just as hard as he could come. And said he'd try to get a-loose from it. He couldn't get a-loose from it a-tall! It stayed with him for about a mile down that creek, and it tore a-loose. And said that horse would just snort and jump and run. Like to have scared him to death then. He never went that creek road again no more after dark."

> Monroe County, 1961 (LM). Informant: black female, born ca. 1881 in Monroe County. This longer account of the ghostly rider contains Motifs *E332.1, "Ghost appears at road and stream"; *E332.3.1, "Ghost rides on horseback with rider"; and *E421.1.2(a), "Ghost scares horse."

Headless Revenant on Horse behind Rider

This man was riding from Summersville to Gabe. He had to ride through a hollow called Milby's Hollow. Right after he started through, he said that he felt his horse jump, and then he felt as if someone was riding with him. He said he turned, and that when he got to the edge of the hollow, the horse became at ease; and he felt that the man had disappeared, and when he looked, he had.

> Green County, 1964 (PP). Informant: male, born ca. 1940 in Green County. Motifs *E272.2, "Ghost rides behind rider on horse," and *E332.3.1, "Ghost rides on horseback with rider," are present as well as Motif *E422.1.1.3.1, "Headless ghost rides horse." A similar account was reported from Barren County in 1958.

Headless Horseman

"The usual ghost stories exist around Greensburg that have existed everywhere, I guess. In numbers of places where I have taught school in Green County I have been told that certain stretches of the road, that that road or along that place was haunted, and that certain times of the year that various and sundry people had seen a headless horseman. They'd just swear up and down that they had!

"I remember that one of the places was near Webbs, Kentucky, because that was the first place where I taught school. Out at Old Salem, there's a stretch of road in there that different people declare that they've seen a horseman riding down the road and that he didn't have a head. And then I've heard people describe all kinds of strange lights in graveyards. They'd say they passed the graveyard at a certain time of night, there was always this light over a certain grave, and there is just these sort of things that you generally hear everywhere."

> *Green County, 1964 (JR). Informant: female, elderly, born in Green County.* The major motif in this widespread legend is *E422.1.1.3.1, "Headless ghost rides horse." The headless ghost motif appears centered in Anglo-American tradition. Baughman lists seven reports from the British Isles and fourteen in American tradition ranging from New England to the Rocky Mountains.

> One of two additional fragmented reports from Barren County in 1958 states: "Once there was a man riding a horse going some place. He had to cross a creek, and he rode in the water to let his horse drink. A man with no head riding another horse came in the water beside him; and every time he would move, the man with no head would move too. The man lifted his bridle reins and took his horse out of the water. The man without a head rode his horse out too; then he disappeared."

> Perhaps the great popularity of this tale can be attributed to Irving's *The Legend of Sleepy Hollow*, which has been popular with school children across the years .

Headless Person (a)

325   A long time ago there was a fellow that lived in Green County who said he was walking home down his lane one night, and he saw a man without a head walking up the other side of the lane. He ran through the field all the way home and never looked back. A few years later it was seen again in this same place.

> *Larue County, 1964 (TS). Informant: male, middle-aged, born in Green County.* The headless man is popular in American folk tradition. This particular narrative contains Motifs *E332.2, "Person meets ghost on road"; *E422.1.1.5, "Miscellaneous actions of headless ghost"; and E783.6, "Headless body vital."

Headless Person (b)

A long time ago people used to walk in groups for many miles to go to church. So there was a bunch of mean boys who thought they would play a trick on the rest of the crowd, so they ran ahead of the group and hid in the bushes to jump out and scare them when they came by. So while the boys were waiting for the group, a man came along in a white shirt without a head, and man, did the boys believe in a crowd from then on!

> Russell County, 1965 (SS). Informant: female, born ca. 1932 in Russell County. The same motifs found in story No. 325 are present here. In a Taylor County report, the ghost is a headless woman represented by Motif *E422.1.1 (b), "Headless woman, appearance only."

The Haunted Woods

My sister had been to Merrimac and had to go through a patch of woods and cross a creek on her way back. It was dark, and she said a thing came out behind her and started screaming; so she started running, and it started running. And we heard her coming but we never did see the thing that was after her. Others also were chased by it. Everybody went out to hunt for it, but they never did find it.

> Taylor County, 1966 (LC). Informant: female, born 1926 in Taylor County. This narrative revolves around Motifs *E272.4, "Ghost chases pedestrian on road," reported only from County York (England), and *E332.1, "Ghost appears at road and stream."

The Musician's Ghost

A man was walking along a road at night. He heard beautiful music, and he stopped to listen to it. He remembered that a musician had been killed here. Then he saw a headless apparition rise from a thicket and come through a fence toward him. He ran. About fifty yards away was a small creek. After he crossed the creek, he looked back, and the ghost had stopped at the bank of the creek.

> Taylor County, 1966 (EH). Informant: female, born 1911 in Taylor County. Although a somewhat fragmented account, this legend is alive with relevant motifs: Cf. *E233, "Return from the dead to

avenge murder"; *E261.4, "Ghost pursues man"; *E332.1(b), "Ghost vanishes at stream bank"; *E402.4, "Sound of ethereal music"; and *E422.1.1, "Headless revenant."

Ghost Chases Boy

329   Walter tells a tale of the ghost around Sano that would chase Sam Hadley at night if he walked by this certain spot. One night Elzie Hadley, Sam's son, was riding his bicycle along, and something dressed in white started chasing him. I know it was a ghost! The faster Elzie would go, the faster the ghost would come. They swear this is the truth!

> *Russell County, 1964 (JiC). Informant: male, elderly, born in Russell County.* Appropriate motifs in this ghost scare story are *E261.4, "Ghost pursues man" (cf. *E272.4, "Ghost chases pedestrian on road"), and *E422.4.5(a), "Male revenant in white garb."

The Dejected Child

330   There were two children and their mother and father. They lived on the Bell Plantation. This was pre-Civil War time. One was an extrovert child, happy and carefree, while the other seemed dejected. And the parents were more partial to the happy child. Neither gave any attention to the dejected child—a daughter. So this kept building up until it seemed she became mad. He began having pains in his head, and the doctor couldn't find out what it was. He died and the blood ran out of his head. So all of them died except the dejected child. So she lived on for several years then passed away. Different people claim they seen her around the house. According to prediction, she is supposed to return this year.

Not too long ago a Greyhound bus driver approached the house with three passengers. Only two got off. He looked back, and the other disappeared. And they have been some disturbances in the cave in the back of the house.

> *Monroe County, 1966 (BP). Informant: male, born 1935 in Allen County.* Story No. 330 contains Motifs *E332, "Non-malevolent road ghosts," and *E332.3.2, "Ghost rides in horse-drawn vehicle which disappears suddenly at certain spot."

336] These stories are all accounts in one form or another of Motif *E599.8, "Ghost vanishes when taken home." This legend, perhaps the most popular folk legend in the United States, generally relates all or portions of the story of two young men traveling along a road on a rainy night in an automobile en route to a dance. They pick up a strange young lady along the route and persuade her to accompany them to the dance. They dance with her, then take her home later that evening. The night air is chilly so one of the fellows places his overcoat around her shoulders. At her house, she departs the car, forgetting to return the borrowed overcoat. Later the boys return to the girl's house to claim the coat. They are told by the girl's mother that she had been dead for several years. She tells them where the girl is buried. They go to the cemetery and there find the overcoat draped over the grave (or gravestone).

The Somerset Ghost

Several years ago a family was traveling toward Somerset late one night on the start of their vacation. As they started down a long hill, the car went out of control and hit the bridge at the bottom of the hill. It killed every person in the car and was said to have been the bloodiest wreck to ever occur in that area.

It is now reported, and every time to be the truth, that when a person driving down this road, being alone, reaches the top of the hill, the door on the passenger side will open, and there will be a figure of a bloody man on the seat. You can see him plainly but cannot touch him. As you cross the bridge the man will then open the door and get out.

Some people have sworn to have blood spots on the seats of their cars.

*Taylor County, 1964 (RSh). Informant: male, born 1937 in Taylor County. This graphic legend has seldom been reported in association with a bloody passenger. It contains Motifs *E332.1, "Ghost appears at road and stream"; *E332.3.2, "Ghost rides in horse-drawn vehicle which disappears suddenly at certain spot"; E332.3.3.1, "The Vanishing Hitchhiker"; and *E334.2.2, "Ghost of person killed in accident seen at death or burial spot."*

The Unseen Rider

Joe's sister was driving along down the highway, and all of a sudden something opened the car door and got in the car and stayed silent.

She said she never seen it, but she could feel the presence of something. It rode with her for a long time, and at a certain spot it opened the car door and got out. She said she never stopped the car. Told to be true.

Russell County, 1966 (SS). Informant: female, born ca. 1932 in Russell County. This tale appears to be an abbreviated version of story No. 331, and it contains two of the same motifs—*E332.3.3.1 and *E332.3.2.

The Vanishing Girl (a)

333   "A man was going down the highway on a motorcycle. It was raining a little. He overtook a girl that was walking. She was thin-looking, and so he stopped and asked her if there was something he could do for her. She said she would like to have a ride down the road a few miles. She didn't have on a coat, so he took off his jacket and let her have it, as it was raining. They went down the road a few miles, and he drove up to a farmhouse. And she told him that was the place where she wanted off. She seemed to be frightened and ran in upstairs. He forgot to ask for his new jacket.

"He went on where he was going and stayed all night somewhere. He got to thinking about his jacket, so he went back to the place where he left the girl. A woman came to the door, and he asked about the girl and described her; also, asked about his jacket.

"She said, 'Mister, you've just described my girl exactly. But,' she says, 'she has been dead seven years.' She told him, though, she would take him to the cemetery and show him her tombstone. And when they got there, there hung his jacket on the tombstone."

Adair County, 1968 (NAB). Informant: female, born 1902 in Russell County. The major theme in this legend is meshed with Motif *E599.8(a), "Person meets girl at dance, dances with her, often drinks with her and takes her home. He goes to see her the next day and finds she has been dead several years. Often a coat he has lent her is found on her grave." The other motifs in this narrative are clearly entwined with those in the "Vanishing Hitchhiker" legend complex: *E332, "Non-malevolent road ghosts"; *E332.2, "Person meets ghost on road"; and *E332.3.3, "Ghost asks for ride in automobile."

The Vanishing Girl (b)

It was raining. These two boys picked up this girl by the roadside, and she was dressed like she was going to a dance. The boys were going to the dance, too. She was dressed in a long formal, and they picked her up. They even danced with her, like all the other girls. When they were going home, they said they would take her home; and she agreed if they would let her out at a certain place. It was still raining, and one of the boys let her take his coat. He would pick it up later.

When he went back to get his coat, he asked for Elizabeth. The lady said she did have a daughter named Elizabeth but that she was killed in an accident. She told them where she was buried. They went to see and found the coat beside the grave.

> *Monroe County, 1969 (RLy). Informant: female, born ca. 1912 in Barren County.* The motifs in this story are the same as those identified in story No. 333 and appear in the same sequential order.

The Vanishing Girl (c)

There were these two boys who came home from college. They were invited to this dance. They came on this young girl on the highway and took her to the dance. It was cold. They loaned her a coat to go on home. In a short time they went back to pick up the coat. The mother answered the door. She told the boys that her daughter had been dead about five years. She told them where to go if they didn't believe her. They went to her grave, and the coat was draped on the tomb rock.

> *Monroe County, 1969 (RLy). Informant: female, born ca. 1910 in Monroe County.* In this somewhat fragmented version the motifs, either stated or implied, remain constant with those identified in story Nos. 333 and 334.

The Vanishing Girl (d)

There were these two boys going from Winchester to Lexington. They were going to a prom. There was this girl in a formal on the road, and they picked her up in a Model A Roadster. It was cold.

Each of the boys danced with her. She danced good, but her flesh was cold. They started home but saw her again on the street and picked her up. She was cold, and they gave her a coat. They took her to her house down this hill and left her. They left his coat, too, but went back to get the coat and told her mother that he left his coat. Her mother told them that she was dead and buried. She then took them to the family graveyard where she was buried. They found the overcoat hanging on the tombstone.

> *Monroe County, 1969 (RLy). Informant: male, born 1905 in Monroe County.* See notes to story No. 333.

Ghost of Man Hit by Auto

337   Two men in England were driving down the road. Suddenly, they saw a man by the side of the street apparently waiting to cross. As they came closer, he came out in front of them before they had a chance to stop. However, they couldn't feel no impact such as a body would generally cause. They turned back to help the man, but when they came to the particular place, they couldn't find no evidence of a man anywhere. They were very curious by this time, so they went back to a town to see if perhaps someone else had found the man. They went to the town described by the men and told what happened. The people looked at one another strangely, and finally one spoke saying, "Yes, we knew the man, but he was run over by a car at that exact spot five years ago today."

> *Russell County, 1964 (RLa). Informant: male, born 1899 in Russell County.* This story is clearly related to the "Vanishing Hitchhiker" complex and shares many of the same motifs. A country song, entitled "Phantom 309," with this theme was composed during the early 1960s. The words of the tune tell of a truck driver who veers off the road to his death to avoid hitting a busload of school children. Each year on the anniversary of the driver's death, a phantom truck with driver stops to befriend a pedestrian along the road.

CRIES OF THE DEAD

Dying Man's Groans Still Heard

338   "Well, this is the way the story goes. Many long years ago—it'uz so far back that people never had—they didn't even have coal oil. The

only lights they had was candles. An' these were very wealthy people that had built 'em a big fine house, an' they entertained a lot—had big balls 'n things, an' these big chandeliers with candles in 'em, an' everything.

"An' said one night they was havin' a big ball, an' everyone had their—lotsa music an' people was all dancin' an' havin' fun y'know. An' one fella came in an' says, 'You all heard about that murder just across the line down in Tennessee?'

"An' they says, 'No, what?'

" 'Well,' says, 'there'uz a girl murdered down there, an' the fella got away though.' Said, 'They haven't been able—they're still searchin' for him, but they haven't found him yet.' Said they knew who killed her, but said they hadn't been able to find him.

"An' so someone said, 'Why Lord no!' Said, 'He's hidin' out somewhere. An' see it's not very far from here to th' Tennessee line, y'know.' An' says, 'He might be here somewhere in Kentucky.'

"Somebody else spoke up an' said, 'He might be in this very house! No tellin'.' Says, 'He's hid somewhere. Nobody hasn't found him yet.'

"An' they all got to jokin' about it, then someone says, 'The bravest girl here will take a candle an' go upstairs an' look under the bed.' An' didn't any of 'em want to do it. The girls said, 'Oh no, no, no!'

"But Mr. Bell—that was the name o' th' people—came in with a lighted candle in his hands, says, 'There never has been a Bell yet that was a coward. So take this candle an' go upstairs an' look under the bed.'

"So, said she was a-shakin', but she took the candle like her father told her an' went upstairs, An' when she stooped over an' looked under the bed, there he laid lookin' out at her. Well, she screamed an' fainted. An' afterwards they knew—course they all— that day an' age people started to go somewhere, they grabbed a candle to go by. They come with more candles, you know when they heard her scream. An' said afterwards they knew she had dropped her candle on the bed was the way the house caught a-fire, but nobody noticed it then.

"They took her downstairs an' bathed her face an' brought her to, y'know. An' took the man an' got a rope an' tied him up in the basement an' went on then with—after while, after they all talked a while—went on with their dancin' an' music till about daylight.

"Along towards morning, why, the first they knew of the fire— y'see they was makin' so much racket, all the dancin' an' music an' everything, they didn't hear it overhead. The first they knew th' ceiling was fallin' in on 'em, an' the house was done too far to save. The whole top of it had done burnt up, y'know. An' everybody commenced gettin' out then to save theirselves, an' they forgot all about the man until the house was cavin' in on him an' they heard him a-moanin' an' a-groanin.' An' it was too late to get him then, cause it had done caved in on him. An' I always tell the children it was no difference anyway, cause he'd a-been hung anyhow, y'know, cause he was th', he was th' man that killed the girl an' he wouldn't— there was no escape for him.

"But they said they built back—now this was a frame house that burnt down, an' they built back a fine brick house. They was wealthy people an' so, perhaps, had insurance. I don't know. I guess they had insurance in that day an' time. But, anyway, they was rich. They was able to build back another big fine brick house. But said every night at the same time that fella burned up in the basement, they could hear him moanin' an' groanin' under that house. They sold it, an' it was sold several times, an' everybody declared they heard that fella down in there groanin' in the basement. So then finally the community went together an' uh—the Christian people— an' bought the old buildin' an' tore it down an' built a fine big church out of it. But they said they still could hear that man under that church a-groanin' every night. [laughs]

"Now that's the story of that."

Adair County, 1964 (VM). Informant: female, elderly, born in Adair County. This unusually long ghost narrative contains Motifs *E275, "Ghost haunts place of great accident or misfortune," and *E402.1.1.3, "Ghost cries and screams."

Cries of a Dead Child

339   "Every February the fourteenth down at Pleasant Hill right beside Flossie Dameron's house, there's a baby that cries. My cousin

she stayed all night up there nights, and she heard it. And my uncle has heard it when he was passing the old house. They say there was a baby that was killed by a soldier during the Civil War. That's the reason that it cries."

> Russell County, 1964 (HD). Informant: (anonymous contributor, except that subject is resident of Russell County). Motif *E402.1.1.3, "Ghost cries and screams," is applicable in this story which is set during the Civil War.

Screams in the Night

Old Granny Irvin told me that somewhere from the creek to the mouth of the lane over here, there was a soldier found dead back during the Civil War. And Aunt Jane Martin and Uncle Ed Smith buried him. And people have heard a woman, or at least a voice, screaming over there in the lane sometimes at night.

> Clinton County, 1963 (SW). Informant: female, born 1919 in Clinton County. This story of the Civil War contains Motif *E402.1.1.3, "Ghost cries and screams."

The Drowned Girl

When one was sitting up with the sick, they would hear loud noises and groans just before the person passed on. One thing I remember was one time when we sat up with the Rafferty family when their daughter drowned and they were dragging the river for her or looking for her, we heard screams that sounded as that of a little girl crying.

> Adair County, 1968 (NAB). Informant: female, born 1912 in Adair County. Motif *E402.1.1.3, "Ghost cries and screams," is present in this account of a drowned child. The screams of a child are also an integral part of a Monroe County narrative which tells of "the fearful sounds of a child screaming and calling for help from an abandoned farm house."

UNEXPLAINED NOISES

Noises on the Stairsteps

Uncle Hoot Wilson and his wife, Ada, moved into this house where Samuel Smith had killed some Blackey man. I forgot his first name.

Uncle Hoot and Ada was lying in bed when they heard this noise, and Aunt Ada wanted Uncle Hoot to go and see what it was. He said it weren't nothing.

Uncle Hoot said all of a sudden he heard a noise that sounded like you had a shoulder load of staves and throwed them down the steps. It scared him to death. He went to see what made the noise. They looked all over that house and never seed nothing that caused the noise.

Russell County, 1966 (JiC). Informant: male, age unknown, born in Russell County. The informant learned this story from his mother. It contains Motifs *E402, "Mysterious ghost-like noises heard," and* *E402.1.8, "Miscellaneous sounds made by ghost of human being."*

Noises in the Night

343   The story which I shall relate is first-hand information since it happened to me and my family. The year was 1943. I was five-years-old and getting very anxious about going to school the next year. The house in which my father, mother, and myself lived was very old; so old in fact that when we had moved into it, it had been completely rebuilt, except for the frame. The upstairs had not been finished, leaving the ceiling joists exposed. There was an old mid-wives' tale associated with the house and barn which frightened me enough to make my blood turn cold every time I thought of it, particularly after dark.

The story went something like this: about forty years prior, a shucking party was being held at this house by the owner of the farm. As it happened he was also owner and father of the prettiest girl in the county. The girl was engaged to the toughest, meanest man in three counties. Sometime during the run of the shucking party the old party game of "pleased or displeased" was started. During the course of the game someone asked whether he was pleased or displeased. He said he was displeased. When asked what it would take to please him, he said, "To see Katy kiss Jim Hathaway (Hathaway was the ex-boyfriend of Katy). Jim, of course, had no choice in the matter but to do the other man's bidding. This broke the game up and in a few minutes people began to go home. Suddenly a piercing scream penetrated the night. The men ran toward the direction of the scream to find Katy standing over the headless body of Jim Hathaway. His head was completely severed from his body and was lying, staring grotesquely at the cold, winter sky. Blood covered the well top on which the body lay. In the legal procedure which followed, a quick conviction was secured against Katy's boyfriend, although he denied it.

We had been living in the Sam Little Hollow for about three months. It was now early winter. A few snows had already fallen. The winter's wood was dry in the old wood shed out back, and the embers cracked until the early hours of morn in the old fireplace on one side of the room—shadows jumping here and there and being built into great goblins by the imaginations of a young boy. Suddenly one night without warning, it began to happen. About eight o'clock one night we heard a noise upstairs on the exposed ceiling joists. At first we thought it was only a rat or possibly a bird. Presently the noise became louder and louder, until at least it sounded like a large dog playing with a ball. Of course, there was no such thing as electricity in the Sam Little Hollow because we lived miles from the closest neighbor. With some hesitation my father took the lamp in one hand and a pistol in the other and began a slow creep toward the stair opening. Up it he crept, slowly and easily, so as to not disturb the noise maker. Suddenly he sprang forward, thrusting himself fully in the upstairs, the lamp fluttered and momentarily died only to regain its flame immediately. What only moments before had been loud noises was now nothing more than an empty upstairs full of silence. Puzzled, my father returned to the living room downstairs. Immediately after having sat down in his old chair, the noise began again, this time it was much louder, becoming loud enough to sound like a yearling calf romping and playing. Again my father crept toward the stairs, more caution exerted, more slowly in step than before. Quickly he flung himself through the opening again—nothing, absolutely nothing, not a sound. Again my father returned downstairs. The night finally passed. This procedure continued for several weeks. All the time we were very quiet about it to the public for fear of being made fun of. Finally one night three men who were on leave from the Army came by the house and were sitting and talking to my father. At a very low intensity it began, at first not noticed. Then they began to perk their ears and ask questions. My father evaded their questions as long as possible but, alas, to no avail. He finally broke down and told all. The three had a good laugh with Dad sitting there with dead seriousness written all over his face. Within minutes the expressions of amusement had changed to expressions of amazement. These three men spent all night sitting there listening to that noise. Every time they attempted to find out what its source was, the noise would cease. I've never known whether they stayed because of curiosity or fright. When they left the next morning, just after daylight, one of the men turned to my father and said, "Clarence, when you move, I'll be back and visit, not until."

We continued to live here for about two years. We set traps, put out poison, bought cats, dogs, weasels, ferrets, nailed everything down, and did everything we could possibly think of. Finally the *coup de grâce* came. The original well top on which the man had been killed still remained. After each rain, large blood-like splotches would appear on the well top. Nothing short of destruction of the well top would do away with the splotches. My father sold the place at considerable loss, and we very thankfully moved out of the Sam Little Hollow.

*Russell County, 1964 (———). Informant: male, born 1938 in Russell County. The collector of this narrative is also the informant. This lengthy and realistic account of the supernatural is recorded as a personal experience, written in 1964. The narrative has two basic motifs: *E402, "Mysterious ghost-like noises heard," and *E422.1.11.5.1(e), "Ineradicable bloodstain as the result of blood shed during murder."*

The Sounds of Running Oxen

344   Lester's dad worked at a sawmill. The boss once brought a friend of his to work with him and told the men not to make fun of him. This man said that he had a farm for sale that he would sell cheap. He said the farm was hainted, that he wasn't afraid but just aggravated. He said the road in front of his house had a sway in it, which

had been left by a team of oxen pulling a wagon. The man who had lived there before had worked with oxen. The man said every afternoon late you could hear oxen running and chains rattling and whips poppin'.

He said, "You could hear them plain as day; and if you got in the road to look for them, you couldn't see them. They would keep comin' closer until they got right up next to you, and then you would jump out of the way just in time for them to go on by. They don't stir any dust up or anything 'cept make a lot of noise. This happens every day; and if anyone don't believe it, they can jist go home with me and stay a day or two."

He also said that while his daughter was writing a letter that someone blew their breath in her face. She turned around quickly but saw no one. It happened again and she still saw no one.

Adair County, 1964 (KB). Informant: male, age unknown, born in Adair County. Three motifs are included in this legend about ghostly beasts of burden: *E402, "Mysterious ghost-like noises heard"; *E402.1.4, "Invisible ghost jingles chains"; *E402.2, "Sounds made by invisible ghosts of animals."

Chains in the Basement

One day Daddy and Tommy were gone to town. I was cooking in the kitchen, standing there by the stove. It sounded like somebody walking across the basement dragging a chain. Whatever it was started up the steps. I wanted to look and see what it was, but I was scared. So I called two friends and told them what happened.

I still heard the sound after I called them, so I went outside. I walked around on the little porch, but I still heard something walking and dragging a chain. I was too big of a chicken to look in the window. Finally, I went to my grandfather's.

When Daddy and Tommy came back, we looked all through the house; but we never found anything.

Monroe County, 1969 (RLy). Informant: female, born 1949 in Monroe County. Motif *E402.1.4, "Invisible ghost jingles chains," is probably applicable here. Accounts of jingling chains are ubiquitous and fairly amorphous.

The Sound of Horses

346   We had been to a party. It had come an awful rain while we were
there. My sister, my mother, and myself were walking back from the
party through a neighbor's field. Even though it had rained hard,
the field still wasn't real muddy.

Our neighbor had horses. There was this sound that sounded like
horses. We ran and got over a fence. After we got over the fence, the
noise sounded like it came to the fence and just stopped. We got
back over the fence and heard it again. We never did know what
it was. It maybe was the rails or something.

That same night Mother went to the bedroom and opened the
door, and there was a round light on the floor. We never figured out
where the light came from.

I don't know if there was any connection between the two happenings or not.

> *Monroe County, 1969 (RLy). Informant: female, born ca. 1910 in
> Monroe County.* Motifs appropriate here are *E402, "Mysterious
> ghost-like noises heard," and *E402.2, "Sounds made by invisible
> ghosts of animals."

Old Knocker

347   "They called them haints then. Now, that's the way they pronounced it. Well, there was this noise that was like something
a-walking. Just a flat noise, I'd say. And we were over there one time,
and if I had of heard of it—not being, you know, expecting it—I
wouldn't have known. It wouldn't have been anything terrifying
to me, and it wasn't then. They said, 'There goes . . . ,' they
called it the Old Knocker—the people that lived there. They said,
'There goes the Old Knocker.' And it was just like something
kindly a-going across the floor—or you might say—something that
was crippled a-going across the floor. And as far as it being anything
outstanding, why, I didn't course, think anything about it. But if I
had heard it of a night, I might have been afraid—I don't know. But
they didn't seem to be! But I heard people say it'd be something,
sound like something a-rolling down a stairstep. And when you'd

go open the door, there wouldn't be a thing there. But I never heard that myself.

"They said, I think, that there was somebody killed upstairs, that the bloodstains were on the floor. But as for who it was or anything about that, I don't know.

"It seems to me like they claimed that it was a soldier, or a soldier had killed somebody, or somebody had killed a soldier there in that house."

Metcalfe County, 1968 (KH). Informant: female, born 1915 in Metcalfe County. Previously unreported. Although this is the first report of a ghost narrative which uses the label "Old Knocker" to identify the supernatural creature, the motifs are no different. Appropriate here are *E402, "Mysterious ghost-like noises heard," and *E422.1.11.5.1(e), "Ineradicable bloodstain as the result of blood shed during murder."

The Heavenly Choir

Back in the early 1900s, there was a hill near to my grandfather's home. As you would ride by on horseback, as my granddad usually did, you could hear the sweet music of the heavenly choir singing sweet songs of long ago. Today the hill has still got the same name. You can ask anyone in the community about that hill, and they will give you the name, "The Haunted Hill." And they still say if you are going by there at night, and the wind is just right you can hear them singing.

Monroe County, 1958 (RMo). Informant: male, born 1943 in Monroe County. The only motif contained in this story of the haunted hill is *E402.4, "Sound of ethereal music," indexed previously from Indiana and Texas.

COMMUNICATIONS WITH THE DEAD

Three Raps on the Table

Mrs. Sims, whose husband had been dead for years, heard something upstairs one day. She asked who it was, but nobody answered. Then she asked that if it was her husband to knock three times, and he did. She asked him if he went to heaven to knock two times, and he did. She was able to talk with him in this way for many years, so she said.

> *Connecticut, 1964 (LS). Informant: male, middle-aged, born in Taylor County.* This brief narrative of spirit communications contains only one motif: *E402.1.5, "Invisible ghost makes rapping or knocking noise," reported previously from Texas and California.

Ghostly Knocks

350   "My old aunt told of talking to a man who got killed and was unsatisfied after death. Back in them days people talked to the dead, especially if they had died but still had some sort of message for the living. They could ask the dead man if what they were asking was true or not. They'd tell him to knock three times, and they'd do it.

"Once this man was killed accidentally by a team. And after they had talked with him about how he had got killed, they got up and went to the front door, and they heard a team coming. The chains on the horses and wagon were rattling very plainly. They listened as the sounds pulled up into the front yard by the gate, but when they looked there was no wagon or nothing."

> *Monroe County, 1961 (LM). Informant: female, born ca. 1915 in Monroe County.* Narratives of this sort are rather uncommon in the Kentucky foothills. This story contains Motifs *E402, "Mysterious ghost-like noises heard"; *E402.1.5, "Invisible ghost makes rapping or knocking noise"; and *E402.2, "Sounds made by invisible ghosts of animals."

Dissatisfied Dead Man Knocks on Wall

351   "Aunt Randy has told the tales that when people would get—you know—killed or anything, something happened—deaths or anything, and you'd say that they died dissatisfied—they would be rackets. And they would hear knocks and hear sounds at houses. And she has told of talking to them. And they'd knock on the wall—you know, talk to the ones that had died—if they died dissatisfied or had got killed or anyway.

"Aunt Randy talked to this person where that I told you about a-knocking three times. She'd ask him questions about things that had happened there at this place. And she'd tell him—whoever she was talking to—if it was all right, why give her three knocks. And she said, 'Plainly, you could hear them three knocks.' That was the answering of her question if he had died dissatisfied, and if things hadn't went right before he died, and so on and so forth.

"When they talked to the man that maybe had got killed and was unsatisfied, they could ask a question. And if what they was asking was true, why'd they tell them to knock [narrator knocks on wall with hand] three times, and they'd do it. And they talked, and he knocked, and they [a few words are unintelligible at this point] they'd do it. After they talked to him, and he knocked, why they got up.

"It was concerning the team somehow that he got killed. And they got up and went to the door, and they heard the team a-coming and the chains a-rattling. And when it got to the yard gate, why the noise stopped, and they's no team either. And no wagon or nothing."

Monroe County, 1961 (LM). Informant: female, born ca. 1915 in Monroe County. The motifs in this story are the same as those identified in story No. 350 and appear in the same sequential order. This is a re-telling with elaboration of the preceding tale by the same informant. An additional Monroe County version of this narrative was collected in 1969.

Ghost of Man Raps to Identify Murderer

A fellow by the name of Jones killed Jim Shuck Peeler. They caught Jones and had him in jail at Tompkinsville. His friends pulled him through bars, a place called the "feed hole." He never was heard of again.

Jim Shuck Peeler lived where Benton [Bowman] used to live. People talked to Jim Peeler after his death. They asked him who killed him. They asked him if Davis Jones did. He would peck to answer.

The news got out. Others didn't believe it and went one night to the house. Got to talkin' to him. He was upstairs, and they wanted him to come down; but they wouldn't ever open the door.

Monroe County, 1969 (RLy). Informant: male, born 1890 in Monroe County. This intriguing tale revolves around Motifs *E402, "Mysterious ghost-like noises heard," and E402.1.5, "Invisible ghost makes rapping or knocking noise." Jim Shuck Peeler, the subject of this account, has also won mention in a local play-party song and in additional tales in the area.

Talking over the Table

353   Someone taught Eva Dover to talk over the table. She would put her hands on the table and talk to the spirits. She could even make chairs walk. People around here thought that it was awful, but people from everywhere came to get her to talk to their dead for them.

Alta Stockton came down and wanted her to call up Ibbie, my uncle's wife. Eva called her up, and she said she'd like to see Alta and Ethel, her mother, and all of them. Alta asked if she wanted to see Lester, my uncle. And she said no that he was going with Jenny Simpson, and he was.

Now, of course, you couldn't hear her talk. Eva just told you what she said.

Clinton County, 1963 (SW). Informant: female, born 1917 in Clinton County. The only recognizable element in this narrative is Motif E385.1, "Husband ignored or discouraged by ghost wife."

GHOSTLY LIGHTS

The Strange Light

354   As I was walking home a few years ago and as I approached a graveyard a light shined in a tree on the left side of the road about eight feet from the ground. It was moving in fast darts back and forth as it moved down the fence row and bushes. It stayed in front of me until I got to the next house. I was so excited I stopped and called my cousin to the door and told her about it. But I didn't see it any more that night.

Later on, a few weeks later, my cousin and I were walking up the road approximately three miles from where I saw it the first time. It stayed along a fence line until we got to his house. It shined on

the barn and went on up in the yard in front of the house and shined
in a tree, and then it returned back to the barn darting back and
forth and disappeared. I saw this myself, but I've never been able to
figure out what it was.

> Russell County, 1965 (SS). Informant: male, born 1923 in Russell
> County. Applicable here is Motif *E530.1, "Ghost-like lights," re-
> ported previously from New York and North Carolina.

Jack-O-Lanterns

"Lawrence says his grandfather Mark has told him of seeing strange
lights at times which seemed to be just dancing around in the
field. He called them 'Jack-O-Lanterns.' He believed these lights
were caused by some mineral or something in the ground. Lawrence
says he has seen them there before."

> Adair County, 1964 (KB). Informant: male, middle-aged, born in
> Adair County. Motif F491.4, "Will-o'-wisp hops about," is present in
> this short narrative from the Eastern Pennyroyal of Kentucky.

Ghostly Streaks of Fire

"I used to walk along the road by that old graveyard there on yonder
side of Aunt Sut's. I've seen streaks of fire in front of me—they'd dart
across in front of me."

> Monroe County, 1961 (LM). Informant: male, born 1918 in Mon-
> roe County. This narrative fragment contains Motifs *E530.1, "Ghost-
> like lights," and *E530.1.3, "Ghost light haunts burial spot."

The Light on the Hill (a)

There was this hill by Skaggs Creek, and when it rained the fog
came in on the creek; and they could always see a light on the hill.
Whenever they saw the light, they wanted to know what it was; and
they went to find out. It moved about on the hill. But whenever they
got near, it disappeared. As long as the people lived there they could
see the light but were never able to figure out what it was. It only
occurred after a hard rain.

> Monroe County, 1969 (RLy). Informant: female, elderly, born in

Monroe County. Motif *E530.1, "Ghost-like lights," is applicable here.

The Light on the Hill (b)

358   "Daddy was walking down the road. They say there was a ghost on that road. People had been telling about seeing a light down there on the hill between his home and the creek. It was scaring everybody to death, so he decided he'd go find out what it was. He started out; and when he left home, he got his pistol. When he got there, there was a little white spot about the size of a ball; and he got out his pistol. And the longer he stood and looked at it, the bigger it got. It got to going up and down. Looked to be about three feet across. He got scared and forgot about his pistol and reached down to pick up a rock to throw at it. He threw the rock, and this thing began coming at him; and he run off and never went back again."

Adair County, 1968 (NAB). Informant: male, born 1925 in Adair County. This story contains Motifs *E272, "Road ghosts. Ghost which haunts road," reported from North Carolina; *E293, "Ghosts scare people (deliberately)"; and *E530.1, "Ghost-like lights."

The Light on the Hill (c)

359   The house where my grandmother and two uncles used to live had always had a name of being spooky. My grandfather while plowing one day had plowed up Indian bowls and cups. Also, he found bones of some kind.

One night as my uncle was coming home from Celina, he saw a light going around the house. Our next-door neighbor said that it was not the only time that someone had seen a light. She said that on some nights you could stand on the front porch and see a light on the hill across from the house.

I was in the house the night my uncle saw the light. I'm glad I didn't know it then.

Monroe County, 1958 (RMo). Informant: female, born 1944 in Monroe County. Applicable in this version of the tale concerning lights on a hill is Motif *E530.1, "Ghost-like lights."

The Fiery Wheel

"Well, one time when I was just a boy, I was a-dodgin' the law to
get out of going before the Grand Jury. Dad studies out a place for
me to go, an' 'fore we knowed the sheriff was a-huntin' the whole
neighborhood a-gettin' all he could to go before the Grand Jury.
So he says, 'Billy, if you will go over to Old Man Davidson's, you
can stay over there; and nobody won't know Old Man Elemental-
lers.' (I've got that wrong. Since I've been sick, I can't remember.)
But anyway, I went to Uncle Jim Elementaller's, and Uncle Jim
was glad I had come. I said, 'Well, I'll go and get'che up some wood,
Uncle Jim, and we'll have a good fire.'

"And he was a-cookin' a big hen and looking for Old Man John
Davidson Place. He had it under mortgage, and he couldn't get mon-
per. They was both old, and I built them a good fire. And long
after supper, why, Uncle Jim and John Davidson got into a little
argument. He wanted to borrow five hundred dollars to go on the
Davidson Place. He had it under mortgage, and he couldn't get money; and he thought that Uncle Jim had the money. And Uncle Jim
told him he had it, but he had it loaned out to different ones; and
he probably couldn't let him have it. And they got into an argument, and they's about to be trouble there. Uncle Jim sorta made a
pass to get his gun. Then later on after the racket started, why, he
fixed pretty soon for me to have a bed. But they wuz different rooms,
hadn't been slept in, in I don't guess a year. He said, 'Would you
sleep with Uncle John Davidson?' 'No,' I said, 'I'd druther sleep
by myself,' fer he'd been in trouble and jail; and I'd druther jest
have a bed to myself.

"After we went to bed, Uncle Jim left, barred up the door where
I went in at. They's no place to get out only go out at the back
door and had to get a lot of things moved before I could ever make
it out that a-way. I got scared in the night. The lights was a-flaming
over Davidson's bed and streaked lights a-crossin' the bed. And I
said, well, 'Can't you see them lights?' He says, 'Billy, don't get
scared. The sheriffs won't come after you tonight.' And I says, 'I
han't scared, I just don't like them lights a-crossin' the bed.'

"About that time I made my way and pulled down a big dogwood fork that forked up the door to hold the door where I went out at. I said, 'Well, I'm a-makin' it out of here now.' And about that time the old door fell, and I crawled out from under it and made my way on out; and I said (in the time of it I forgot my hat or my cap one, and I says), 'Would you pitch me my cap?' And he says, 'Yes.'

"Well, through the old orchard of Uncle Jim's, I saw the awfullest big wheel of just nothing, just a-rolling, just great big, well, as big as a barrel was a-coming from that wheel and just sounding like a big snowball and a-lightnin' up the whole plantation in that thar place till you could see all the way back to Shepherd Place. I made a jump to run, and I run and jumped a fence down thar that I guess was seven or eight rails high and just kept a-runnin'!"

> *Russell County, 1964 (HD). Informant: (anonymous contributor, except that subject born 1888 in Russell County). This lengthy narrative about the fiery wheel contains Motif *E530.1, "Ghost-like lights."*

The Flashing Light

361   It was one summer day early in June. It had been raining that day. The water was dripping off the house, and the fire flies were buzzing. I kept seeing something pass by the window. It was like a big light flashing. I closed my eyes, but when I opened them, it came again. Finally, I laid there with my eyes open. I got scared to death and went and told Daddy. I thought of a flying saucer and maybe people with flashlights. I never saw it again.

> *Adair County, 1968 (NAB). Informant: female, born 1945 in Monroe County. Motif *E530.1, "Ghost-like lights," is found in this brief narrative.*

The Light over the Bed

362   One night I saw a light. Me and two of my brothers was sleeping upstairs. Later on, they saw the light. We would see the light often. We thought it might be a car light, but it would take turns at night over my bed, then, the next time over one of my brothers' beds. We never did find out what it was. Also, at the same house about

The coffin, as with the grave, is the point of departure for many tales of the supernatural. Tompkinsville undertaker Charles Strode, shown here, can recall a number of stories involving the coffin that are known in his nearby home community of Old Mt. Herman.

Left: Nature reclaims the grave headstone of this early resident of the Eastern Pennyroyal, which was settled only a few years before her birth in 1815. *Above*: Famous for the appearance of ghosts at the turn of the century was the old Strode homeplace, as well as the entire Forkton community near Tompkinsville.

Left: A storyteller and retired schoolteacher, Mrs. Margaret Edith Tucker, stands in the doorway of the haunted Hiestand house located two miles southwest of Campbellsville in Taylor County. *Above*: The ghostly cries of a baby have been reported from this deserted cabin in Russell County.

Above: Croy Fish, Monroe County storyteller, peers into the bewitched Lon Frazier house near Cedar Hill as he relates one of the many ghost legends about it to Lynwood Montell. *Right*: This house in Mt. Gilead community (Monroe County), home to at least four generations of tellers of supernatural legends, was itself specter-haunted in earlier years.

every month, we would hear a loud stomp or a big noise upstairs. It never did happen while we were upstairs. When it happened, we would run upstairs; and it wouldn't be anything. We never did solve this mystery either.

> *Monroe County, 1959 (LM). Informant: male, born 1944 in Barren County.* In this account of mysterious happenings, there are motifs which are related both to strange noises and to strange lights. Motifs *E338.1(ad), "Occupants hear ghost fall on floor of room above them," and *E402, "Mysterious ghost-like noises heard," refer to the noises. The only appropriate motif for strange lights is *E530.1, "Ghost-like lights," since there is no mention of a death subsequent to the appearance of the light

The House by the River

"There was this farmhouse on the river. Nobody couldn't live there. There was an old stage crossing there. The family that lived there at that time used old spinning wheels and looms. A bunch of travelers came along and wanted to spend the night. They let them stay, and they killed the girls that night. One of them was churning, and one of them was weaving. They say that the house still lights up of a night, and one can hear the churn going and the weaving loom going."

> *Adair County, 1968 (NAB). Informant: male, born 1904 in Adair County.* Applicable here are Motifs *E281, "Ghosts haunt house," and E530.1, "Ghost-like lights." Cf. E534, "Phantom spinning wheel makes noise."

Moon Hovers over Men's Heads

I never have understood a light I saw once. There was this place close to Little Barren where several men have been killed. Well, me and these two others were coming up through a woody section. One of the men looked back over his shoulder right into this tree and said, "Look at that moon."

I said, "Hold on a minute." I knew this would never do. I looked straight up and saw the moon right over my head.

I still don't know what it was. It was as big as a hogshead.

Green County, 1964 (JPo). Informant: male, elderly, born in Green County. The only discernible motif in this legend is *E530.1.0.1, "Ghost light as ball of fire," reported previously from Florida, Kentucky, Illinois, and Iowa tradition. One black Monroe County informant also compared a ghostly ball of fire with the size of a hogshead. In 1959 a Barren County subject reported that on the night of his grandfather's death, balls of fire rolled out of the barn loft. Attempts to catch them before they disappeared were unsuccessful.

The Strange Light

365   This story was told about the graveyard at Palestine Baptist Church in the colored section. When Aunt Lucy and Grandmother were little girls, at night when it got pitch dark and there was no moon or stars, they could see a light looking like a lantern would move over the graveyard. This light was so bright that Aunt Lucy and Grandmother, who lived not quite a quarter of a mile across the field from the graveyard, could see well enough to write their names on the house.

Just why this light did occur is not completely known, except the first time that the light was seen was when one of the neighbor men was riding home on a donkey, and the light came upon him as he was crossing the graveyard. The light was so bright, he lost his way.

From then on my Aunt Lucy and Grandmother and a few other folks would come out on the porch on a moonless and starless night after twelve and watch the strange light circle over the top of graveyard.

Taylor County, 1969 (BS). Informant: female, born 1948 in Taylor County. This story of lights in the graveyard contains Motif *E530.1, "Ghost-like lights."

STRANGE DOORS AND LATCHES

Stairway Door Refuses to Stay Closed

366   There was a real old lady who would come to our house when I was a child and would tell old haint tales. And she told once about hearing a voice upstairs. The house was haunted, and there was a

rumble and a roar upstairs. And then it went bump-bump down the stairs, and the stair doors came open. After the rumble there was a swish sound. And the old witch came down the stairs on a broomstick, through the house, and out the door. And away she went. And the stair door could never be kept closed any more.

   Metcalfe County, 1968 (WB). Informant: female, born 1903 in Metcalfe County. Included are Motifs cf. *E338.1(c), "Ghost opens doors and windows repeatedly"; *E402, "Mysterious ghost-like noises heard"; and G242.1, "Witch flies through air on broomstick."

The Voice from the Cedar Tree

I moved here from Hominy Creek, Jim Brown's Place, over at the mouth of the holler. I lived there for two years in a house that had four rooms and two doors. Now this didn't happen every night, but no matter how many buttons or locks you put on the door, it would open at night. One night the old lady [informant's wife] went to her niece's and left me and the kids there. My bed stood beside the door, and a chair sat by the bed, and a gun was on the chair.

I had two dogs, and they wuz rough. They'd just as soon eat a man as look at him. I woke up in the night, and the kids wuz snoring like hogs a-dying. And I just felt like something was going to happen.

I opened the door, and there was two elm trees on each side of the door; and the dogs lay at the roots of the trees. The moon was a-shining, and I couldn't hear a thing. I started to shut the door, and a voice spoke to me from out of the top of a cedar tree out there in the yard. I forgot what it said first, but the last thing it said was, "Don't be scared or surprised. You've done nothing, and no one'll hurt you." I didn't say a word, and I went to bed.

When the door would open, it would crack just like you had turned a lock. And if it had button, it would be turned up straight.

   Clinton County, 1963 (SW). Informant: male, born 1896 in Clinton County. This supernatural legend of the voice from the tree includes Motifs *E338.1(c), "Ghost opens doors and windows repeatedly"; *E360, "Friendly return from the dead"; and *E402, "Mysterious ghost-like noises heard."

The Lady in Black

368   My father's brother had just moved into this house and was going
to bed for the first time there. When he got in bed, the door to the
bedroom opened. This happened three times after he locked it
each time. The next time it opened, he said, "This time I am going
to find out what is doing it." And in the hallway was a lady dressed
in black, so he closed the door hard. But this time the door didn't
open, and he never saw the lady dressed in black again.

> *Taylor County, 1964 (LS). Informant: male, age unknown, born in
> Taylor County.* There are two motifs present in this brief narrative
> from the Kentucky foothills: *E338.1(c), "Ghost opens doors and
> windows repeatedly," and *E422.4.4(e), "Female revenant in black
> dress," reported previously from Lincolnshire (England).

GHOSTLY FURNITURE AND UTENSILS

The Ghostly Sewing Machine

369   One time we started living in what they always called a haunted
house. My sister, Aunt Dollie, and I went up into the attic and
brought an old sewing machine down to use for a lamp table. Dollie was staying by herself that night. When she had gone to bed for
a while, she saw a light in an old house not too far away. It was so
bright that it lit up the whole house. Then it kept getting dimmer,
dimmer, dimmer, and dimmer until it went out. Well, Dollie was
never afraid of anything, so she just turned over and tried to go to
sleep. About that time she heard something that sounded like
footsteps walking around that old sewing machine. She sat up in
bed, and the walking stopped. When she laid back down, it started
again. Dollie got up and went into the boy's room and crawled up
on the end of the bed and slept there the rest of the night. She
woke up sometime early the next morning and thought how silly
she was being and went back to her room. She had no sooner laid
down again than she heard that walking sound again.

Well, the next day, the old sewing machine went back to the
attic.

Green County, 1966 (TB). Informant: female, born 1899 in Green County. This mysterious tale revolves around Motifs E421.2.1, "Ghost leaves no footprints"; *E530.1, "Ghost-like lights"; and *E530.1.0.1(c), "Building seen to light up strangely at night when unoccupied," a motif known in New York and in the Isle of Skye.

The Strange Floor

"Belle Holland had a large family of young children and they were so much trouble that she had to wait until they got in bed to wash them off. She set her teakettle of hot water on the floor one night, and it began to move.

"The floor was laid directly on the ground in such a way that nothing could get between the ground and the floor. The floor boards moved in such a way that one board was raised upon another.

"Belle never could find out what was moving the floor, so she told me that it must have been ghosts."

Taylor County, 1964 (GS). Informant: male, age unknown, born in Taylor County. The moving kettle in this account may be related to Motif D1646.3, "Dancing kettle."

Bed Moves Up and Down

Once when Aunt Belle's baby was small, she thought she heard him cry. She walked upstairs to see about him, and when she reached the top of the stairs and looked into his room, he was sleeping soundly. Another bed in the room was moving up and down. She fainted, and other people in the house ran to see what was wrong. When they saw the bed move, also, another woman—Alma Froedge—fainted.

Green County, 1964 (SM). Informant: female, born 1944 in Green County. D1646, "Magic dancing object," is the closest motif to the one contained in this concise narrative.

The Jumping Skillet

Grandma West told me about the Frank Billings place. It's burned now. Richard Hagan used to live there. It's up in Meadow Creek. Grandma was getting supper for Bertie, and the skillet begin to jump up and down. It scared her to death, and she had to hold the skillet down to fry the meat.

Then they went to bed, and they heard something roll down the stairs. And the door was closed. But it sounded like it would roll through the door and out into the yard. You couldn't see anything, but it just sounded like a barrel. I wouldn't stay all night in that house for nothing. And a lot of people have heard it, too. It wasn't just Grandma.

> *Clinton County, 1963 (SW). Informant: female, born 1888 in Clinton County. Only one motif, *E402, "Mysterious ghost-like noises heard," is applicable.*

The Lighted Lanterns

373   Years ago there was once a family who was somewhat poor, for they had quite a lot of children. They decided to move to Campbellsville but couldn't find a house to live in that was suitable for their income. One day the man of the family came upon this big, old, abandoned house that had been vacant for some time. He asked the owner of the house if he and his family could move in it for a small amount of rent. And, of course, the man said he could because the house was doing no good just sitting there vacant.

After the family moved in, they started to notice funny happenings. Every Sunday night they'd turn out all lanterns and lock all doors before going to church. When they came home from church, all the lanterns were lit and the doors were still locked.

> *Taylor County 1969 (BS). Informant: female, born 1946 in Taylor County. The only identifiable motif in this narrative is *E530.1, "Ghost-like lights."*

The House over the Graveyard

374   There was this old house, the Wilson home in Russell County, built over a graveyard. At night the furniture would rock back and forth and nearly fall over. People who slept there said that when you went to bed at night, something would pull the covers off

you. Also, a pillow would come down and go back up the stairs.

Adair County, 1968 (NAB). Informant: female, born 1912 in Adair County. Motifs *E279.3, "Ghost pulls bedclothing from sleeper"; E280, "Ghosts haunt buildings"; and *E334.2, "Ghost haunts burial spot," are applicable here.

HORSES SENSE HAINTS

Emma Saw the Ghost

John Haskins lived in Green County with his wife and twelve children, where Virgil Holloway now lives. Three of his children—Tom, Sam, and Emma—had heard that there was going to be a big square dance at Mr. Hammerhill's Place at the Levelwoods community in Taylor County, since they went to all the square dances. They got ready and left on horseback.

When they got to where they thought Mr. Hammerhill lived, they found it was a deserted house. Chains began to rattle all around their horses, and the horses began to rear up and snort; but the brothers could never see anything. The girl was so badly frightened that they had to hold her on her horse. This noise of chains followed them about three miles on their way home.

When they got home, they called the doctor for Emma. She was having chills. She died about three months after this event and never walked during these three months. Before she died Emma told them that she had seen what had been after them that night, but she wouldn't tell them what it was.

Green County, 1967 (KP). Informant: female, born 1914 in Taylor County. Motif *E402.1.4, "Invisible ghost jingles chains," is applicable here as well as *E421.1.2, "Ghost visible to horses alone."

Horse Balks at Hainted Spot

"When I was younger, I would borrow this horse from Willie Montell and would ride through these woods where this man was killed. This horse would snort and cut all sorts of shines when I would get near the spot where the death occurred. I'd go on to church up there at Pleasant Hill. Late at night when I was returning home, the horse would act the same way. This was the place where a limb fell on Johnny Vibbert and killed him."

> *Monroe County, 1961 (LM). Informant: male, born ca. 1918 in Monroe County.* The only identifiable motif in this narrative is *E421.1.2, "Ghost visible to horses alone," reported mainly from northern European tradition. In addition to the present text, I collected three other versions from Monroe County in the Eastern Pennyroyal, but found no American versions in print. Cf. White (ed.), *The Frank C. Brown Collection of North Carolina Folklore*, I, 678.

The Stench of Human Flesh (a)

377   One time this man was coming home on his horse. There was a terrible odor that smelled like dead human body. (The odor of human body is so terrible that you just can't imagine it. If you ever do smell it, you'll never forget it.) The man's horse began to shy. He whipped his horse to get it past this certain place in the road. (Horses are frightened from the odor from a dead body.) He never knew where the odor came from.

> *Monroe County, 1969 (RLy). Informant: female, born ca. 1918 in Monroe County.* The motif most closely associated with this story about the smell of death appears to be *E421.1.2, "Ghost visible to horses alone."

The Stench of Human Flesh (b)

378   At Sulphur Lick, Fred's mother had a gathering for all the young people. They were called candy breakings. Clem was in a hurry and came on. I stayed longer to come home by myself. I rode a big horse, and at top of Skaggs Creek Hill I smelled something like a corpse. The horse liked to have never come on. I never come on. I never knew what it was.

> *Monroe County, 1969 (RLy). Informant: male, born ca. 1895 in Monroe County.* The motif in this narrative is the same as the one in story No. 377. That account is the daughter's version of her father's experience, recounted in this text.

FRIGHTFUL CREATURES

Ghostly Creature

I stayed all night with Uncle Ike Ritter once. I slept in a room in that wing that runs out toward the graveyard. I hadn't gone to sleep when something jumped up on the window sill, gave one jump into the middle of the floor, and the next jump it landed on the bed with me.

Maybe it could have been a big cat; but if it was, it was standing on two legs. It felt like it was about the size of a big monkey, and it stood up like one on two legs. But whatever it was, it sure could pull cover. For some reason it wanted to get my bed cover. I fought for my quilt for I guess just seconds, but it was like hours to me.

All of a sudden it just turned loose, hopped onto the floor, give one jump onto the window sill, and was gone.

The next morning I was going to look at the window it had used to come in and leave the room. There just wasn't a window there.

Barren County, —— (——). Informant: female, born ca. 1932 in Barren County. The collector of this narrative is the informant, who learned it from her father, also a native of Barren County. This supernatural legend contains two motifs: *E279.3, "Ghost pulls bedclothing from sleeper," and F500–529, dealing with "Remarkable persons." Motifs F500–529 mention the basic descriptive motifs found in this tale, but none contain reference to parallel accounts.

Ghostly White Creature

My Granddaddy Russell, he claimed he had seen a good many things as unaccountable for.

Well, let me see now. Well, now I'll tell you this about him. Now this has been handed to me. I didn't hear him tell it, but he was a firm believer in it.

One night him an' another man was out a'huntin'. He was a hunter. An' he was all kinds of a hunter, an' that day 'n time he was a fox hunter, I reckon. He was out one night with a gun, I reckon. I don't know what they was doin' with a gun of a night huntin'. Him an' another man had hounds, I reckon, don't know. Anyway, there was a place down in the neighborhood called the hainted house. An' they come by that house. An' they said sump'm big, white—sump'm come outa that house an' rared up on the fence. An' he shot at it. An' he was a—he was a—he was one o' the best shots that 'uz ever in this country, an' he started runnin' then. That other man jumped on his back [the informant laughs], an' he had to carry him in.

　　Adair County, 1964 (VM). Informant: male, elderly, born in Adair County. This narrative contains two basic motifs: *E421.5, "Ghost seen by two or more persons; they corroborate the appearance," and E422.4.3, "Ghost in white."

Raw Head and Bloody Bones

381　There was a house that everybody said was haunted, and no one would have anything to do with. A lady said she was not afraid to stay all night in it. She took her lamp and a book to read and went to the house. During the night, she heard a noise and went to see just what it was. It was two legs coming down a stairs for a few seconds, and then there were two more legs that appeared. Then a body was added to the four legs. After the body was joined, a head appeared and was put on the body. Big eyes were added to the head with blood shooting out of them.

　　(As the persons telling this story got to this, they would jump at the kids and about scare them to death.)

　　Lincoln County, 1965 (DP). Informant: female, born 1907 in Lincoln County. Appropriate motifs are E402, "Mysterious ghostlike noises heard," and E422.1.10.1, "Dismembered corpse reassembles."

The Dismembered Corpse

382　There was this haunted house. A human leg came down the chimney, then another leg came down the chimney. After a few minutes an arm came down, then a few more minutes another arm. Then a head came down. About this time the body came down. The legs and arms kept joining, and the man didn't hang around to see if the body got joined or not.

Monroe County, 1969 (RLy). Informant: male, born ca. 1916 in Monroe County. The only discernible motif in this narrative is E422.1.10.1, the same as in story No. 381.

The Big Toe (a)

There was this woman whose big toe was cut off. She would bury it and dig it up. She would take it from one place then bury it somewhere else. One day when she went to get it, it wasn't there. She went moaning through the hills: "Who stole my big toe? Who stole my big toe? Who stole my big toe? Who stole my big toe?

"You stole my big toe?" [The storyteller would then jump at a person in the audience.]

Monroe County, 1969 (RLy). Informant: male, age unknown, born in Monroe County. For this well-known supernatural narrative, cf. *E235.4, "Return from dead to punish theft of part of corpse."

The Big Toe (b)

One time a man was plowing, and he plowed up a big toe. He took the toe to the house. The woman cooked it for supper, and they ate it. When they started to bed, something said, "Where's my big toe?" They looked everywhere under the bed, in the cabinets. They looked up the chimney and saw the awfullest looking thing ever was. The man looked at its eyes and said, "What you got them big eyes for?"

It said, "To look you through."

"What you got them big claws for?"

It said, "To tear you all to pieces."

Monroe County, 1969 (RLy). Informant: male, born ca. 1915 in Monroe County. This story is similar to story No. 383, but the motif (*E235.4) is more direct.

"Who Stole My Money?"

Long ago when there were no undertakers, neighbors took care of all the arrangements. They put money on the eyes of the dead person to keep them closed. When the man who did the last for this one man (they had put quarters on his eyes) got ready to close the casket, he took the money off and put it in his pocket. He took it home and put it in a tin can on the shelf in his little hut. That night after he went to bed, he couldn't sleep. He heard a "Tinkle, tinkle" on the shelf. The wind started blowin' real hard—"Woo, woo." And the money went "Tinkle, tinkle." The wind blew harder and harder. The man pulled the cover up over his head, but he still heard the "tinkle, tinkle." The wind blew so hard that it blew the door open. The man peeped out from under the cover and saw a long white robe blow into the room. The wind went, "Woo, woo, woo." The money went, "Tinkle, tinkle, tinkle." The voice said, "Who stole my money? Who stole my money?" The wind went, "Woo, woo, woo." The money went, "Tinkle, tinkle, tinkle." The wind went "Woo, woo, woo." The money went, "tinkle, tinkle, tinkle." The voice said, "Who stole my money? Who stole my money?

"You stole my money!"

> *Monroe County, 1969 (RLy). Informant: female, born 1910 in Barren County.* In this humorous account from the Kentucky hillcountry dealing with the dead haunting the living, only two motifs are present: *E236.8, "Ghost seeks repayment of stolen money," and *E279.2, "Ghost disturbs sleeping person."

The Creature in the Canoe

386   "My mother's sister, she used to ferry across the river. And so my grandmother kept telling her, says, 'Now you better quit that setting people across the river every night.' Says, 'Somebody will fool you some of these nights, and you are liable to get drowned or something another.'

"Said she said, 'No, I ain't afraid.'

"Said one night something another called her, 'O'Fertil, O'Fertil.'

"She said, 'What?'

"Said, 'I want to cross the river-r-r-r-r-r-r.'

"Said, well, she went down. Said she got down there, and said she didn't see nobody. Said she said, 'Where are you?' Nobody didn't answer. And said she said, 'Where are you?'

"Said they answered on the other side of the river then, 'Who-o-o-o-o.'

"Said she went on across the river, got up there; and said something another hopped on the other end of the canoe. Said it had a head as big as a half-bushel. Said its teeth was as big as your fist. And said its neck was, said its neck was, wasn't big as a broomstick. And said it was just a-gritting them teeth, 'Eeehhhhh, eeehhhhhh,' and said it was a-setting on the other end of the canoe. And she paddled backwards plumb across the river. And said in reason, it looked just like a ghost.

"Said when he, when this thing hopped in the river, why this thing hopped in the river to leave just something another like a ghost. And it hopped in, too. Said she fell backwards, right backwards across the river in the skift. Said when she got to the bank, she jumped out backwards. And said she shoved the skift out in the river. And said this thing hollered, 'Toodleopp, toodleopp'—made two of the funniest noises ever she heard in her life. And that skift just as far as she could see it, said he was gritting his teeth going on down the river out of sight."

Monroe County, 1961 (LM). Informant: (anonymous contributor, except that subject born ca. 1912 in Cumberland County). Motifs F500–529, "Remarkable persons," contain mention of the basic descriptive motifs found in this tale, but none contain reference to similar accounts. People of medieval times believed that the devil often assumed hideous forms, according to George Lyman Kittredge, Witchcraft in Old and New England (Cambridge, Mass.: Harvard Univ. Press, 1929), 175ff. Despite the association of motifs in this tale with Satan motifs, the narrator referred to the strange looking creature as a ghost. For that reason the story is included here.

Horse with Firebreathing Nostrils

There were two people out hunting for someone that was lost one snowy night. The people got about a mile away from home close to a big pond, and something just like a horse with a man on it was there. And when they asked who it was, it screamed real loud and fire came from its nose and mouth. But it never did move. They went back over there the next morning, and there wasn't anything there like that. This happened to my grandmother and my great-grandmother.

Monroe County, 1959 (LM). Informant: female, born 1944 in Barren County. Motif B15.5.1, "Horse with fire-breathing nostrils," has been reported previously from Danish and Icelandic tradition only.

Unseen Creature

388   "This man who was mean to his wife drank a lot. And one day he was coming home walking, and a thing picked him up and carried him up to the top of a very big and tall hill which no one had ever been up before. He told his wife about it and some others, but no one would believe him. So one day his wife told him to bring her some yarn. So he got drunk again and was walking home, and the thing picked him up again and was taking him up to the top of this hill; and the yarn came loose and strung all the way up the hill. And by that the people believe him. They thought since he was so mean and evil was the reason for him being carried up the hill. He was never saw again."

Russell County, 1966 (SS). Informant: female, born ca. 1929 in Russell County. The informant learned this tale from her parents. The unspecified creature mentioned in this story is probably related to Motif F585, "Phantoms."

The Creature

389   Around 1895, there used to be a lot of talk about a creature coming out of the woods in South Campbellsville. Many people swore they had seen it.

My dad used to go to school at Smith Ridge, called Carthelidge, as a boy. Him and some buddies came riding by this area one evening coming home from school. Every horse stopped with no command. They couldn't get the horses to move for half an hour. They couldn't explain it. A couple of them said that they had seen the monster.

Taylor County, 1966 (TD). Informant: male, born ca. 1944 in Taylor County. "The Creature" contains Motif *E421.1.2, "Ghost visible to horses alone," although Motif F585, "Phantoms," is probably also applicable here.

The Hooded Figure

I lived in this house, and it was told that it was "hainted." Even children knew it. Old people had experienced strange happenings and peculiar sounds very often. It was late one afternoon, and two children were playing in the yard. Now this house stood in the holler with woods coming almost down to the house. There was an old, stone chimney at one end of the house, and near the top of the house in the gable end was a small window. A noise attracted one of the children, and when they both looked toward the small window, they saw a hooded person or figure. Frantic, the children fled as if they had seen death.

> *Taylor County, 1969 (BS). Informant: male, born ca. 1919 in Magoffin County.* Although it is of minor significance, the only motif here is *E281, "Ghosts haunt house." The hooded figure does not carry a motif assignment.

When John Gets Here

"Once there was this feller down in South Alabama who had this big ol' house he's tryin' to get rid of. Nobody wouldn't buy it 'cause they thought there wuz haints there.

"Finally, he talked this ol' nigger boy to spend the night there to prove it weren't hainted. He promised him a hunnert dollars. The nigger took a big cauldron of grease and some catfish and some RC's to snack on while he's waitin'.

"Along about ten o'clock the door opens up, and this little-bitty feller comes in. He's about six inches high. He says, 'Is you gonna be here when John gets here?' The nigger thinks to hisself, 'I ain't gonna be scairt. I gonna stay here an' make that hunnert dollars.'

"Along about elebun o'clock another little feller about three feet high comes in. He sez, 'Is you gonna be here when John gets here?' The nigger's gittin' worried now, but he's still thinking about that hunnert dollars.

"Right at the stroke of twelve the door opens up real slow an' this bad, mean-lookin' feller comes in. He's about nine feet tall, with eyes that look like fire coals. He's got chains on, an' he's draggin' 'em. He takes the big cauldron of fish an' grease and drinks it all down, an' it don't even burn him. He picks up a double-handful of fire coals an' wipes his mouth with 'em, points his finger over at the nigger and says in a voice jest like thunder, 'Is you gonna be here when John gets here?' The nigger looks at him an' says, 'Man, if you ain't John, I'se gone!' "

> *Casey County, 1964 (WP). Informant: female, middle-aged, born in Casey County.* This story contains two basic motifs: *E293, "Ghosts scare people (deliberately)" and *H1411, "Fear test: staying in haunted house."

Wait for John

392　　　There was a house down in Russell County in Kentucky which was said to be haunted. One man decided to stay all night in this house to show that the house was not really haunted. He built a fire in the stove and settled down for a peaceful night.

As night came on a cat came in and sat on one side of him, and then another cat came in and sat on his other side. The cats looked at each other, then looked at the man and then looked back at each other. Then one cat said to the other, "Shall we eat him now or wait until John comes?" The man did not wait for the other cat to answer.

> *Adair County, 1964 (PA). Informant: male, born 1894 in Adair County.* Only two motifs are applicable: *H1411, "Fear test: staying in haunted house," and *E423.1.2, "Revenant as cat."

Wait for Caesar

393　　　There was an old haunted house. It was a two-story building. Nobody could live there, and there was a feller in the neighborhood. He wasn't afraid of anything. So he went there one night to spend the night. Winter time, got him some wood, built him a fire. There was stairs going upstairs, and the door was closed. All at once the door popped open, and this cat walked down, went over, and sat by the fireplace and started licking his paws. The man got up and shut the door. But no sooner had he sat back down when the door popped open again, and a second cat walked down and went over to the fireplace and sat down on the other side and started licking his paws. The man thought this was too much, but he was determined to stay the night. So he got up and shut the door again and sat back down. For the third time the door popped open, and the third cat walked down to the fireplace, sat down in the middle, and started licking his paws. One of the cats said to the others, "Should we eat him now or wait for Caesar?" Upon hearing this, the man jumped up and ran for home.

> *Adair County, 1968 (NAB). Informant: male, born 1904 in Adair County.* This narrative contains the same motifs as story No. 392 and in the same sequential order.

A Good Race

My grandfather's twin sister's husband—she is alive—she's got a good mind and ninety-four years old. She is the only one living of the original seven children of that particular family.

During the time of about 1915, in the neighborhood of Pitchford Ridge, there used to be one house that stood across the farm of Jeffrey Skaggs, my great-grandfather, which was apparently to be haunted by a ghost. This was the common joke of the neighborhood. Everyone seemed to add or detract about the ghost and different things he would do. One time, as a suggestion, my grandfather, James S. Skaggs, suggested that Dr. Ray spend the night in the old haunted house to prove no such a ghost existed there. Then everyone proceeded to kid Dr. Ray about the haunted house. They said he shouldn't be afraid to go because everyone knew there was no such thing as a ghost. And Dr. Ray accepted the challenge. He would stay in the haunted house with no one else with him.

So Dr. Ray entered the old house approximately 7:30 and observed any actions of any peculiar being or being unknown. Long toward the bewitching hour of 12:00, Dr. Ray became drowsy and fell asleep sitting at the table with only a candle to light. Dr. Ray awoke. He heard something coming down the staircase from the old attic toward where he was resting. It was a blurrish figure vaguely resembling a human figure.

Dr. Ray leaped through the door and ran down toward the road two miles away. Dr. Ray was running as fast as he could! At his great astonishment he ran faster than he ever had in his natural life. After about a mile of this, Dr. Ray became exhausted and proceeded to rest on a stump in the woods. While he was resting on the stump, the figure or ghost came up behind him and said, "That sure was a good race." Dr. Ray replies, "Yes, and we're fixin' to have another in just a few minutes."

> *Monroe County, 1966 (BP). Informant: male, born 1934 in Allen County.* In this somewhat lengthy narrative, Motifs *H1411, "Fear test: staying in haunted house," and *E293, "Ghosts scare people (deliberately)," are applicable. Additional versions of this very popular tale were gathered from Taylor, Russell, and Metcalfe counties.

It Sure Was a Hard Race

395 There once was a man who always wanted adventure. He wanted to find a ghost. He searched far and wide but couldn't find a ghost. He had just about given up all hopes. Back in them days it was just a wilderness, and there were very few roads. This man was on his way home and got lost just about dark. He went to a cabin on the side of the road and asked to spend the night. The old man of the cabin was kind but said he didn't have room for him because his family was so big. A storm was coming up, and the old man told him to go to the deserted cabin down the road.

The man went to the cabin and went in and found a few furnishings. The storm ended, and the moon came out brightly. The old man had told him that a man had been killed about five hundred yards from the cabin and carried his head in his hand. The man decided he would see if he could find his ghost. He walked outside and soon a man without a head was walking beside him. The man stepped up his pace and so did the haint. The man began to run and so did the haint. The man soon gave out and had to sit down on a log to rest. The haint said, "It sure was a hard race." The man said, "You haven't seen a race yet until I get my breath back!"

> *Taylor County, 1965 (CC). Informant: male, born 1893 in Taylor County.* The motifs in this story are the same as those in story No. 394 and in the same order. This is a variant of the previous tale, but the details are sufficiently different to merit a separate printing.

ANIMAL GHOSTS

The Ghost Bull

"A hired hand that works on our farm—we own a farm over the rock quarry in Green County. There's an old house on that farm—it's a pretty weird place. And we have cattle up there, and our hired hands feed the cattle late in the afternoon. And uh, this man—this hired hand—went up there by himself late in this afternoon. And, uh, about ten or fifteen minutes he came back to the house as white as a sheet, driving the old car, and got out.

"My grandfather, who owns the farm, asked him what was the matter. His name is Dolphus. He said, 'Dolphus, what's the matter?' And, uh, his story was that he'd heard an awful sound two or three times, repeat, repeating you know, like the bellow of a bull, and something similar to the bellow of a bull. And my grandfather told Dolphus, 'We haven't a bull in two miles of that place have we?'

"And he said, 'No.'

"And it was true that we didn't have a bull on the place, and there weren't any bulls on any other farms near there. And it was a bull or something similar to a bull. And Dolphus was white. Said he'd seen something. And uh, he didn't go up to that farm for a month, for some odd reason, and it was because he was scared—his imagination—or maybe it was because he had seen something, but he wouldn't go up to that farm for a month after that. And he always went with someone else when he did go up."

Green County, 1964 (JR). Informant: male, born ca. 1910 in Green County. This mysterious narrative revolves around Motifs *E402.2, "Sounds made by invisible ghosts of animals"; *E423.1.8, "Revenant as cow, bull, calf, or steer"; and *E520, "Animal ghosts."

Ghostly Apparitions

"Now George Ab Jones' sister, Mrs. Bivin, she was Dr. Graham's mother-in-law. (The first school ever taught at Webb, Mrs. Bivin was living—an old lady—she was about eighty-years-old then.) She firmly believed in ghosts; at least she told a lot of stories. I don't recall any of them very well, except that I remember that she told us one morning that she waked up and looked up. Well, she told us in the morning, but it had been some time during the night that she waked up and looked out across the field between the house and the store out there at Webb, and that there were white things moving around all over the field, just like, well, she said you could tell what it was. It was dark, but there was enough light that you would tell there were white objects. And they were moving like there might be a whole field full of geese. Of course, there were none there—or sheep. She didn't know what it was, but she just declared there was something out there that was unusual and that it was all moving around.

"But, of course, Dr. Graham said, 'Mrs. Bivin, you never did no such of a thing!'

"She'd just declare, 'Now, Dr. Graham, I know I did. I saw it!' "

Green County, 1964 (JR). Informant: female, born ca. 1888 in Green County. The informant learned this tale from another resident of Green County. The only identifiable motif in this story is the very general *E520, "Animal ghosts."

The Old Man and His Dog

398   There was this old man who lived in a place called Bluebird Hollow, and he was said by the townspeople to have a lot of money. He had a big, white dog which he took with him everywhere he went. The story must have gotten around about the old man having all that money. Anyway, both he and his dog were found dead, and their house was a mess.

There are people who say that they see the old man and his dog every once in a while looking for the money.

Taylor County, 1964 (LS). Informant: male, age unknown, born in Taylor County. This brief narrative contains three motifs: *E422.4.5, "Revenant in male dress"; *E423.1.1.1(c), "Ghostly white dog"; and *E521.2, "Ghost of dog."

Ghost Dog

399   There was this old swinging bridge out near home, and there was an old saying that a ghost dog appeared every night at midnight in the

middle of the bridge when the moon was right. Well, one man didn't believe it and went out one night to see. Sure enough there was a dog in the middle of the bridge. He went out to pat it, but it disappeared!

> Oldham County, 1964 (HB). Informant: male, born ca. 1944 in Adair County. In this very brief narrative, Motifs *E423.1.1.1(a), "Ghostly dog of unspecified color," and *E521.2, "Ghost of dog," are present.

Bullets Go through Dog Ghost

"We don't hear and see things nowdays like we did back yonder in olden days. There's this Kirk man I was telling you all, said about that old scorpion and him killing it—lizard or whatever it was.

"They's a graveyard over yonder—Center Point. And they said everybody that would pass that graveyard at night would see a dog —a litty, bitty, black fith. Had a ring around its neck and feet, just a little, old, bitty thing. Said when it got right even with that graveyard, this here little dog would come out and just run around your feet; and you couldn't kick it. And you could hit it, kick at it, and your feet would go through it.

"They had a party over there at Uncle Andy Kirk's one night. It broke up at midnight, on Saturday night. Uh, there was a passel of young girls and boys, you know. Well, just before they got to this graveyard, they all begin to grab the men, you know, and take them by their coats and hold them.

"Walter Kirk, he said, 'Now that goddamn dog comes out on me tonight, I'm killing that son-of-a-bitch.' He had a pistol [that] shot six times. Said they got up about even in the graveyard, said here it came through the fence. And said it went right straight to Walter. Oh, just a-running around his feet! And Walter said he was just a-shooting at it, 'Bang, bang, bang.' And said couldn't look like you couldn't hit it a-tall. All the women just a-screaming and hollering. It scared them to death. And said it run around his feet there, and said he emptied his pistol and never could hit it. And said all at once it just started back toward the fence. Said it went up in the air; said it just like a puff of wind, like a whirlwind, 'Shr-r-u-u-u-u.'

And said it was gone.

"I don't know how many did tell me that they'd seen that there. My sister was in that crowd, too, Sister Mary."

Monroe County, 1961 (LM). Informant: black female, born ca. 1884 in Monroe County. Although a ghostly dog complex is known all over northern Europe, the tradition of Motif *E423.1.1.1(b), "Ghostly black dog," is found mainly in the British Isles, Canada, and the U. S. To Baughman's extensive index, add Henry L. Trice, "Lore of the Hopkins-Webster Line," *Kentucky Folklore Record* 2:3, 92; Helen Creighton, *Bluenose Ghosts* (Toronto, 1957), 231–32; Barbara Allen Woods, *The Devil in Dog Form, A Partial Type-Index of Devil Legends*, Folklore Studies No. 11 (Berkeley: Univ. of California Press, 1959); J. Mason Brewer, *Dog Ghosts* (Austin, 1958), 3–4; Richard M. Dorson, *Negro Folktales in Michigan* (Cambridge, Mass., 1956), 163; and Richard M. Dorson, *Negro Tales from Pine Bluff* (Bloomington, Ind., 1958), 192.

The Black Dog Ghost

401   "They was a Crawford man. He killed a man. His name was a Crawford, and he had a dog. This man had a dog when he killed him. And so he couldn't step out or go to eat or nothing but what he didn't see this man. Every night when he'd step out in the yard, said this [ghost] would be out there with this little dog. This dog would be all come around this man—this dog that that man had. Said he killed the dog, too.

"Well, he left this country and went to Missouri. Thought he would get shut of this dog. And said the second night after he got to Missouri, he stepped out in the yard; and the dog and this man was following him. Just worried him to death nearly. Well, he stayed around there so long, and he couldn't rest; and he came back to this country.

"(Said he killed this man near a pond. And I reckon he must have put him in this pond.) And he said he went and stayed all night with a man. And said they was a-riding along. (This man took him up and was a-riding him along, talking to him.) Said this little dog come up, and they didn't know where the dog come from. And said this dog went wading out in this pond. When he come out, said he come out with a bone, with a bone in his mouth. And said he stopped,

This man had, this man killed this man. Said he said, 'What's that dog carrying that bone for, around for?' And said everywhere they would stop, said this dog would drop this bone at this man's feet, 'Thud.' [Narrator makes noise by hitting floor.]

"And said that man looked like he [was] just about to sink every time that dog would come around with this bone. And they didn't know where that little old dog come from—a little black dog. And said this man said to this other man that killed that man, 'I don't understand that dog a-carrying that bone around.' Said 'Do you know what he's carrying it for?'

"He said, 'No, I don't.'

"He said, 'He come out of that pond with that bone.' Said, 'Something has been put in that pond, or somebody has killed somebody; and that's somebody's bone.' Said, 'That ain't a hog bone or nothing.' Said that old man said just sunk down. And said he said, 'Well, what's the matter with you?'

"Said he couldn't talk. He just give down. Broke down over it, you know. And finally he said (he told this man's name; I forgot just who it was he said he killed) and said, 'I can't get shut of him. I've been plumb to Missouri.' And said, 'This dog, every time I go,' said, 'he'll be around my feet, and I can't get shut of him.' And said, 'That's one of his bones.'

"And said they went back over there and dug around, pulled all that man's bones out where they did it. And I think they give him a whole lot of time, maybe life in the pen, for killing this man and hiding him in the pond."

[After concluding the story, the informant summarized the tale, adding only that the murder was committed eight or ten years before the crime was discovered.]

Monroe County, 1961 (LM). Informant: black female, born ca. 1884 in Monroe County. See note for story No. 400.

The Horse with No Track

When my father was a little boy, he and his father and mother were sitting in the house talking. And they looked out the window and saw a man on a white horse riding through the yard.

It had been raining that day so my grandfather went out in the yard and looked for the man but could not see him anywhere. Also, he could not find any tracks in the place where the man rode by. This mystery was never solved.

> *Monroe County, 1959 (RMo). Informant: female, born 1944 in Monroe County.* This brief narrative contains Motif E521.1, "Ghost of horse."

The Ghostly Spotted Cow

403   "I'd heard them tell about this spotted cow that they'd see over here by the graveyard at Wendell Bowman's. Well, one night I was going home from church at Skaggs Creek. Laying right there on the side of the road just this side of that old house was a big spotted thing that looked as big as a cow. Of course, I thought it was a cow for a while! But directly, it just stood straight up—looked big as a mule. It just disappeared there right in front of my eyes! I saw that!"

> *Monroe County, 1961 (LM). Informant: male, born 1918 in Monroe County.* No motif number has been assigned to the appearance of a cow ghost. Trice, "Lore of the Hopkins-Webster Line," 92, gives the only known account in print of a cow ghost. There is a 1961 account of a cow ghost from Arizona Negro tradition. I recall a Monroe County report of several years ago in which the informant saw a whole herd of cattle disappear before her eyes. In Dorson, *Negro Folktales in Michigan*, 124, the appearance of a ghost with a cow head was an omen of death.

The Belled Sheep

404   "My daddy used to be over at the Old Johnny Copass Place a lot. Of a night when he'd go out into the yard for a few minutes and then start back for the house, there'd be a little sheep with a bell follow him. That sheep would run along at his heels, the bell just ringing! When he'd get to the door and start in, the little sheep would be gone."

> *Monroe County, 1961 (LM). Informant: female, born ca. 1920 in Monroe County.* Previously unreported. A sheep ghost, in the sense that it occurs in this story, has not been given a motif number. I have

included it here because the tale is already in second-generation tradition. Cf. Motif *E423.1.6, "Revenant as lamb," reported only from Hampshire (England).

GHOSTS REVEAL MONEY

The Hidden Money

If someone is killed, they'll be something left at the place where he is killed. If he is killed in the house, the house is haunted after that.

People used to hide money in their houses. Once a man was killed because this other man couldn't find the money he had hid. Everyone was afraid to come around the house after that. Then some men decided they would go to the house and stay and see what happened. While they were there, something said, "Come go with me." This happened at the time he was killed. It was a big dark somebody that said it. It went upstairs and told the men to look under the boards. When they did, they found thousands of dollars that the man who had been killed had hid. The men had been afraid to go that night, but when they went back the next day, they found it.

  Barren County, 1967 (BAk). Informant: female, born ca. 1880 in Barren County. This mysterious narrative revolves around several motifs: *E281, "Ghosts haunt house"; *E334.4, "Ghost of suicide seen at death spot or near by"; *E371, "Return from dead to reveal hidden treasure"; *E411.1.1, "Suicide cannot rest in grave"; and *H1411, "Fear test: staying in haunted house."

The Stranger in the Room

There is a place in Dry Hollow, in the southeastern part of Wayne County, which people who live in that section said was haunted for many years. They can always see a man, with a dark suit and dark hat somewhere near this particular house. Sometimes he will be near the spring house, sometimes around the barn, and again nearby or in the house. He never speaks, and when anyone tries to touch him, he very suddenly disappears. Those who try to sleep in the house are kept awake by him walking over the bed and around the room.

On one occasion, myself and two other men were to stay over

night at this house. As there was only one bed in the room where we were to sleep, two of us were to sleep in the bed, and the other fellow was to sleep on a feather bed, which had been placed on the floor. This bed on the floor was placed directly across the door, and if anyone should come through there, the fellow who was in that bed would have to move before the door was opened. We two, who slept in the bed, soon went to sleep; but my friend on the floor said that as soon as everyone about the house got quiet, something very quietly unlatched the door and began to push against his body, trying to open the door. He tried to hold the door by putting his whole weight against it. But in spite of his efforts to keep the door closed, a man, or what he thought was a man, stepped over him and walked all about the room, then stepped over him again and went out. In a few minutes he came to the door again and pushed his way in. This time the fellow on the bed tried to grab his legs, but it was just like grabbing thin air. He again passed out of the room after he had walked all around. This same thing happened four times when our friend on the floor could stand it no longer, so he roused us up and demanded that we make room for him in the bed.

Well, I just thought he had been dreaming or had imagined all this; so I let him take my place in the bed, and I slept on the floor. I got all settled and was almost asleep, when the door opened very quietly, and something began to push against my body. I tried to hold the door shut, but found it was no use. The man, just as my friend described him, came over my bed and walked around the room several times, then stepped over me and went out. Very soon the door opened again and the pushing started. I did not wait to see what would happen this time, but immediately informed the fellows that I thought there was room enough for three of us in the bed. We remained in the room all night, but the form of that man with his dark suit and hat on kept walking about the room all night and would even step across the bed where we lay.

On another occasion, I sat with a group of men on the porch of this house late one afternoon, when we were all startled by a loud noise like someone beating on the clapboard roof of the old spring house which stood one hundred yards from the house. Soon the beating stopped, and we all saw the man in the dark suit come from the springhouse and pass on through the barnyard. There was only one old cow with a bell on her neck in the barnyard, but such ringing of that old bell you never heard. It seemed that there must have been forty or more cows there instead of only one.

Many of the people who live in that community believe that there is some hidden treasure somewhere near there, and if someone would follow this ghost, it would lead to it.

Wayne County, 1937 (GV). Informant: male, age unknown, born in Wayne County. "The Stranger in the Room" is used by permission of the Folk Music Division, Library of Congress. Quite a few motifs are present in this lengthy narrative: *E281, "Ghosts haunt house"; *E338(a), "Male ghost seen"; *E338.1(c), "Ghost opens doors and windows repeatedly"; *E422.4.5, "Revenant in male dress"; and *E425.2, "Revenant as man." Implied also is the presence of Motif *E371, "Return from dead to reveal hidden treasure."

Hidden Treasure Revealed (a)

A preacher, caught out late in the evening, stopped at a house and asked to stay all night. The family didn't have room for him, but told him there was a big haunted house up on a hill. Nobody lived at the house.

The preacher went to the house, lit a fire, and started to read his Bible. He heard a noise upstairs. Then he heard it come down the stairs. A woman dressed in white came to the bottom of the stairs. The preacher said, "What have I done that you appeared to me?"

She said, "I have appeared to many people, but all of them were afraid and ran. Do not run. I will not harm you. I was murdered for my money. It is buried in the cellar. Go and get my brother and divide the money with him."

The preacher got her brother and divided the money with him. The ghost never appeared again.

Taylor County, 1964 (EH). Informant: female, born ca. 1910 in Taylor County. This story contains Motifs *E281, "Ghosts haunt house"; *E371, "Return from dead to reveal hidden treasure"; *E371.5, "Ghost of woman returns to reveal hidden treasure"; *E402, "Mysterious ghost-like noises heard"; *E422.4.4(a), "Female revenant in white clothing"; *E451.5, "Ghost laid when treasure is unearthed"; and *E545.12, "Ghost directs man to hidden treasure." Cf. *E545.19.2

(b), "Proper means of addressing ghost: person must ask, 'In the name of the Lord, why troublest thou me?' "

Hidden Treasure Revealed (b)

408   There was an old man who died. He had lots of money, but before he died he buried it.

Many people went to hunt the money. Everyone that went said that they saw a ghost and got scared and ran away. It went on like that for a long time. No one had the nerve to talk to the ghost of the man.

One day there was man came to town from another state. He went by the old house and saw the ghost. He had the nerve to talk to it.

The ghost told him where the money was and what he wanted done with it, and gave the man part of it. And after that day, no one ever saw the ghost again.

Monroe County, 1959 (LM). Informant: female, born 1946 in Monroe County. Motifs are *E281, "Ghosts haunt house"; *E371, "Return from dead to reveal hidden treasure"; *E425.2, "Revenant as man"; *E451.5, "Ghost laid when treasure is unearthed"; *E545.12, "Ghost directs man to hidden treasure"; and *H1411, "Fear test: staying in haunted house."

Hidden Treasure Revealed (c)

409   This house in Barren County was haunted. And this man who owned it told these three boys that if they would sleep there all night, they could have the farm.

So that night about twelve o'clock they woke up and seen this figure in front of their bed. Two of the boys ran and the other one just froze. This figure motioned for him to follow him, so he did.

They went upstairs, and the figure disappeared in front of a fireplace. The boy went back to bed and slept the rest of the night. The next morning this man and woman gave the place to him. A few days later he went back upstairs and started cleaning the fireplace and while doing so, he found a big box of money which had been there years. So this boy was now rich and owned his own farm.

Monroe County, 1959 (LM). Informant: female, born 1944 in Bar-

ren County. Contained in this story are Motifs *E281, "Ghosts haunt house"; *E371, "Return from dead to reveal hidden treasure"; *E451.5, "Ghost laid when treasure is unearthed"; and *H1411, "Fear test: staying in haunted house."

Hidden Treasure Revealed (d)

Now Mamie Alexander told me this, and I know it to be true. She lived right down here, and she was as fine a lady as ever lived. She lived in Burkesville before she moved up here, and this happened down there. It happened for a fact, for it happened to one of her neighbors.

Anyway, they wuz this house down there that nobody could live in. And the man that owned it told anybody that they could have the house if they could stay in it all night. A lot of people had tried it, but none of them could stay there all night. The place was haunted. This new preacher moved into town and when he heard about it, he said that he would like to have the house; for he was new, and he hadn't found no place to stay.

So he went to see the man, and he told him the same thing. And he went to the house and built him up a fire and was sitting there reading his Bible when the stair door fell open, and clothes fell out; and then a dog came down and sat by the fire.

The man just went on reading his Bible like nothing had happened. And a man came down, and the preacher said, "What in the name of the Lord do you want?"

And the man said, "Come with me." And he took him to the cellar and said, "Dig here!"

And the man dug and found a pot of money, and he got the house and the money both. And I think that he started a church with some of the money. That was a good thing to do with it. So many people would just have wasted it, but he started a church with it.

(Notes incomplete on collector, informant, and locale of this story.) Present are Motifs *E281, "Ghosts haunt house"; *E371, "Return from dead to reveal hidden treasure"; *E425.2, "Revenant as man"; *E451.5, "Ghost laid when treasure is unearthed"; *E545.12, "Ghost directs man to hidden treasure"; *E545.19.2(b), "Proper means of addressing ghost: person must ask, 'In the name of the Lord, why

troublest thou me?' "; and *H1411, "Fear test: staying in haunted house."

HAUNTED DEATH SPOTS

The Ghost at Hole in the Wall

411   A few years ago people would go out to a place called "Hole in the Wall." They would have the car windows rolled up and the doors locked, and the little blue light would appear; and there would be a slight wind inside the car. The little blue light would sit on the hood of the car, and the front of the car would raise up all the way off the ground.

There used to be a little girl and boy, and the little boy disappeared and the little girl got killed. They found her three or four weeks later, raped and murdered at this place called Hole in the Wall; and she still had her little doll in her hand. And they say the blue light is her ghost.

Taylor County, 1966 (FD). Informant: male, born 1945 in Taylor County. The only identifiable motif in this brief narrative from the Kentucky foothills is *E530.1, "Ghost-like lights."

The Ghost of the Murdered Man

412   There was this place over on the other side of Albany, where that sometimes early of a morning when there was a fog on, you could be walking through there, and you would come up on this old bearded man that was sitting leaned up against this old tree; and he had a cane laying across his lap. He would just sit and look at you as long as you didn't get too close to him and if you did, he would go up the tree and disappear.

I always heard that somebody was going through there early one foggy morning, and some other feller killed him; but I don't know if that's right or not.

Russell County, 1964 (HD). Informant: male, born ca. 1915 in Russell County. This fragmented narrative contains Motifs cf. *E334.2.2, "Ghost of person killed in accident seen at death or burial spot"; E425.2.1, "Revenant as old man"; and E744.1, "Soul as mist." Also noted is Motif *E422.1.9.1, "Living corpse: appearance only."

Return of the Hanged Chicken Thief

There was a Negro man who was hanged in Columbia a long time ago for stealing chickens. It was later learned that this man was not the one who stole the chickens. Some people say that this man's ghost comes back and haunts the hollow where he was hanged.

   Adair County, 1964 (PRA). Informant: female, born ca. 1932 in Adair County. This extremely brief narrative contains only one recognizable motif, cf. *E334.2.2, "Ghost of person killed in accident seen at death or burial spot."

Deserted House Lights Up

There had been a family of people that had been killed at this house, you know. And after they buried them, nobody else ever did move in that house and they just left all the furniture—beds and everything—in the house just like the family had when they lived there. And the people got to noticin' this house at night. It'd be lit up just like there wuz somebody living in it. And they went and investigated, you know. And there was a bunch of men that was hauling timber, and they stopped there that night; and they was going' to stay all night there. They took the teams out and fed them, and they all eat their supper. And all at once the house just lit up all over. They just had the teams hitched outside, and the teams got to cuttin' up; and some of them, I think, broke loose. And these men wan't very scared. And they searched the house all over, and they couldn't find anything, nobody. And they finally just got their teams and hitched them back up. They liked to of not got them hooked back up, and they pulled out in the night and left there. The house was still lit up.

   This was up next of Columbia, Adair County. It was a fine home, they said, but nobody lived there. Finally, just tore the house down. It happened about 1900. This is true because Nellie's daddy told it; and he was one there with them. A bunch of Hartfields were along, too.

   [The following details were added by Mrs. Nellie Judd.] Somebody killed the family, and the ax that they was killed with was still there. Everything just exactly like when they were killed—furniture, even the dust.

It was raining, and the river was up. And these men thought they could stay anywhere, but they found out they couldn't. Them old Hartfields was never afraid of nothing. Them was old men forty, fifty years old. They wan't no boys. All was just as peaceful. They were asleep. And in the other room they heard a racket—went from room to room. Said Mr. Hartfield said, "I'll see what it is. I'll just shoot it out of there!" Said he didn't see anything. Said the longer they stayed the worse it got—dishes rattled and everything. And said the racket got so bad, and children wuz screaming, women hollerin', and blood everywhere just like when they were killed. Said they looked back after they got to the barn, and there was lights in every room in the house.

> *Green County, 1963 (MP). Informant: male, born 1898 in Green County.* The informant learned this tale from his father-in-law. This narrative contains Motifs *E281, "Ghosts haunt house"; *E337.1.1, "Murder sounds heard just as they must have happened at time of death"; and *E402, "Mysterious ghost-like noises heard"; cf. *E402.1.1.3, "Ghost cries and screams," and *E530.1.0.1(c), "Building seen to light up strangely at night when unoccupied."

The Haunted Tree

415   There was a girl that lived in a town, and one day she was standing out in the yard under a small tree. She died all of a sudden with a heart attack. The legend goes that this tree grew into the shape of the girl's face, and every year at the time of her death, the leaves would die. People came from miles around to see this tree.

> *Russell County, 1964 (RLa). Informant: male, born 1900 in Russell County.* Previously unreported from oral tradition is the motif that leaves die each year at the time of a person's death. Somewhat related, however, are Motifs *F974, "Grass refuses to grow in certain spot," and *F974.1, "Grass will not grow where blood of murdered person has been shed."

River Haunted by Slave's Last Words

416   "Now down there where I lived at, you know, where, uh, you know where Gordon Boswell lives. Well, I was raised there till I was nine,

twelve year old. That'uz my daddy's place. My daddy built that
house. He sold out'n come here. Well, now you know where the
river's at now. Well, it'd always run there since I can recollect, but at
one time, you know where them hills are over the far hill. In the ol'
days, back in the days of slavery, it run over there. An' that road,
that road'uz public passway. That was a—that'uz the Springfield
Road. That'uz the Springfield Road. You've heard o' the Springfield
Road ain't you? Well, that'uz the Springfield Road. There was a
tavern or inn—or whatever y' wanta call it—right acrost the road.
You know, where Watson lives. Well, it was right down below Watson's place there about three or four—[although distance is implied,
the narrator never finished the statement] they called it the Black
House. That was an old tavern there. Travelers—that was a public
passway.

"Well now, right over there, the river forded right over there at
the hills then. There was a river ford there. Well, then wagoners,
wagoners, you know they wagoned then like they truck today. Well,
now they was a man lived over on Wilson Creek, five miles through
them hills. An' there was a man lived over on the other side of Wilson Creek over there—Robinsons Creek it is. An' there was a man
over there by the name o' Thompson that owned a team an' wagon
an' some slaves. An' he had a, he had one, uh, in partic'lar goin'
over to, carrying freight over to Columbia an' bringin' back whatever they wanted—Columbia or wherever they went to. An' one
day he made the trip across there, an' ther'd been a rain up the river
that he didn't know anything about. An' now that'uz called over
there—right across the river from Boswell—is called the Ferguson
Place. An' the Ferguson family settled there, I reckon. An' so he
got over there at the Ferguson place, an' he seen the river was up.
An' he turned around an' drove clear back through that five mile
o'hills there. That's rough country through there. Pulled the load
back an', he got over there; an' Thompson told him, why says
'There ain't been no rain. That river ain't up. You just 'fraid. Go
on back over there an' go acrost that river like I tell you.' An he
sent that slave back. An' th' slave got over there, an' he put that—
he had four mules in there—an' he put them mules in there, an' he
put them mules in, made 'em go in the river.

"You know, they used to people drove teams. You remember, they'd 'gee' an' 'haw' a lot. I do myself, yeah, I do today. I drive a team o' mules myself an' I use 'gee' an' 'haw' quite a bit. An' so when he, see he'uz comin' north, wudn't he? Be comin' this way all right an' the river flowin' west or south or whatever it was'ud make the river comin', you know pullin', pushin' his mules to the right. An' they said that he went into the river. An' them Ferguson people lived up there said he kep' a-hollerin', 'Haw, George!' That was his lead mule. 'Haw, George! Haw, George!' Y'see it'uz pushin' him down. He wanted the mule to, you see the river got so swift an' said the last ever heard of him sayin' was, 'Haw, George!' An' he drownded there.

"An,' I heard people say (now, I never did hear this. I lived there all my life). But they said that you could hear that in there, hollerin', 'Haw, George!' for years on an' on an' on."

Adair County, 1964 (VM). Informant: male, elderly, born in Adair County. Only two motifs are present in this lengthy account of a haunted river: cf. *E334.2.2(c), "Ghost of drowned person haunts spot of drowning," and cf. *E337.1.2, "Sounds of accident re-enact tragedy."

The Bare Spot

417   There was this sissy boy murdered up on the creek above home. Nobody couldn't figure why he was killed because he didn't bother anybody. His daddy came down the hollow looking for him the morning after he didn't come home, and he found him dead in the creek. He started screaming and several people went down there. I went myself. They got him out and laid him there on the bank. In a little while the grass died just like you had laid a board or something on the ground and left it. I don't know why, but I know that it did because I saw it!

It wasn't long 'til people started talking about seeing a light out in the middle of the creek. It was just a little flame, and when you went up the road by it, just as you got even with it, it would go out. People thought it was a gravel or a piece of glass, but they waded around in the creek and couldn't find a thing. One night Dad and your Uncle Ezra were coming home from the mine. It was about three o'clock in the morning. After they crossed the bridge, Ezra says, "I seen it, Fish."

Dad says, "I seen it, too!"

Not long after that, this boy and me were coming home from church. As we crossed the bridge, I looked up the creek, and there it was—a little light right in the middle of the creek. I was afraid to ask him, but I think he saw it, too, because we flew the rest of the way home.

> Green County, 1963 (MK). Informant: female, age unknown, born in Green County. The only identifiable motif in this account is *E530.1, "Ghost-like lights." Another motif here apparently refers to F974, "Grass refuses to grow in certain spot." This form of the narrative was reported from Barren County tradition in 1958. Cf. also *F974.1, "Grass will not grow where blood of murdered person has been shed." There is a fragmented Barren County account (1959) of the bare spot motif.

Ghost Walks at Night

Some years before I ever moved to Kentucky—about a mile above Elk Horn—there is a place where you come down a real rocky field and hill, and the rocks stuck out in a washboard effect in the road.

In a house over on the side of the road, a man committed suicide and hanged himself. On a very dark night he can be seen out in the road coming down that rocky hill next to Elk Horn Cemetery with the hang rope still around his neck.

> Taylor County, 1964 (GS). Informant: female, born ca. 1925 in Taylor County. The informant learned this tale in her childhood in the Eastern Pennyroyal. In this fragmented narrative are Motifs *E334.4, "Ghost of suicide seen at death spot or near by"; *E411.1.1, "Suicide cannot rest in grave"; and *E425.2, "Revenant as man."

The Head

This was supposed to have happened during the Civil War. There was these two men who were fighting one day, and one of them got mad and cut the other man's head off and put it on a fence post.

Now when you pass the spot where they had the fight, on the day they had the fight, you can hear them fighting.

> *Wayne County, 1965 (LH). Informant: male, age unknown, born in Wayne County.* The only recognizable motif in this short narrative is *E337.1.1, "Murder sounds heard just as they must have happened at time of death."

The Haunted Spring

420   Through the hillcountry of Kentucky often came peddlers. Some of these were foreigners, and they were chiefly Italians. These peddlers would carry their merchandise in satchels or in rags tied to the end of a stick.

On one cool, gloomy, gray day in October, a peddler, having departed from this house, was followed by the man of the house to whom he had sold the merchandise. It all happened at a spring near the road that led by a dark holler. The body of the peddler was found the next morning.

Ever after this, people were afraid to pass the spring anytime during the day. The reason for this is that when anyone would look into the spring, they would see blood and could hear the dying screams of a man. It is said his ghost haunted the spring ever after.

> *(Notes incomplete on collector, informant, and locale of this story.)* Two motifs are found in this fragmented narrative: *E402.1.1.3, "Ghost cries and screams" (Midlothian and York [England], New Hampshire, and Texas), and *E422.1.11.5, "Revenant as blood."

Ghost of Man Seen at Death Spot

421   Winn Schoolhouse, now extinct, was located in a very isolated section of Barren County. After a certain man had been murdered out front of the schoolhouse in the road, horses would shy away from this spot at nighttime, and the rider could see the dead man's body standing by the side of the road. The murder weapon, a knife, was easily seen there in the road also.

> *Monroe County, 1958 (LM). Informant: male, born 1936 in Barren County.* The informant learned this tale from his grandfather. This story probably belongs with Motif *E275, "Ghost haunts place of

great accident or misfortune," a Finnish-Swedish narrative in which the ghost is malevolent. Motif *E334.2.2, "Ghost of person killed in accident seen at death or burial spot," of Anglo-American tradition, may also be related.

SHAM GHOSTS

The Woman in White

"I spent most of my time when I was a youngster in the little town of Buffalo down here. I would go to school in the day time, and at night we would go down there and would have a bunch of those Niggers from Georgetown come down; and we would get them singin' and a-dancin' around there till ten or eleven clock up in the night. Then I would play around town, and then comin' home (naturally I cut across the fields comin' home), and up here in the field there was a cabin and a fella by the name of Tom Wellman lived in it. And I come by Tom's house and just before I got about a quarter of a mile from home, I saw this woman comin' down the path to meet me all dressed in white. Well, I couldn't figger what a woman would be doin' out there at that time of night walkin' around. I kept lookin' at it as I walked towards it and, begorra, when I got up close to it where I could see it real good, the thing had no head. It was comin' on towards me, and immediately the first thing I thought of was self-preservation, and I took off. And I'll be honest with you, I never felt the ground under my feet. I don't know whether I touched the ground or just took one great big jump to George [Tom] Wellman's house.

"Just before I got to George's house, I slowed up. I thought, well, it wasn't nothin,' but I'll get it anyway; so I looked around George's woodpile for his axe. I was goin' down and kill that thing, and immediately one of George's boys came out and said, 'Who is that out there?'

"I told them, and they said, 'Ah, Clarence, you're scared.'

" 'Well,' I said, 'I'm not scared. I was, but I'm not now.'

"And they said, 'Well, you just leave that axe alone, and we'll go and show you there is no ghosts.' So we walked around, and we didn't see nothing. They said, 'See you didn't see nothin'.'

"Well, they didn't fool me. I knowed I seen something, and I finally figured it out. Tom had had some visitors, and he had put one of them up to going outside like that and give me a scare when he heard me come a-whistlin'.

"Well, Old Emile Lewis had left an old pistol here when he was here visiting my brother. So I slipped that pistol out the next night and went on back to town the next night. Goin' by George Wellman's house, he asked if I was goin' out again. He was curious about that ghost, so I told him I wasn't scared of no ghosts. Evidently they suspicioned something because that ghost never showed up again. If he had, I was sure plannin' on findin' out who that ghost was."

> *Taylor County, 1966 (———). Informant: male, born ca. 1890 in Larue County.* The collector of this narrative preferred anonymity. This ghost-like narrative contains Motifs *E422.1.1, "Headless revenant," and *E425.1.1, "Revenant as lady in white."

The Ghost in the Churchyard

423   "Now this happened a long, long time ago before there was any railroads or anything like that between Greensburg an' Louisville. An' men with wagons an' four-horse an' six-horse teams hauled goods from Louisville to the merchants around here.

"Now, my grandma—that was your great, great grandma—had a cousin that was a wagoner. That's what they called the men that hauled. His name was Bob Proctor, an' I've heard my father say lotsa times that Cousin Bob Proctor wasn't afraid of the Devil himself.

"Well, one night Cousin Bob was later than usual and trying to make up time. He asked a man he met on the turnpike about a shortcut he had heard about. The man told him he could save several miles that way. But said, 'I wouldn't go through there at night for no amount you could name.' And there was a haunted church right where you had to pass, an' plenty of folks had seen the ghost.

"An' like I said Cousin Bob wasn't easy to scare. He took that short cut an' had just about forgot about the ghost when his team begin to prance an' snort an' rare up. An' sure enough, there was a church. An' in the moonlight he could see a tall, white ghost goin' into the graveyard. Well, Cousin Bob stopped his team an' tied 'em tight to a tree an' took his blacksnake whip an' started after the ghost. The ghost went back towards the church gettin' faster as Cousin Bob got closer an' went in an' right on up the ladder to the little bell house on the roof with Cousin Bob follerin' him. When Cousin Bob overtook him an' had him cornered, he begin whipping that ghost with the butt of his blacksnake whip, tellin' him to take off that sheet an' tell his name an' be quick about it. An' he was in a big hurry to do as he was told.

"I don't remember what they said his name was, but he said he'd been comin' there at night an' scarin' people for the last ten years. An' Cousin Bob told him that if he ever heard of a ghost in that church again, he would come back an' whip him within an inch of his life."

> *Adair County, 1964 (VM). Informant: female, born ca. 1895 in Adair County.* "The Ghost in the Churchyard" revolves around Motifs *E421.1.2(a), "Ghost scares horse," and *E422.4.5(a), "Male revenant in white garb."

The Sheet Scare

Back over here at Chestnut Grove, there was a Ford boy who got killed. They was cutting timber when he got killed. My brother-in-law was afraid to come by Mt. Poland Cemetery. He would come about dusk and bring the children. He took off his hat and would run as fast as he could by the cemetery.

One time my brother-in-law came by himself, and he was afraid to go by the graveyard. My dad was planning on scarin' him. When my brother-in-law got to the road near Mt. Poland, he got scared. My dad slipped and got a big white sheet and took two big sticks and put the sheet on the sticks and raised it when Tom got near the graveyard. He put the sheet up, and Tom took out runnin' and told his wife that there was somethin' in the graveyard. She said there was not and made fun of him. He never came back by this graveyard way again. He would always go clear around. Finally, they told him what they did.

> *(Notes incomplete on collector, informant, and locale of this story.)*

The motif in this narrative is *E422.4.5(a), "Male revenant in white garb."

The Rope

425   A graveyard at Broughtown was a place for boys to scare people as they came passing by at night. One boy was coming home from his girl's, and boys had a rope stretched across the road where it could not be seen. Some of the boys made a racket in the graveyard and scared him. The others jerked the rope up in front of him, and he liked to have broken his neck. He got to his feet and never slowed down until he got home.

Western Kentucky, 1964 (DP). Informant: male, born 1910 in Lincoln County. Appropriate here is Motif *E402, "Mysterious ghost-like noises heard."

Strange Noises

426   This man had moved into a new house and had taken his family with him. It was way out in the woods, and the children were rather scared almost every night. But one night they were sitting around the fireplace, and they heard this peculiar noise upstairs, draggin' a chain. They all begin gettin' up closer to each other, huddling up in their chairs. Finally, they heard whatever it was coming down the steps. And it came so many steps, and the chain would come so many steps. That's the way it sounded to them, "Merrily call call comes a demo demo demo." And the children were really frightened by now. In a few minutes it opened the door, and here was the object with no head at all—the children thought. It came up closer and put its hands over their eyes, "Mae e you call e moll e mengo dengo dengo dengo."

The father, quite wise, realized that this was someone trying to fool them so they would leave the place. So he went to the object and pulled the sheet off of it and found it was a man who was trying to get them to believe in ghosts so they would give up claim to the new house.

Taylor County, 1964 (EH). Informant: female, born 1911 in Taylor County. The narrative elements utilized to give cohesion to this story are Motifs *E402.1.2, "Footsteps of invisible ghost heard"; *E402.1.4, "Invisible ghost jingles chains"; *E422.1.1, "Headless revenant"; and *E422.4.5(a), "Male revenant in white garb."

Perils of Sleepwalking

Around 1890, Uncle Lee Brown was troubled with sleepwalking. He was in the habit of walking all over the countryside in his sleep. One night when he was asleep, my grandfather and several uncles got up to bring Lee back to bed before he walked over the edge of the bluff. Lee woke up and saw all the men chasing him in nightgowns, and he thought they were ghosts. Poor Uncle Lee nearly ran himself to death that night.

> *Taylor County, 1966 (JPi). Informant: female, born 1925 in Cumberland County.* This brief, humorous narrative from the Eastern Pennyroyal draws upon Motif *E421, "Spectral ghosts," for its substance.

The Ghost and the Fool

"Over at Tom Gresham's there was a gatherin'. And my daddy was a young man at that time, and he was there at the gatherin'. There was a man there about half-idiot, and they wanted him to go to the spring and get a bucket of water.

"When he started out to the spring, there was a man by the name of Harrison there at the gatherin'; and he said he was going to scare that fool. So he put a counterpin [bedspread] over him and went to lay down by a fence the fool had to climb over before he could dip up the water. Old Man Tom Smith took a bed quilt and said he was going to scare Harrison, so he slipped up to the fence and laid down close to Harrison.

"The fool got up and saw them laying there, and he said, 'Hi, there, Mr. Devil.' And then said, 'Why there's two devils, a black devil and white devil.' Then Harrison looked around and saw Smith laying there, and Harrison got scared.

"Harrison jumped up to run, and Smith jumped up and grabbed Harrison by the counterpin. The fool laughed and shouted, 'Hold to him, Black Devil, hold to him.' The fool wasn't a bit scared, but

Harrison ran back to the cabin where all the people were and fell down in the middle of the floor, he was so scared."

(Anonymous collector and informant.) This is Tale Type 1676(a), *Big 'Fraid and Little 'Fraid,* and cf. Motif *K1682.1, "Big 'Fraid and Little 'Fraid." Man decides to frighten another person or his son or servant; he dresses in a sheet. His pet monkey puts on a sheet and follows him. The person who is doing the scaring hears the victim say, "Run Big 'Fraid, run. Little 'Fraid'll get you." The scarer sees the monkey in the sheet, runs home.

Dividing Up the Dead (a)

429   One dark night a slave walked into his master's room and said, "The Lord and the Devil are up at the graveyard dividing up the dead." (What really was going on—two men had been gathering hickory nuts and had gone into the graveyard to divide their nuts. As Sam had passed the graveyard, he did hear their voices mumbling, "One for me and one for you. One for me and one for you.")

"Now, Sam, you know that can't be true," said the master. "If I could just walk, I would go up there and see for myself." (The old man had been crippled for many years and couldn't walk.)

At last Sam persuaded his master to let him carry him on his back up to the graveyard. As they stopped at the gate to listen, they heard the mumbling, "One for me and one for you. One for you and one for me."

Finally, the counting stopped. One voice said, "That is all." Another said, "No, there are two more down at the gate." (The nut hunters each had dropped one as they went in.)

As the story goes, this old crippled master, who hadn't walked in many years, outran the strong slave back to the house.

Lee County, 1966 (LF). Informant: female, middle-aged, born in Taylor County. Cf. Tale Type 1791, *The Sheep Thief in the Graveyard,* and Motif *X424, "The Devil in the cemetery."

Dividing Up the Dead (b)

430   Once there was a Negro walking through a cemetery. And at the same time two small boys had stopped in this same cemetery and

were sitting behind a tombstone, dividing walnuts which they had collected during the day. The boys' way of dividing the walnuts went like this: "One for you, one for me. One for you, one for me," and so on.

As the Negro passed by the tombstone which they were behind, the boys were down to their final walnut. They began to fight over this walnut. The Negro man had heard the boys dividing the walnuts, and he thought it was the Devil and God dividing the souls of the people buried in this graveyard. As the little boys continued arguing over the one odd walnut, which was larger than any other walnuts, one of the boys said, "It's only fair that I should get this black son-of-a-gun." The Negro man thought that the walnut was his soul, and he quickly removed himself from the cemetery.

Adair County 1964 (PRA). Informant: female, born 1923 in Adair County. The notes for this narrative are the same as for story No. 429.

Dividing Up the Dead (c)

"There were two boys picking up walnuts in a graveyard, and it began to get dark. So they stopped to divide their nuts and to sack them up. They were saying, 'Here's one for me, and one for you,' while they were dividing the walnuts.

"An old man passed the graveyard and heard them, and he swore what he heard was God and the Devil dividing up the people there."

Taylor County, 1964 (GS). Informant: female, born ca. 1920 in Taylor County. The notes for this narrative are the same as for story No. 429. There are additional reports of the story from Monroe County (two in 1969), and Barren County (two in 1959). A Monroe County variant (1969) claims that two men had gone fishing and stopped in the cemetery to divide the fish.

GHOSTS THAT WERE NOT GHOSTS

The Men in the Open Grave (a)

There were three men who were worthless when it comes to work. Their names were John, Joe, and Jack. They would meet every day at a fishing hole and would stay there until time to go home.

One day Jack failed to show up, so John and Joe went down to see what was wrong. They found that Jack had died.

They asked Jack's wife if there was anything they could do. She said that they could dig the grave, so they dug the grave.

That night Joe decided to go and get him a few drinks so he could forget about the death of his buddy, while John (kindly shook up) decided that he had better go to church and get right with the Lord and pray his buddy into heaven.

Late that night Joe was on his way home, and he had all he could drink—in fact a little too much. He said, "I want to go to the funeral tomorrow, and it is late, so I will take a shortcut across the graveyard." He did, but he stumbled into the grave that he had helped dig that day. He tried, tried, and tried to get out but couldn't. So he decided to just sit down and wait until morning, and when missed someone would come looking for him.

He hadn't much gotten settled until John decided he would take the shortcut, because it was getting late. He, too, fell into the grave. He tried to get out and didn't have any luck until Joe said, "You just might as well make yourself comfortable, because you can't get out."

But you know something, he did!

Mercer County, 1965 (JS). Informant: male, middle-aged, born in Lincoln County. The only identifiable motif in "The Men in the Open Grave" is *X828, "Drunk person falls in open grave with humorous results," found only in Kentucky and New Mexico.

The Men in the Open Grave (b)

433   Over near where my grandfather and grandmother lived, there was a graveyard. Someone who lived in the community died, and they dug his grave and left it open without putting a tent over it. Earl Crowe walked through there and fell into the open grave, and he kept trying to get out. He kept falling back in, and finally he gave up and just sat over in the corner of the grave. Not very long afterwards another man came by, and he fell in, too. And he kept trying to get out and could not. And the man sitting in the corner had not said anything but finally said, "You can't get out.

There is no use trying." Then the man got out of there faster than he got in.

Monroe County, 1958 (LM). Informant: female, born 1944 in Monroe County. Although the chief actor in this story from the Kentucky hillcountry is not a drunk person, the motif is similar to *X828, "Drunk person falls in open grave with humorous results."

The Men in the Open Grave (c)

I heard this once about this grave being dug in a graveyard. People lived on both sides of the graveyard and crossed it to visit each other now and then. Well, late one night this guy started across to visit Bill, his neighbor, and crossing the graveyard, he accidentally fell into this grave that had been dug the day before.

Well, this guy fought and fought and climbed and climbed to get out. Finally, he just saw it was impossible to get out. So he just sat in the corner of the grave waiting for daylight.

A little later here comes this other man. He stepped in the same grave, and when he straightened up, he fought and fought to get out but couldn't. Finally, this guy, sitting over in the corner said, "You can't get out." But he did!

Green County, 1964 (JPo). Informant: male, age unknown, born in Green County. The motif in this narrative is the same as in story No. 432.

The Men in the Open Grave (d)

There was an old colored fellow that would get drunk every weekend. One Saturday night he cut across a cemetery to take a shortcut home. He fell into a freshly dug grave. He tried and tried to get out, but the sides just kept breaking as he tried to climb out. Finally, he gave up and laid down in a corner and went to sleep.

Shortly, another fellow came through the cemetery and fell into the same grave. He tried to get out for some time and couldn't make it. He began to cuss and scream and woke up the other fellow. The colored fellow, still about half asleep, said in a low husky voice, "It's no use. You can't get out."

But he was fooled, because this other fellow went over the side of the grave like a rabbit.

Clark County, 1964 (VB). Informant: male, born 1942 in Muhlenberg County. The motif in this narrative is the same as in story No. 432.

The Sheep in the Open Grave

436   "Lucian Coleman had been out and was coming in. He'd been gone for three or four days, and a person in the neighborhood had died. He had to come by the grave they had just dug to bury the person in. He looked out towards the grave and saw somethin' white. It would jump up in the air and then vanish. He said it done it several times.

"It turned out the next morning when he went back to look that it was a white sheep that fell in the open grave and was jumpin' and trying to get out."

Adair County, 1965 (CB). Informant: male, born 1908 in Adair County. Only one motif is present in this narrative: cf. *E423.1.6, "Revenant as lamb."

The Goose in the Open Grave

437   Several gathered around one night and began to tell ghost and tramp tales. One night as one of the men was goin' home from seein' his girl, he had to pass through this graveyard. Before he got there, he saw something white jumping up and down there. He got so scared that he turned his horse around and turned back another way. The next day they found a white goose that had fallen into an open grave and couldn't get out.

McLean County. 1966 (AJS). Informant: female, born 1943 in Adair County. The closest motif to the episode described in "The Goose in the Open Grave" is *E520, "Animal ghosts."

The Pet Coon

438   "Lucian would come in sometimes driving an old rig. Said one time he needed to rent a house. Well, he rented one, and they told him

the one he had rented was haunted. But he moved in anyway. At night something would go out and in, dragging log chains or tha's what he said it sounded like. Finally, he caught it. It was a coon somebody had had for a pet, and it had an old chain on it."

> *Adair County, 1965 (CB). Informant: male, born 1908 in Adair County.* This brief narrative contains only one motif: *E402.1.4, "Invisible ghost jingles chains."

The Pet Animal

There was this argument about this haunted house. The people argued that nobody could live there. They offered so much money to get somebody to live there. Finally found out that it was a pet fox that made it haunted. Then another person argued that it was a pet coon.

> *Monroe County, 1969 (RLy). Informant: male, born ca. 1908 in Monroe County.* The only identifiable motif in this brief narrative is *E281, "Ghosts haunt house." This narrative appears to represent an explanation for the tale type containing the fear test. It is interesting to note that disagreements came even in explaining away the belief in ghosts.

Fox Fire

Years ago there was a sheriff who traveled all over the country. He went through the woods for a shortcut and was never afraid. One time it was dark, and he was in the woods and all of a sudden saw two big eyes peering at him. And he hid behind a tree. He picked up some rocks and threw them at the eyes. The eyes didn't move, so he looked a little closer and saw that it was fox fire on a tree.

> *Western Kentucky, 1965 (DP). Informant: male, born 1906 in Lincoln County.* The closest motif to "Fox Fire" is *X916(m), "Remarkable eyes."

Dog Scares Man to Death

"There was a man that worked away from home, and he would— it was so far it would be after dark when he would get in. And he'd always be comin' in singin'. And he owned a big white dog, and this dog heard him a-singin' way off. And he run to meet him, but he run, happened to run in behind him. And so this man looked back and saw this big white dog a-runnin' after him, and he started runnin' just as hard as he could run. He just thought it was a ghost, you know, or something, and this dog was a-runnin' after him. Ever time he'd look back, he'd see this great dog comin' after him. So he run and run till he got to the door almost. And this dog caught up with him and reared up on him, and he fell dead."

Taylor County, 1964 (BH). Informant: female, born 1887 in Taylor County. Present here is Motif *E423.1.1.1(c), "Ghostly white dog."

The Graveyard Dog

442   My daddy taught writing school. He rode horseback and sometimes had to stay a week at a time. When riding the horse to school, he had two ways to go.

He never believed in haints. He always said he would see what it is coming from school. One place was a graveyard nobody could pass, but he said he was going to pass. He was coming back from school, and it was dusky dark. And he said he prepared himself for what came out. His horse got scared and backed back. He spurred the horse and finally got him closer. Something came and scared the horse to death. He couldn't control him. He said he would see what it was, and there was a vicious dog. He got his knife out and got off the horse. When he got ready to use his knife, he opened it with his teeth. The dog came on toward the horse. And when the dog came again, my father turned the horse loose and stayed close by. He grabbed the dog, and all he could do was hold it. He cut the dog and afterwards said he never heard anyone say that this graveyard was hainted.

Monroe County, 1969 (RLy). Informant: female, born ca. 1892 in Monroe County. No motifs are appropriate for this narrative; however, the episodes contained in it may be compared with *E421.1.2(a), "Ghost scares horse"; *E423.1.1, "Revenant as dog"; and *E423.1.1.1(a), "Ghostly dog of unspecified color." This story begins as though it were another variant of the ghostly hitchhiker, but then trails off into the simple appearance of a dog which is tamed by the man with a slashing knife.

Just Before Hog-Killing

We were sleeping upstairs one night with our meat box set out in the yard for killing hogs. All of a sudden we heard someone sharpening knives. The sound seemed to get closer and closer. Finally, just before we died of fright, we heard the cow's bell. And we later learned that what we thought was someone sharpening knives was really our old cow licking the salt box.

Adair County, 1964 (PRA). Informant: female, born 1883 in Adair County. *E402, "Mysterious ghost-like noises heard," is the only applicable motif for this narrative.

The Cow in the Graveyard

I was coming in home and was passing through a strange place. And it was dark, and I came to a cemetery out in front of me. Something or other dressed in white was going up and down. My hair went up, and I had to reach up and put my hat down. I had to go on down to the place—cemetery—and I aimed to see who it was. I got up so close to it. It was an old white-headed cow rubbing her neck on a tombstone.

I had to pull my hat down on my head two or three times. If I hadn't, I would have left my hat there.

Monroe County, 1966 (BP). Informant: male, born 1887 in Macon County, Tennessee. The only applicable motif in this narrative is related to *E421, "Spectral ghosts." A Monroe County informant related a very similar personal experience of passing through a cemetery after dark: a ghost with a long, white beard and a walking stick turned out to be an old, gray mare with a stalk of corn in her mouth.

The Resined House

A Negro family lived at the Old Toll Gate House on the Lincoln Wells Farm. Nearby was the church and cemetery. Stories had been told of seeing ghosts in the cemetery. One night a white boy put a nail on a weather board with a long fifty-yard string attached and ran resin over the string. This produced a weird sound inside the house, and the entire family fled in night clothes in an opposite direction to the cemetery. Several white neighbors brought them back at gunpoint, and upon finding the nail and string, concluded that they were the victims of a "ticktacker."

Taylor County, 1966 (NS). Informant: male, born 1905 in Casey County. This narrative revolves around Motif *E402, "Mysterious ghost-like noises heard." Although this narrative from the Eastern Pennyroyal is concerned with the prank custom of resining a house to frighten the inhabitants, it does, nonetheless, contain mention of Motif *E273, "Churchyard ghosts." "Ticktacker" is defined in *A Dictionary of American English on Historical Principles* as "a contrivance for making a rattling sound on a window or door"; the term is very rare in the Kentucky foothills.

The Voice from the Grave

446   "Where I used to live on a farm before I married, there was an old family cemetery near our house. The people who lived there first told us, when we moved there from the city, that if you would go there on a new moon and close your eyes and stand near a grave and put your hand on a headstone, you could say, 'What are you doing down there?' And they would always answer.

"I didn't believe it but being very brave, I got a girlfriend to go with me and when the time came that the moon was new, we went there. My girlfriend was afraid to shut her eyes, but I shut my eyes and put my hand on the headstone, And I said, 'What are you doing down there?' A voice down below said, 'Nothin-n-n-n.'

"We took off in a run, and we never went back again after dark."

Taylor County, 1964 (GS). Informant: female, born ca. 1920 in Taylor County. Present here is Motif *E402.1.1, "Vocal sounds of ghost of human being." This story appears to be one told to children in much the same vein as accounts of the Golden Arm and the Big Toe, i.e., to evoke initial fright and then laughter.

The Chained Mouse

447   There was a man who was sort of a bum, and he was trying to find a place to sleep. As he was walking along the road, he saw this old, old abandoned house and asked the owner if he could stay there. The owner said he could but that it was told that people had seen and heard ghosts inside the house. The sound that was heard was

of chains being dragged across the floor. The bum said he didn't mind because he wasn't afraid of anything.

That night the bum saw bats flying around, and the wind was really blowing hard through the house. And he heard a chain being dragged across the floor upstairs. He looked and looked but could find nothing. Finally, he found a pasteboard box, and lo and behold, there was a mouse in it with the chain around its tail. And as it would go across the floor, the sounds would be made.

Taylor County, 1969 (BS). Informant: female, born 1944 in Taylor County. The only applicable motif in this story is *E402.1.4, "Invisible ghost jingles chains." This is another of the narratives which begin on the fear test note. This one ends on a rather ridiculous note of having a mouse with a chain tied to its tail.

A Ghost and Church Story

A great uncle of mine, Bud Ferguson, always rode a horse when he would go to church and other places. One night he had been to church with his girlfriend. And on the way home, he and the girlfriend had a big surprise. All at once the horse raised up on his back feet, and down they both came on the ground laying upon something hainty.

Both said, "Oh, no, it got me!" They jumped up and ran as fast as they could because they did not know what kind of animals they were up against.

The next day Uncle Bud went back to see what it was, and to his surprise a dead dog was laying in the road. This, people knew about the rest of his life.

Lincoln County, 1966 (BJ). Informant: male, middle-aged, born in Lincoln County. There are no motif numbers assigned to this narrative from the Kentucky foothills.

A Cow and the Bell

A man died. And in those days they had no undertakers, so they had him at home with a sheet over him. During the night, the sheet started to move a little; and then it started moving rather fast. And this scared the people very badly. Then, all of a sudden, a bell started to ringing. When the people looked under the sheet, they found it to be a cow with a bell around its neck and her head stuck through the window by the bed, pulling on the sheet.

> *Russell County, 1968 (DDab). Informant: (anonymous contributor, except that subject born in Russell County).* There are no motif numbers assigned to this narrative.

The Dog and the Chain

450   One night when I was in bed and nearly asleep, I heard what sounded like something dragging a chain across the yard. I got up and found the flashlight. But by the time I got outside, it was gone. I went back to bed, but I took the flashlight with me. I heard the noise again and immediately got up to see about it. I ran out in my gowntail and barefooted. I kept hearing the noise and ran over the hill to see what it was. I found a dog dragging a chain.

> *Monroe County, 1969 (RLy). Informant: female, middle-aged, born in Monroe County.* The applicable motif is *E402.1.4, "Invisible ghost jingles chains."

The House over the Grave

451   There was this fellow going through the graveyard, and he was half-drunk. He had a friend who was buried with a house over his grave. He stopped and asked his friend if he didn't want a drink. When he didn't get an answer, he kicked the house, and a rabbit ran out. The man left scared to death.

> *Monroe County, 1969 (RLy). Informant: male, born ca. 1908 in Monroe County.* The only identifiable motif in this narrative is *E334.2, "Ghost haunts burial spot."

The Sounds on the Steps

452   There was a huge farmhouse located about one-half mile off the road. There were no neighbors. Especially in the winter, the people could hear what sounded like a marble rolling down the steps. It would go to the bottom and just stop. They heard this two or three times in the night, but not every night.

They never found the source of the noise, but decided it must have been made by rats.

> Monroe County, 1964 (RLy). Informant: female, born 1946 in Monroe County. Only one motif is present in this story: *E402, "Mysterious ghost-like noises heard."

The Low Limb

I had gone to my mother's grandmother's to get a setting of eggs. Of course, I stayed till dark to play and had to go back by this grave-yard. I had always been told that something would reach out and get your hat. I was scared to death. I got beside the graveyard, and there was this low limb that knocked my hat off. At the time I didn't know what it was. I knew that I wasn't supposed to shake the eggs, but I left out of there and quick!

I went back the next morning to see what had happened. I saw the low limb and got my hat, but I was scared to death at the time that it happened.

> Monroe County, 1969 (RLy). Informant: male, born ca. 1920 in Monroe County. Motif *E334.2, "Ghost haunts burial spot" is the only applicable motif.

Only Boards against the Wall

Now, we had a ghost down here! Mother had her new house built. We moved down there, and some nights you couldn't sleep hardly. And we couldn't find nothin'. And you—but if you'd open a door it would stop, that door that went into the dining room. And one night it's just terrible, and the moon was a-shining almost bright as day. And they's two stacks of boards. They had more boards than it took to cover the house, and they's stacked up there against the kitchen. They liked just a little bit bein' against the wall, just a little. Well, when the wind would get in such a place, they'd rake that wall. Well, it'd make the awfullest racket in the house ever you heard, and we found it that night.

Now, they's ricked up aside of the wall. And they liked just a little bit touching the wall. But when there's just a little bit of weave there, they'd screek there. You've never heard such a racket.

If you'd open that door that went into the dining room, you couldn't hear it.

> *Metcalfe County, 1969 (KH). Informant: male, born 1882 in Metcalfe County.* Present is Motif *E402, "Mysterious ghost-like noises heard."

Headless Body Is Really a Sack

455   A man was riding through Milby's Hollow, and he saw a headless body lying at the side of the road. He didn't stop, but later he decided he would go back the way he came. When he went back, he stopped. And much to his surprise, he found the headless body to be an old sack that had been washed white by the rain, and the wind had left it by a fence post.

> *Green County, 1964 (PP). Informant: male, born 1940 in Green County.* Motif *E422.1.1, "Headless revenant" is the only motif in this story from the Eastern Pennyroyal.

The Reflection of the Moon

456   My mother was teaching school. She rode a little mare to school. On her way to and from school, she had to pass a graveyard. And she was always afraid to look at the graveyard. About the time she passed it, she glanced over into the graveyard and thought she saw something. She finally realized it was just the reflection of the moon in a mud puddle, but it made the horse shy, too.

> *Monroe County, 1969 (RLy). Informant: female, born ca. 1920 in Monroe County.* Present in this narrative is Motif *E334.2, "Ghost haunts burial spot."

The Falling Picture Frame

457   Down at our old house, Daddy was gone with a load of tobacco. He would have to be gone two nights. He left Mother with five children.

One time when he was gone, we were sitting around the fire telling ghost stories like we used to do, and all at once we heard a thud upstairs. All of us were scared and grabbed Mother. We couldn't imagine what it was. We decided we would have to find out because we'd have to stay there all night.

None of us could shoot a gun. One got a stick of wood, another the butcher knife, and so on. Mother said she'd lead, if the rest of us would follow her. We all started, one behind the other. We all stopped at the head of the stairs because we dreaded opening the door. Mother was holding a lantern. In the dim light we saw a picture frame that had fallen.

Monroe County, 1969 (RLy). Informant: female, born ca. 1920 in Monroe County. This narrative contains Motif *E402, "Mysterious ghost-like noises heard."

GHOST RELATED STORIES

Fork in Skirt (a)

At a party in a mountainous region of Virginia, the young people were making dares as to who would go up the hill to a graveyard nearby. Finally, a young girl said she would. Everybody didn't think she would do it. They wanted her to prove she would for sure, so they gave her a fork to stick in a grave when she got there and leave it. She said, "All right," and headed for the graveyard.

She was gone a long time, and everyone became worried. They all went up to the graveyard to find her. They found her laying on the grave, fainted. When she had stuck the fork in the grave, she had caught her dress in the dirt, also. When she started to leave the grave, the dress had been pulled; and she thought something in the grave had her.

Western Kentucky, 1965 (DP). Informant: male, born 1907 in Lincoln County. In this story the following references are evident: Tale Type 1676B, *Clothing Caught in Graveyard*; Motif *N384.2, "Death in the graveyard; person's clothing is caught, the person thinks something awful is holding him; he dies of fright"; and Motif J2625, "Coward is frightened when clothing catches on thistle."

This legend is widespread throughout North America and most of the world. A logical archetype runs as follows: in an unspecified setting, a group of people are telling scary stories at a get-together. Because a young girl boasts that she is brave, the group dares her to

go to the graveyard and stick a plain fork in a certain grave as proof
that she did in fact carry out her act of bravery. Unknowingly, she
sticks the fork through her skirt. When she begins to move, she
thinks that some sort of haint has grabbed her. The next morning,
the group finds her dead of a heart attack at the grave.

Fork in Skirt (b)

459   My grandfather use to tell about a group sitting around one night
telling ghost stories and things that had happened in cemeteries.
One woman in the group pretended that such talk did not scare her.
Someone said, "All right, if you are not scared, you take this stick.
And as you go by the cemetery alone, you stick this stick in Uncle
Joe's grave."

The woman accepted the challenge and started home. It was
back in the days when women wore dresses down around their
ankles. The woman never arrived home, so they started out in
search of her. They found her in the cemetery by Uncle Joe's grave.
She had stuck the stick through the hem of her dress as she put it
down in the grave. They assumed she died with a heart attack, when
she found she was pinned to the ground.

> *Lee County, 1966 (LF). Informant: male, born ca. 1910 in Taylor
> County.* This story contains the same tale type and motifs as story
> No. 458.

Fork in Skirt (c)

460   My mother always told us kids never to take a dare to do anything.
She told us of this girl that her mother told her about who took a
dare to go to this graveyard at midnight. There was this curse or
something that would cause something to happen to you. This girl
took the dare and went to the graveyard at midnight. She was supposed to stick a fork in the grave, but when she stuck the fork in
the grave, she caught her dress with the fork. When she started to
stand up, she thought something had hold of her dress; and she fell
over dead. This is why mother always told us kids never to take a
dare to do something.

> *Russell County, 1964 (JiC). Informant: female, middle-aged, born*

in Russell County. The tale type and motifs are the same as in story No. 458.

Fork in Skirt (d)

Once there was an old house in the neighborhood that my grandfather lived in that everybody said was hainted. A young feller laughed at these old beliefs and said he was going to spend the night in it by hisself. So he took some sandwiches along. And because there was some loose boards in the floor, he put on his carpenter's apron an' took a hammer and some nails along.

Next morning he didn't come out, and some men went to see what had happened. What it was, was while he was nailin' the boards down, he accidentally nailed down his apron. When he couldn't get up he thought a haint was holding him down, so he fainted. That cured him.

Casey County, 1964 (WP). Informant: female, age unknown, born in Casey County. The tale type and motifs are the same as in story No. 458. Also note that this tale has basic similarities at the onset to Type 326, *The Youth Who Wanted to Learn What Fear Is.*

Fork in Skirt (e)

Once there was a bunch of young folks gathered at someone's house having a party. The house was close to a graveyard, and they were talking about being afraid to go to the graveyard and it dark. One girl said that she wasn't afraid to go and that she would go. They said that if she would go that they would give her a dollar and a half. She said she would stick a stob in a certain grave so that they would know she had been there.

So when she got to the graveyard, she bent over to drive the stob in the ground, and she caught her dress under the stob. And when she started to get up, it caught her dress and scared her so bad that she died. After she didn't come back for a long time, the others went to look for her and found her dead.

Monroe County, 1959 (LM). Informant: female, born 1944 in Barren County. The tale type and motifs are the same as in story No. 458. Two additional Barren County versions in my files are very similar to this account, except that one specifies $50 for the reward.

Corpse Sits Up in Coffin (a)

463 "I've heard the story of one of the older Vaughns that died. And that was before the day of embalming, and they were sitting up with him. Now, this wasn't in the parlor. This was in the vault room of the house, they called it. And some of the men in the town were sitting up with one of the older Vaughns. And, uh, sometime during the night, the contraction of his muscles, something, caused him to make a noise or sit up in the casket. And that's actually supposed to be true. Everybody ran out and left him by himself."

> *Green County, 1964 (JR). Informant: female, born ca. 1890 in Green County.* There is not a motif number assigned to this legend complex, unless we accept Baughman's *J1769.2, "Dead man thought to be alive." Additional accounts of the story can be read in Richard M. Dorson, *American Negro Folktales* (New York, 1967), 329, 330, 440, and John A. Lomax, *The Adventures of a Ballad Hunter* (New York, 1947), 182.

Corpse Sits Up in Coffin (b)

464 "A man who lived near Summerville made an agreement with a man to make his coffin when he died. And he asked this man if he would—when they took him to the graveyard, if he was living—open his casket and see if his pillow was straight. And this man got sick and died. The doctor pronounced him dead. They sat up with him all night, and the next day they packed him to the graveyard. It was closed.

"This man that made his coffin, he opened the casket. When he did, this man just said, 'Boo!'

"And this man that opened the casket come might nigh fainting. They packed him back to the house, but this man that made the casket wouldn't help them pack him back. And he lived fifteen years after that.

"This really happened. Nellie's daddy helped pack him there and watched them open the casket.

"The dead man said he knew all the time what was going on, but he couldn't speak a word till they opened the casket.

" 'Gorsh, I helped pack him down there, but I'd never helped pack him back. I'll never drive another nail in his coffin and make him another one neither.' "

Green County, 1963 (MP). Informant: male, born 1898 in Green County. See note to story No. 463.

Corpse Sits Up in Coffin (c)

This story is told for the truth. Mrs. Miller said that when she was a girl that the colored man that lived across the street had died. She and her mother went over to sit up with the body. When they arrived, all of the family were in the kitchen eating supper. They were in the room by themselves. All at once this body raises up and says, "Huh," and fell back.

She said, "You talk about two people getting out of there, we did." She said, "I guess they buried the poor man alive, but neither one got courage to go back and tell them."

Mercer County, 1965 (JS). Informant: female, middle-aged born in Taylor County. See note to story No. 463.

Corpse Sits Up in Coffin (d)

A man died, and he was hump-shouldered. They laid him in bed, but finally they had to lay him on a flat board to straighten him out. A cat got in the house and got under the place where the corpse lay. The strap that held the shoulders flat broke while they were trying to get the cat out. The corpse sat up, and the man who was chasing the cat told the corpse, "You lay back down. I'll get the cat out."

Monroe County, 1969 (RLy). Informant: male, born ca. 1910 in Monroe County. There is not a motif number assigned to this legend complex, unless we accept Baughman's *J1769.2, "Dead man thought to be alive." This version from the Kentucky foothills seems to be related both to the stories about the corpse which sits up in the coffin and to the legend cycle dealing with the live substitute for the corpse discussed in the note for tale No. 468.

Corpse Sits Up in Coffin (e)

467   Once there was this ol' mountaineer up around Bell or Harlan or somewhere up in there, an' his wife died.

Well, him an' some of the neighbors made a coffin an' laid her out in it. And they was taking her to the cemetery to bury her. They were taking her in a ol' road wagon. An' they hit a bump in the road. So she comes around and sits up in the coffin, so there's nothin' else to do but take her home again.

Well, about two weeks later she dies agin', an' they're taking her back the same as before. Well, they come to the rough place agin', so the ol' man tells the driver, "Slow down! Slow down! Take it easy! Take it easy! Remember what happened here the last time."

    Casey County, 1964 (WP). Informant: male, born 1915 in Casey County. See note to story No. 463.

A Live Substitute for the Corpse (a)

468   There was a man who was afraid of the dead. A bunch of fellows or men made it up to really scare him. They told him that this man had died and wanted him to go with them to sit up. One of the men was going to play dead. All the men, except the one that was afraid, left the room. The one that was left turned his back on the dead man. As he turned around, the man that was playing dead had raised up to a sitting position. This frightened the other man, who grabbed a nearby poker and began beating what he thought was a corpse. He almost killed the man. The next morning the other men apologized for leaving him alone. He said, "That man you all left me with wasn't dead, but by hell, he's dead now!"

    Lincoln County, 1964 (JWi). Informant: female, elderly, born in Lincoln County. Appropriate here is Motif *J1769.2, "Dead man thought to be alive." Tales about the dead are many and varied. This particular cycle deals with a trickster who substitutes himself for the corpse, thereby frightening friends or random acquaintances. The old custom of sitting up with the corpse provided ample opportunity for the trickster's antics. Stories of this variety are especially popular in oral traditions in the southern part of the United States. In most instances, the stories are set in private homes in those areas where distances involved and the lack of funeral homes made it imperative that the corpse be displayed and cared for at home. It was an easy matter for friends, relatives, and the curious to pay their last respects to the dead one. Such a complete acceptance of the unburied corpse was typical of the conditions of a raw, frontier society.

A Live Substitute for the Corpse (b)

Back in the old days, there was this old colored man who worked at a funeral home. And his job was to dust out coffins. One of the morticians decided to play a trick on the poor, old, colored man. So the mortician climbed into one of the coffins just before the old colored man was to dust it. When the colored man started to dust the coffin, there the man was. And the old colored man was so scared that he ran and busted through the glass, and they never saw him again.

> *Taylor County, 1969 (BS). Informant: female, born 1944 in Taylor County.* See note for story No. 468.

A Live Substitute for the Corpse (c)

One time in West Virginia there were some men who decided to play a joke on a half-wit in a funeral home. They saw the man coming, and one of the men climbed into a coffin. As the half-wit passed by the coffin, the man raised up. The half-wit turned around and whopped the man in the head with a wrench and said, "Lay down, you're dead."

> *Adair County, 1964 (PRA). Informant: female, born 1893 in Adair County.* See note for story No. 468.

The Grave Robbers

This is a Barren County story. It would have been somewhere in around Eighty-eight [an Eastern Pennyroyal community], somewhere in that country in there. It was sometime about the time of the Civil War or prior.

A young couple were engaged, and she had her wedding dress made. She contacted something—typhoid, I'd guess—and died. Instead of getting married, she was buried on her wedding day. And they buried her in her wedding dress. The boy she was to have married went home with her parents after the funeral.

It was coming up a storm as he went back home after supper. He had to pass the church on the way. By the time he got to the church, it was storming and doing so bad he dashed in to get out of it. Just as he went in the door, there came a real bright flash. And he saw something sitting down the aisle on the front seat. He just thought someone had already taken shelter in the church, and he would go down and talk with them.

As he got almost there, another flash came. And he saw the girl he was to have married sitting there. It almost scared him out of his mind, and he turned and started to run. Just as he started to go out the door, hands grabbed him and someone stuck a gun in his back.

Grave robbers had come and stolen the body, but before they could get away, this big storm came up. They'd carried her in the church with them and propped her up on the front seat.

They wouldn't let him leave until he promised he'd never tell what had happened, but he did tell.

> *Clinton County, 1966 (MLB). Informant: male, born 1933 in Barren County. There are no motif numbers assigned to this narrative from the Kentucky hillcountry.*

The Grave Robbers (b)

472   "Orville Kingery and his associate were riding horseback from a pie supper at Slick Rock School in Monroe County several years ago. As they passed by Pleasant Hill Church, it began storming and raining. They went inside the church to take shelter from the rain. After an hour or so, upon seeing that the rain was not going to cease, they chose a back bench each and lay down and were soon asleep. Suddenly, they awakened with a start at the same time. Coming toward them from the front of the church, not even making the slightest noise, was a dim, robed figure. The men swear that they actually saw something and that it was coming toward them when they darted out into the storm."

> *Monroe County, 1960 (LM). Informant: male, born 1931 in Mon-*

roe County. There are also no motif numbers assigned to this version of "The Grave Robbers." The corpse is missing in this text, but it appears to be related to the grave-robber legend.

The Grave Robbers (c)

Two men came close to a graveyard, and it came up a storm. It was thunderin' and lightnin'. He was afraid to go in the church house, but he went in anyway. Every time it lightninged, he saw someone else in there. He did not know what to do. He didn't know whether to talk to the other person. He eased out and did not say another word to the other person. Later they found out they knew one another and could have had a good time together.

Monroe County, 1969 (RLy). Informant: female, born 1890 in Monroe County. No motif numbers assigned to this narrative. The story, too, appears to be an incomplete version of the grave-robber legend, although there is nothing really out of the ordinary in the near meeting of two rural friends in a church house.

The Jewelry Thieves (a)

I have heard of the wealthy woman that died and was buried with her diamond rings on. That night some men dug up her body to get the rings. When they opened the casket she was alive. She got up and went home, and when she knocked on her door, the old colored man went to the door. When he saw it was his mistress, he went and told her husband. He didn't believe the old Negro, so he went to the door; and there she was in person.

Taylor County, 1965 (CC). Informant: female, born 1900 in Adair County. No motif numbers have been assigned to this narrative from the Eastern Pennyroyal of Kentucky. This is Type 990, *The Seeming Dead Revives*, a tale which probably originated in Europe. It may have been brought to America by German immigrants. The tale was recorded in Philadelphia by Ruth Benedict in 1923. In virtually all known examples of this popular story the item of jewelry was a ring. Although the girl may wake up during the funeral or when the casket lid is opened, she generally is awakened when the thieves cut her finger.

The Jewelry Thieves (b)

475   My mother told me that they thought this woman was dead, and they buried her. This was before doctors checked on dead people, before they embalmed them and buried them. Well, she was buried with a ring on her finger, and that night two men came and dug her up to get the ring off her finger. But it wouldn't come off, so they tried to cut off her finger. And when they cut her finger, it started bleeding. And she woke up and scared the robbers nearly to death. She got up and went home and nearly scared her relatives to death too.

    Taylor County, 1965 (JPi). Informant: female, born 1925 in Cumberland County. See note for story No. 474.

476   I heard another story about a girl that died. She had a valuable ring, one which could not be removed. A Negro went that night and opened the grave. He started to cut off the finger, and the girl started to moan. She sat up in the grave and asked where she was and to take her home. The Negro was so scared, but he finally promised he would return her to her family, which he did.

    Adair County, 1968 (NAB). Informant: female, elderly, born in Adair County. See note for story No. 474.

The Jewelry Thieves (d)

477   A beautiful girl died. Her people buried her in beautiful clothing and with quite a bit of jewelry. After she was buried, a robber opened the grave to take the jewelry. He found that the girl was turned over on her face with both hands in her hair.

    Nearest dwellers to the cemetery swear that they had heard screams in the night.

    Adair County, 1968 (NAB). Informant: female, elderly, born in Adair County. Although the motif is the same as in the variants of this tale—Nos. 474, 475, and 476—this story was apparently not considered a part of the jewelry-thieves complex—at least not in the view of the narrator who also related story No. 476.

The Jewelry Thieves (e)

This story starts one morning when a man found a woman dead in her bed. The man called the parents of this woman and told them what had happened. The parents rushed over to see their daughter because they just could not believe that she was dead. But when they got there they indeed saw that she was dead. They called the funeral director and made arrangements for the funeral. He went and got the body and prepared it for the funeral.

The parents of the woman who died had a beautiful ring that they put in the casket the day she was buried. The family was real poor and couldn't pay the funeral director for his services. A year or so later the family found out that the ring that they had buried with their daughter was worth a lot of money and would make them rich. So they dug up the grave and opened the casket and saw that the girl had turned over on her stomach and pulled the hair out of her head.

Russell County, 1964 (RLa). Informant: male, born 1899 in Russell County. See note for story No. 474.

The Golden Arm

One time there was this man who had a wife who had a golden arm. His wife died, and the day they buried her it was cold and rainy and the wind was blowin'. So the man was real greedy and that night he went back to the graveyard and dug up his wife and cut off her golden arm. So he took it back home with him and put it under his pillow. So, like I said before, it was rainy and windy and the wind would just blow. He hadn't been asleep very long when something would reach up and slap his face, and it would say, "Where's my golden arm? Who's got my golden arm? Who's got my golden arm?"

Then you jump at the person and say, "You've got it!"

Monroe County, 1969 (RLy). Informant: female, born 1947 in Monroe County. The only identifiable motif in this narrative from the Kentucky foothills is *E235.4.1, "Return from dead to punish theft of golden arm from grave." The tale type is No. 366, The Man from the Gallows.

John A. Burrison, *The Golden Arm: The Folk-tale and Its Literary Use by Mark Twain and Joel C. Harris* (Atlanta, 1968), 3, says: "The underlying folk belief or superstition from which the motif and tale type spring is ancient: a dead man or animal can find no rest until its physical remains are intact. The ghost must search out its lost member. Punishment is bound to be severe for anyone who has removed or disturbed a part of the deceased body or an object buried with him and meant to accompany him in the other world. This revenge is just one of many motivations (most of them concerned with something left undone) causing a revenant to enter the world of the living. It is important to note that this basic theme remains intact even in the modern variants of 'The Golden Arm' told by American children. In the few cases in which this theme has been modified or corrupted, it is obvious that the tale has undergone considerable degeneration and may not survive in this new form."

Ineradicable Bloodstain (a)

480   Mom always said our house must have been haunted with the ghost of a person who had been killed at our place a long time ago, for everytime it would rain, there would be a spot just outside our door that would turn as red as blood; and the rain mixed with it was blood. When it stopped raining, the blood would go away.

    Russell County, 1966 (SS). Informant: female, born 1911 in Pulaski County. The informant learned this tale from her mother. Only one motif is present in this narrative: *E422.1.11.5.1(e), "Ineradicable bloodstain as the result of blood shed during murder."

Ineradicable Bloodstain (b)

481   I remember this house where we used to live. Before we moved there, when I was a little girl—I can't hardly remember it—somebody was killed there. And it was back then before we had rugs. And his blood was in the bedroom there on the floor. And when we moved in, the stain couldn't hardly be seen. But when it would rain, it would raise up there just as plain as could be. And when it rained, I couldn't go in that room. I was scared to. You just couldn't drag me in that room with the blood there on the floor just as plain as could be.

The blood of a dead person will not wash off wood without
leaving a stain.

*Clinton County, 1963 (SW). Informant: female, born 1918 in
Clinton County.* The only identifiable motif in this narrative is
*E422.1.11.5.1(a), "Ineradicable bloodstain in stone or wood floor
after bloody tragedy at spot."

Ineradicable Bloodstain (c)

A married couple moved into a house. They were cleaning the
house. Upstairs in a closet they tried to wash the spot off the floor.
When the floor was wet, it looked like the spot was gone. But when
the floor dried, the spot seemed to become brighter as if it were
boiling up or had been polished. About a week later, they heard
noises upstairs as if someone were trying to get out of the closet,
banging and kicking the closet door.
They moved out of the house.

*Taylor County, 1964 (EH). Informant: female, born 1911 in Tay-
lor County.* Three motifs are present in this narrative: *E402, "Mysterious ghost-like noises heard"; cf. *E402(d), "Ghost-like noises cause
owner to abandon farm"; and cf. *E422.1.11.5, "Revenant as blood."
Additional versions of the ineradicable-bloodstain complex are le-
gion, and my own files contain several other unpublished accounts.
For a study which includes this motif in its historical perspective,
consult D. K. Wilgus and Lynwood Montell, "Beanie Short: A Civil
War Chronicle in Legend and Song," in Wayland G. Hand (ed.),
American Folk Legend: A Symposium (Berkeley, 1971), 133–56.

Stopping the Coffin

"Once there was this family consisting of a father, mother, brother,
and sister. One night at exactly midnight, the telephone rang downstairs. The son went down to answer the phone. Suddenly, the
stillness of the night was rent with a scream. The family ran downstairs to see what had happened, and there they found the boy
dead. His head had been cut off, and his hand was still clutching
the receiver of the telephone.

"Exactly one year later at the stroke of midnight the telephone
sounded again, and the father insisted that the daughter go down

and answer the phone this time. Once more the stillness of the night was disturbed by a mournful scream and then silence. The father and mother ran downstairs only to find that the daughter, too, had been killed and decapitated.

"The next year at precisely the same time, the same thing happened. This time he forced his wife to go down to answer the phone. Again the scream, again he went down and found her body. Her hands which had been cut from her body were clutching the dangling receiver. With the death of the other three members of the family, only the father survived.

"Again, on the anniversary of the others' death at exactly midnight, the telephone sounded. With fear, the man got out of bed, descended the steps and headed for the telephone. At the moment when he picked up the telephone receiver, he could see a form in the far corner of the room materialize and began getting larger and larger and started easing slowly across the room toward the man. As it came closer the man recognized it as a coffin. It came closer and closer. And when it was almost upon him, he reached into his pocket, took out a cough drop, and stopped that coughin' (coffin)."

Warren County, 1971 (LM). Informant: male, born 1931 in Monroe County. The informant learned this tale in Taylor County. A similar story was published as "The Walking Coffin" in Indiana Folklore 2:2 (1969), 3, by William Clements. This story also gave reference to the motifs included in the narrative—*E281, "Ghosts haunt house," and *E538.1, "Spectral coffin"; cf. *Z13.4(j), "Man chased by coffin which follows him."

The basic format of this short "ghost" story puts a person or persons in a face-to-face situation with a threatening coffin. Just as the coffin makes its final lunge toward the victim, someone pulls out some type of medication designed to stop the "coughin' " (coffin). The story leading up to this punch line is given in such a manner and in such an appropriate setting that the tale is very believable to the listeners.

The Russellville Girl (a)

484   There was a young girl who was sitting near the window looking at herself in the mirror. It was a very stormy night, and lightning was flashing all around. She had been waiting for her boyfriend.

But the night was too bad, and he would never come. As she went to get up from her seat, lightning struck her and killed her. They say that every once and awhile you can see her image in the window.

Taylor County, 1964 (LS). Informant: male, born 1935 in Hamilton County, Tennessee. Motifs involved in this migratory legend and its attendant subtypes include C984.5, "Disastrous lightning for breaking tabu," and *E532(a), "Ghost-like portrait etched in glass."

The legend of the girl whose image was imprinted on a window-pane by electrical photography is still quite lively in Russellville and in oral circles across the state, the Upper South, and the Midwest. The house in which the incident supposedly occurred is located in Russellville on the Clarksville Road and now serves as the residence for the caretaker of Maple Grove Cemetery. In desperation the owner of the structure has tried both painting the window and boarding it over.

Mildred Barnett Mitcham published accounts of the legend as "A Tale in the Making: The Face in the Window," in *Southern Folklore Quarterly* 12:4 (1948), 241–57. D. K. Wilgus added some additional variants of the legend in "The Girl in the Window," *Western Folklore* 29 (1970), 251–56, and Ronald L. Baker called attention to a distinctly related legend complex, "The Face in the Wall," in *Indiana Folklore* 1:1 (1969), 29–46.

The Russellville Girl (b)

This girl was in her home, and she was getting ready to go out on a date. Her mother came up to her room and told her that if it rained, she couldn't go out with the boy. She really wanted to go out with the boy. It started raining when the boy came after her. So she went to the window and looked at the rain and cursed. And the lightning struck her and killed her. Now every time it rains, her face appears in the window.

Russell County, 1964 (RLa). Informant: male, born 1899 in Russell County. This variant of story No. 484 includes three motifs: C984.5, "Disastrous lightning for breaking tabu"; *E532(a), "Ghost-like portrait etched in glass"; and M414.1, "God cursed."

The Russellville Girl (c)

There was a young girl dressing to go to a formal dance. She had to go back upstairs because she had forgotten something. It began to rain. The girl felt the evening was ruined, so she cursed God. Lightning struck her because she cursed God. She died, and her image was said to be seen on the window of her room. Her window was painted to hide the image. Still people said they could see the girl's image on the window.

> *Adair County, 1964 (PRA). Informant: female, born 1907 in Green County.* See note to story No. 485.

The Russellville Girl (d)

487   There was a little, twelve-year-old girl that lived near our farm at White Rose who was yelling and cutting up something awful. It had just started storming outside, and she ran to the door and said that she wished lightning would strike her. It did almost as soon as she finished saying those words.

> *Taylor County, 1965 (JPi). Informant: male, born 1943 in Taylor County.* The only identifiable motif in this narrative is C984.5, "Disastrous lightning for breaking tabu." This account is localized in Taylor County.

The Russellville Girl (e)

488   Well, this girl was wanting to go to a dance, but her parents wouldn't let her go. And she was fussing. Anyway, she was standing in front of a window. And it came up a storm, and lightning flashed. And her picture was in the window. It was supposed to have been in color. I believe it happened in Greensburg.

> *Taylor County, 1965 (JPi). Informant: female, born 1925 in Cumberland County.* The two motifs found in this variant are C984.5, "Disastrous lightning for breaking tabu," and *E532(a), "Ghost-like portrait etched in glass."

The Russellville Girl (f)

489   This slave owner would watch his slaves from the attic window as they worked on his farm so he could make sure they were working hard enough. One day a storm came up, and lightning struck him

and killed him. And ever after that, they say you can see his image in the window.

Taylor County, 1964 (LS). Informant: male, born ca. 1905 in Western Kentucky. See note for story No. 488. This legend is previously unreported in association with the institution of slavery. It could represent an earlier form of the tale, but it is unlikely because of the total lack of specifics in this variant.

GLOSSARY

Bedside coffin. A container, generally made of wood, which was designed to rest on a stand by the bed of the deceased or in the parlor.

Belief. See *Folk belief.*

Belief tale. A narrative, generally brief, which documents or validates a folk belief or practice in the mind of the teller.

Booger. Folk synonym for *ghost* and *haint.*

Butter and eggs day. A local expression derived from the days of a barter economy when farm families took home-produced items to town to exchange for groceries and notions. Saturday was the traditional butter and eggs day in the Kentucky foothills until livestock markets were opened in the county seat towns in the 1920s; after that, the day of the livestock auction tended to become the butter and eggs day.

Casket. See *Coffin.*

Coffin. The chest-like container in which a corpse is interred. The folk primarily use this term rather than casket.

Collector. The person who seeks out and records accurately an item of oral folklore from an informant.

Custom. See *Folk custom.*

Dark of the moon. The period from the full moon to the new, the decrease or waning of the moon.

Death bell. Tinkling sounds in one's ear before the death of a friend or relative.

Death watch. The custom of sitting up with the corpse until time for the burial.

Family legend. See *Legend.*

Folk belief. A belief maintained in oral tradition among a people whose lives are shaped by folkways, practices, and customs. A folk belief is learned informally, not through formal education and religious indoctrination. A folk belief may be congruous, thus the term *belief* implies rational thinking and positive action. *Superstition,* on the other hand, is based on irrational fear and a system of negative taboos. It connotes ignorance of the laws of natural science.

Folk custom. Any traditional practice or event which is generally observed as a part of a daily or seasonal rhythm, such as a quilting bee, funeral ceremonies, planting and harvesting, the observation of Decoration Day or labor swapping during grain-threshing periods.

Folk tradition. Folk tradition reflects a sense of real historical continuity; the tradition helps to create a lifestyle that is based on example and imitation of one's elders and peers, a lifestyle which treasures cultural stability rather than social change. In a more narrow sense, a folk tradition may consist of one item or text of folklore that can be isolated and studied apart from the culture which produced it.

Ghost. The disembodied soul of a dead person which may reappear in bodily likeness of the deceased, or which may be manifested in the form of unexplained cries, screams, or other unnatural sounds. See also *Haint.*

Haint. Virtual synonym for *ghost.* Haints, generally, may be classified as that body of ghosts which are heard but not seen by the living.

Hogshead. A large wooden barrel capable of holding liquid but designed especially for the storage and shipment of agricultural commodities such as tobacco.

Informant. The person who transmits an item of oral folklore to the collector.

Laying out the body (corpse). The washing, dressing, and grooming of the corpse at home by friends and neighbors.

Legend. A traditional narrative, set in the recent past, believed to be true by the narrator, and generally by the listener. On the one hand a legend deals with supernatural characters such as ghosts, or it may be a recounting of local historical events whose chief characters were real human beings.

Malevolent ghost (creature). Supernatural creature with a disposition to do evil or bodily harm to the living.

Memorat. First-person tellings of experiences with supernatural or unnatural creatures and happenings.

Motif. The smallest unit of a story which has the capability of an independent existence. It may occur in identical form in other stories under a different set of circumstances. An example of a motif would be "the ineradicable bloodstain."

Mummy coffin. An early commercial casket, as well as a product of local wood craftsmen. Its shape resembled Egyptian mummy cases.

Mystic. A person who possesses magical powers.

Narrator. See *Informant.*

Omen. Any unnatural event, real or imagined, which takes place just prior to the death of a friend or relative.

Portend. See *Omen.*

Revenant. Synonymous term with *ghost* to identify the visible *spirit* or *soul* of a dead person returned from the grave.

Seance. A group meeting for the purposes of communicating with the spirits of the dead.

Shotgun house. A common type of an urban one-story, one-room-wide folk house with its front door in the gable end. It is said that one can stand in the front door with a shotgun and shoot through the house and out the back door.

Shroud. Burial garment.

Sign. See *Omen.*

Slatter-wire fence. Colloquial for a fence constructed with wooden slats, pickets, or palings woven together by criss-crossed wire.

Spectral. Ghostly.

Spirit. In folklore, a supernatural being such as a ghost or the soul of the deceased; generally non-malevolent.

Superstition. See *Folk belief.*

Text. Any item of folklore is a *text*—legend, song, riddle, epitaph, and so on. The text is important in understanding folklore, but it is no more important than the *context* which spawned or nurtured it.

Token. Synonym for *omen,* but especially of wide popularity in the Eastern Pennyroyal of Kentucky.

Variant. Any traditional item of folklore which varies, even in minor proportions, from others of its kind. The "fork in the skirt" legend complex is an excellent case in point.

Wake. See *Death watch.* The term *wake* is not generally used in the Eastern Pennyroyal.

Weaning house. Small dwelling built adjacent to the parents' home for newlyweds who are apprehensive of an immediate total break from the safety and security of parental care and guidance.

Winding sheet. Burial clothing.

Wraith. The spectral appearance of one who is about to die.

SELECTED BIBLIOGRAPHY

The bibliography of ghostlore in the United States is not very extensive, especially when scholarship is the essential criterion. Ghosts, like witches and necromancers, have been the topics of outpourings of literary drivel across the years. Most of this material is useless to the serious student of folk tradition and indicates, at best, the ebbs and flows of the popular mind at given periods in history. In the present century, for example, the period from 1900 to 1913 represented the zenith of articles appearing in *The Reader's Guide to Periodical Literature*. Ninety-two entries appeared under ghosts or apparitions during those years. Only forty-one were listed between 1914 and 1927. The number has declined rather steadily since then.

Although scholarly articles on ghostlore have appeared in learned journals from time to time, serious books on the subject are surprisingly few in number. The following selection of publications should prove helpful in a quest for additional ghost narrative texts, supportive data, but not even all of these have sufficient scholarly trappings.

Books

Baughman, Ernest Warren. *Type and Motif-Index of the Folktales of England and North America*. Indiana University Folklore Series No. 20. The Hague: Mouton, 1966; New York: Humanities Press, 1966.

Bendann, Effie. *Death Customs: An Analytical Study of Burial Rites*. London: Dawsons of Pall Mall, 1969.

Bowman, Leroy. *The American Funeral: A Way of Death*. New York: Paperback Library, 1964.

Brand, John. *Observations on the Popular Antiquities of Great Britain: Chiefly Illustrating the Origin of our Vulgar Customs, Ceremonies, and Superstitions*. London: H. G. Bohn, 1849; rpt. 1913.

Brewer, J. Mason. *Dog Ghosts, and Other Texas Negro Folk Tales.* Austin: Univ. of Texas Press, 1958.

Briggs, Katharine M., and Ruth L. Tongue. *Folktales of England.* Folktales of the World. Chicago: Univ. of Chicago Press, 1965.

Browne, Ray B. *Popular Beliefs and Practices from Alabama.* Berkeley: Univ. of California Press, 1955.

Burrison, John A. *The Golden Arm: The Folk Tale and Its Literary Use by Mark Twain and Joel C. Harris.* Research Paper No. 19 (June 1968). School of Arts and Sciences Research Papers, Georgia State College, Atlanta.

Campbell, Marie. *Tales from the Cloud Walking Country.* Bloomington: Indiana Univ. Press, 1958.

Christiansen, Reidar Th. *Folktales of Norway.* Folktales of the World. Chicago: Univ. of Chicago Press, 1964.

Coleman, Marion Moore. *A World Remembered: Tales and Lore of the Polish Land.* Cheshire, Conn.: Cherry Hill Books, 1965.

Creighton, Helen. *Bluenose Ghosts.* Toronto: Ryerson Press, 1957.

Danaher, Kevin. *In Ireland Long Ago.* Hatboro, Pa.: Folklore Associates, 1967.

Davidson, Hilda Roderick (Ellis). *The Road to Hel: A Study of the Conception of the Dead in Old Norse Literature.* New York: Greenwood Press, 1968.

Dégh, Linda. *Folktales of Hungary.* Trans. Judit Halász. Folktales of the World. Chicago: Univ. of Chicago Press, 1965.

De Gubernatis, Angelo. *Storia popolare degli Usi Funebri Indo-Europei.* Milano: Fratelli Treves, 1873.

Dorson, Richard M. *American Negro Folktales.* New York: Faucett World, 1967.

———. *Jonathan Draws the Long Bow.* Cambridge, Mass.: Harvard Univ. Press, 1946.

———. *Negro Folktales in Michigan.* Cambridge, Mass.: Harvard Univ. Press, 1956.

———. *Negro Tales from Pine Bluff, Arkansas, and Calvin, Michigan.* Bloomington: Indiana Univ. Press, 1958.

Frazier, Sir James George. *The Golden Bough: A Study in Magic and Religion.* New York: Macmillan, 1951.

Gardner, Emelyn Elizabeth. *Folklore from the Schoharie Hills New York.* Ann Arbor: Univ. of Michigan Press, 1937.

Gennep, Arnold van. *Manuel de Folklore Français Contemporain.* 4 vols. in 9 parts. Paris: Éditions A. et J. Picard et Cie, 1937–58. Vol.

I, pt. 2: "Les Funérailles," 649–824. This volume deals systematically with the customs connected with death and burial, but there are folk beliefs listed in connection with some of these customs.

———. *The Rites of Passage.* Chicago: Univ. of Chicago Press, 1960.

Habenstein, Robert W., and William M. Lamers. *The History of American Funeral Directing.* Milwaukee: Bulfin Printers, 1955.

Hand, Wayland D., ed. *American Folk Legend: A Symposium.* Berkeley: Univ. of California Press, 1971.

Hastings, James, ed. *Encyclopaedia of Religion and Ethics.* 13 vols. New York: Scribner's; Edinburgh: T. & T. Clark, 1925–35.

Hazlitt, W. Carew, ed. *Faiths and Folklore. A Dictionary of National Beliefs, Superstitions and Popular Customs, Past and Current, with their Classical and Foreign Analogues.* 2 vols. London: Reeves and Turner, 1905.

Henderson, William. *Notes on the Folk-Lore of the Northern Counties of England and the Borders.* London: W. Satchell, Peyton and Co., 1879.

Hole, Christina. *Haunted England: A Survey of English Ghost-Lore.* London: Batsford, 1940.

Hyatt, Harry Middleton. *Folk-Lore from Adams County, Illinois.* New York: Memoirs of the Alma Egan Foundation, 1935.

Jones, Louis C. *Things That Go Bump in the Night.* New York: Hill and Wang, 1959.

Lomax, John A. *The Adventures of a Ballad Hunter.* New York: Macmillan, 1947.

Mitford, Jessica. *The American Way of Death.* New York: Simon and Schuster, 1963.

Møller, J. S. *Fester og Højtider i gamle Dage.* Holbaek, Denmark: Amtstidendes Bogtrykkeri, 1929. Vol. 1, Pt. III, "Død," 239–491. Customs and beliefs connected with death and funeral practice. Excellent on revenants, ghostlore, etc.

Musick, Ruth Ann. *The Telltale Lilac Bush.* Lexington: Univ. of Kentucky Press, 1965.

Neely, Charles. *Tales and Songs of Southern Illinois.* Menasha, Wis.: Banta, 1938.

O'Súilleabhain, Seán. *Folktales of Ireland.* Folktales of the World. Chicago: Univ. of Chicago Press, 1966.

———. *A Handbook of Irish Folklore.* Dublin: Folklore of Ireland Society, 1942. "Death," 215–50.

————. *Irish Wake Amusements.* Hatboro, Pa.: Folklore Associates, 1961.

Parsons, Elsie Clews. *Folk-Lore of the Sea Islands, South Carolina.* New York: Memoirs of the American Folk-Lore Society, 1923.

Puckett, Newbell Niles. *Folk Beliefs of the Southern Negro.* Chapel Hill: Univ. of North Carolina Press, 1926.

Puckle, Bertram S. *Funeral Customs, Their Origin and Development.* London: T. W. Lannie, 1926; rpt. Detroit: Singing Tree Press, 1968.

Randolph, Vance. *The Devil's Pretty Daughter.* New York: Columbia Univ. Press, 1955.

————. *Ozark Superstitions.* New York: Columbia Univ. Press, 1947; rpt. Dover, 1964, as *Ozark Magic and Folklore.*

————. *Sticks in the Knapsack and Other Ozark Folk Tales.* New York: Columbia Univ. Press, 1958.

————. *The Talking Turtle.* New York: Columbia Univ. Press, 1957.

————. *We Always Lie to Strangers.* New York: Columbia Univ. Press, 1951.

————. *Who Blowed Up the Church House?* New York: Columbia Univ. Press, 1952.

Ranke, Kurt. *Folktales of Germany.* Trans. Lotte Baumann. Folktales of the World. Chicago: Univ. of Chicago Press, 1966.

Roberts, Leonard. *South from Hell-fer-Sartin.* Lexington: Univ. of Kentucky Press, 1955.

————. *Up Cutshin and Down Greasy.* Lexington: Univ. of Kentucky Press, 1959.

Rush, Alfred C. *Death and Burial in Christian Antiquity.* Washington, D.C.: Catholic Univ. of America Press, 1941.

Sabatier, Robert. *Dictionnaire de la Mort.* Paris: Éditions Albin Michel, 1967. A treatment in dictionary form of ideas, customs, beliefs, etc., dealing with death in terms of history, religion, art, poetry, folklore, etc.

Sackett, Samuel J., and William E. Koch. *Kansas Folklore.* Lincoln: Univ. of Nebraska Press, 1961.

Samter, Ernst. *Geburt, Hochzeit und Tod. Beiträge sur vergleichenden Volkskunde.* Leipzig: B. G. Teubner, 1911. Modern German and other European beliefs and customs connected with death treated with reference to analogues in classical antiquity.

Sartori, Paul. *Sitte und Brauch* (Handbücher zur Volkskunde, Vols. V–VIII). Leipzig: Verlag von Wilhelm Heims, 1910–14, Vol. V: "Die Hauptstufen des Menschendaseins": C. "Tod und Bergräbnis,"

123–86. The material on death and other aspects of the life cycle is part of a larger treatise on folk customs that encompass the whole of life and human activity. Folk beliefs underlying customs are often included.

Stevens, William Oliver. *Unbidden Guests* [:] *A Book of Real Ghosts.* New York: Dodd, Mead, 1946.

Thiselton-Dyer, Thomas Firminger. *British Popular Customs, Present and Past: Illustrating Their Social and Domestic Manners of the People: Arranged According to the Calendar.* London: George Bell and Sons, 1876; rpt. Detroit: Singing Tree Press, 1968.

————. *The Ghost World.* London: Ward & Downey, 1893.

Thomas, Daniel Lindsey, and Lucy Blayney. *Kentucky Superstition.* Princeton: Princeton Univ. Press, 1920.

Thompson, Stith. *Motif-Index of Folk Literature.* 6 vols. Rev. ed., Bloomington: Indiana Univ. Press, 1955.

————. *The Types of the Folktale.* Helsinki: Suomalainen Tiedeakatemia Academia Scientiarum Fennica, 1961; rev. edition, Hatboro, Pa.: Folklore Associates, 1961.

Von Hoffmann-Krayer, Eduard, and Hanns Bächtold-Stäubli. *Handwörterbuch des deutschen Alberglaubens.* 10 vols. Berlin: Walter de Gruyter, 1927–42. Dictionary treatment of all phases of beliefs and customs connected with death and funeral practice, the realm of the dead, etc. Covers not only Germany, but contains much other material.

White, Newman Ivey, ed. *The Frank C. Brown Collection of North Carolina Folklore.* 7 vols. Durham, N.C.: Duke Univ. Press, 1952.

Woods, Barbara Allen. *The Devil in Dog Form, A Partial Type Index of Devil Legends.* Folklore Studies No. 11 (Berkeley: Univ. of California Press, 1959).

Writers' Project—Georgia. *Drums and Shadows, Survival Studies Among the Georgia Coastal Negroes.* Athens: Univ. of Georgia Press, 1940.

Articles

Baker, Ronald L. "The Face in the Wall," *Indiana Folklore* 1:1 (1969), 29–46.

Brumbach, Paul D. "Funerals in My Childhood Days," *Pennsylvania Folklife* 14:1 (1964), 30–34.

Christiansen, Reidar Th. "The Dead and the Living." *Studia Norvegica* 2 (1946).

Clements, William. "The Walking Coffin," *Indiana Folklore* 2:2 (1969), 4–10.

Cornett, Elizabeth B. "Belief Tales of Knott and Perry Counties," *Kentucky Folklore Record* 2:3 (July–Sept. 1956), 69–75.

Hand, Wayland D. "California Bells Legends," *California Folklore Quarterly* 4 (1945).

Jones, Bryan H. "The Dead Coach and Ghost Funerals," *Folk-Lore* 19 (1908), 320–21.

Lee, J. Frank. "The Informal Organization of White Southern Protestant Funerals: The Role of the Arranger," *Tennessee Folklore Society Bulletin* 33:1 (March 1967), 36–40.

Mitcham, Mildred Barnett. "A Tale in the Making: The Face in the Window," *Southern Folklore Quarterly* 12:4 (1948), 241–57.

Montell, W. Lynwood. "Belief Tales from Barren County," *Kentucky Folklore Record* 8:1 (Jan.–March 1962), 11–17.

Montell, Ruth. "Tales from Monroe County Children," *Kentucky Folklore Record* 4:4 (Oct.–Dec. 1958), 145–48.

Owens, Ethel. "Ghost Tales from Breathitt County," *Kentucky Folklore Record* 5:3 (July–Sept. 1959), 81–86.

Trice, Henry L. "Lore of the Hopkins-Webster Line," *Kentucky Folklore Record* 2:3 (July–Sept. 1956), 91–97.

Wilgus, D. K. "The Girl in the Window," *Western Folklore* 29 (1970), 251–56.

Wilgus, D. K., and W. Lynwood Montell. "Beanie Short: A Civil War Chronicle in Legend and Song," in Wayland D. Hand, ed., *American Folk Legend: A Symposium*. Berkeley: Univ. of California Press, 1970.

INDEX OF COLLECTORS

This index refers to item numbers assigned to the various beliefs and tales. The counties or cities following names of collectors are their addresses at the time of collection. Unless otherwise indicated, all counties are in Kentucky.

INDEX OF TALE TYPES AND MOTIFS

This index refers to page numbers within this volume. References accompanying the beliefs and tales are keyed to the numbering systems employed in Stith Thompson's *The Types of the Folktale* and his *Motif-Index of Folk Literature*. All items marked with an asterisk (*) are found in Ernest Warren Baughman's *Type and Motif-Index of the Folktales of England and North America*, a work which more closely corresponds in scope with the narratives in the present book.

GENERAL INDEX

Adair County, vii, 20–21, 23–25, 29–30, 35–38, 41–44, 57–58, 66–67, 69, 84, 87, 96, 98–99, 101–102, 104–10, 115–16, 120, 126, 130–31, 135, 141–42, 144–45, 151, 154, 160–61, 165, 175, 178, 183, 187, 190–91, 193, 205, 207–208, 214
Afternoon, mentioned in ghost narratives, 91
Ailments, 17
Allen County, vii, 124, 162
Animals: in belief expressions, 34–42; in ghost narratives, 92–93, 95–215 passim; see also especially Horse and 163–69, 190–96, for dogs and other ghostly animals
Ashes, 30

Baby: exceptional, in a belief expression, 18; in a funeral procession, 77; ghost cries of, 130–31
Barren County, vii, 22, 40, 68, 96, 98, 104–105, 108, 114, 118–19, 122, 127, 145, 153, 156, 158, 169, 172, 179–80, 201, 206
Bat, 34
Bear tales, defined, 87–88
Bees, telling the, 63, 69
Belief in the supernatural, 89–90
Beliefs and practices: tenacity of, 15; about impending death, 17–42; veracity of, 63–64; surrounding the hour of death, 66–69; about the dead, 69–84; about the return of the dead, 87–94; see also Folk belief
Belief tales, 14; death omen narratives as, 43–60; ghost tales as, 95–215; defined, 217
Bells: ringing, 21; tolling to signal a death, 64, 68; passing bell, 68; toll bell, 68; see also Death bell
Big 'Fraid and Little 'Fraid, 185–86
Big Toe, The, 98, 155–56

Birds: unspecific, 37–39; dove, 39; owl, 39; crow, 40; mockingbird, 40; redbird, 40; whippoorwill, 40–41
Birth: sign of, 19; dream of, 20
Birthmarks, 17
Bloodstain, ineradicable, 134, 210–11
Booger, 95–215 passim; defined, 217
Burial; see Funerals
Buried alive, 73
Butter and eggs day, ix; defined, 217

Campbellsville, ix, x
Campbellsville College, vii
Cars, 77
Casey County, vii, 18, 22, 42, 77, 160, 194, 201, 204
Caskets: in death beliefs, 28, 41, 63, 68; in death omen narratives, 45, 49–52; utilization of for burial, 70, 73–76; construction of, 73–76, 84; in ghost narratives, 95–215 passim; defined, 217; see also Coffins
Cat, 34, 71
Cemetery, mentioned in ghost narratives, 91
Chair, 25, 26
Child: care of, 17–18; exceptional, in a belief expression, 18
Chills, 23
Christmas, 29–30
Clinton County, vii, 17, 21–24, 28, 30, 32–33, 38, 41, 48, 50, 63, 71–72, 74, 76–77, 81–83, 108, 131, 140, 147, 150, 206, 211
Clock: gonging or striking, 24; ticking noises of, 28; stopping, 67
Cloud, shaped like a coffin, 28
Coffins: spectral, 14, 57, 104; bedside, 75, 217 (defined); mummy, 74–75, 219 (defined); in ghost tales, 112–14; see also Caskets
Colic, 17